SolidWorks 2009 Tutorial

David C. Planchard & Marie P. Planchard CSWP

ISBN: 978-1-58503-494-9

SDC

PUBLICATIONS

Schroff Development Corporation

www.schroff.com

Trademarks and Disclaimer

SolidWorks® Corp. is a Dassault Systèmes S.A. (Nasdaq: DASTY) company that develops and markets software for design, analysis, and product data management applications. Microsoft® Windows, Microsoft Office® and its family of products are registered trademarks of the Microsoft Corporation. Other software applications and parts described in this book are trademarks or registered trademarks of their respective owners.

Dimensions of parts are modified for illustration purposes. Every effort is made to provide an accurate text. The authors and the manufacturers shall not be held liable for any parts or drawings developed or designed with this book or any responsibility for inaccuracies that appear in the book. Web and company information was valid at the time of the printing.

Copyright© 2009 by D & M Education LLC

Examination Copies

Teacher evaluation copies for 2009, 2008, 2007, and 2006 SolidWorks books are available with classroom support materials and initial and final SolidWorks models. Books received as examination copies are for review purposes only. Examination copies are not intended for student use. Resale of examination copies is prohibited. All assemblies and components for the final ROBOT assembly displayed on the cover are located on the enclosed CD under the *Chapter 5 models* folder. SolidWorks 2009 Tutorial with Multi-media CD is targeted toward a technical school, two year college or four year university instructor/student or industry professional that is a beginner or intermediate user who is looking for a step-by-step project based approach with an enclosed 1.5 hour Multi-Media CD with SolidWorks model files. The physical components and corresponding Science, Technology, Engineering, and Math (STEM) curriculum are available from Gears Educational Systems [www.gearseds.com]. Visit www.schroff.com or www.dmeducation.net for additional information.

Electronic Files

INTRODUCTION

SolidWorks 2009 Tutorial with Multi-media CD is targeted toward a technical school, two year college or four year university instructor/student or industry professional that is a beginner or intermediate user who is looking for a step-by-step project based approach with an enclosed 1.5 hour Multi-media CD.

The book covers the SolidWorks User Interface and CommandManager, Document and System properties, simple machine parts, SimulationXpress analysis, simple and complex assemblies, design tables, configurations, multi-sheet, multi-view drawings, BOMs, Revision tables using basic and advance features, and a section on the Certified SolidWorks Associate CSWA program with sample exam questions and models.

Follow the step-by-step instructions and develop multiple assemblies that combine over 80 Extruded machined parts and components. Formulate the skills to create, modify and edit 2D sketches and 3D features. Learn the techniques to reuse features, parts and components through symmetry, patterns, copied components, design tables, and configurations. Learn by doing, not just by reading!

Desired outcomes and usage competencies are listed for each project. Know your objectives up front. Follow the step-by step procedures in Project 1 - 5 to achieve your design goals. Work between multiple documents, features, commands, and custom and document properties that represent how engineers and designers utilize SolidWorks in industry. Note: Project 6 provides a basic introduction into the curriculum and categories of the Certified SolidWorks Associate CSWA exam.

The authors developed the industry scenarios by combining their own industry experience with the knowledge of engineers, department managers, vendors, and manufacturers. These professionals are directly involved with SolidWorks everyday. Their responsibilities go far beyond the creation of just a 3D model.

LINKAGE Assembly
Courtesy of Gears Educational Systems
www.gearseds.com

About the Cover

Create the final ROBOT assembly illustrated on the cover. The physical components and corresponding Science, Technology, Engineering, and Math (STEM) curriculum are available from Gears Educational Systems www.gearseds.com. *Note: All assemblies and components for the final ROBOT assembly are located on the CD under the Chapter 5 models folder.*

Pneumatic Components Diagram
Courtesy of Gears Educational Systems
www.gearseds.com

About the Authors

David Planchard is the President of D&M Education LLC. Before starting D&M Education, he spent over 27 years in industry and academia holding various engineering, marketing, and teaching positions and degrees. He holds five U.S. patents and one International patent. He has published and authored numerous papers on equipment design. He is a member of the New England Pro/Users Group, New England SolidWorks Users Group, and the Cisco Regional Academy Users Group. David holds a BSME, MSM and a Certified SolidWorks Associate (CSWA) Certification. David is a SolidWorks Solution Partner and an Adjunct Instructor at Worcester Polytechnic Institute.

Marie Planchard is the Director of World Education Markets at SolidWorks Corporation. Before she joined SolidWorks, Marie spent over 10 years as an engineering professor at Mass Bay College in Wellesley Hills, MA. She has 14 plus years of industry software experience and held a variety of management and engineering positions. Marie holds a BSME, MSME and a Certified SolidWorks Professional (CSWP) Certification.

David and Marie Planchard are co-authors of the following books:

- **A Commands Guide for SolidWorks® 2009**, 2008

- **A Commands Guide Reference Tutorial for SolidWorks® 2007**

- **Assembly Modeling with SolidWorks® 2008**, 2006, 2005-2004, 2003, and 2001Plus

- **Certified SolidWorks® 2008 Associate CSWA Exam Guide**

- **Drawing and Detailing with SolidWorks® 2008**, 2007, 2006, 2005, 2004, 2003, 2002, and 2001/2001Plus

- **Engineering Design with SolidWorks® 2009**, 2008, 2007, 2006, 2005, 2004, 2003, 2001Plus, 2001, and 1999

- **SolidWorks® The Basics with Multimedia CD 2009**, 2008, 2007, 2006, 2005, 2004, and 2003

- **SolidWorks® Tutorial with Multimedia CD 2009,** 2008, 2007, 2006, 2005, 2004, 2003, and 2001/2001Plus

- **The Fundamentals of SolidWorks®: Featuring the VEXplorer robot, 2008**, 2007

- **Official Certified SolidWorks® Associate CSWA Exam Guide 2007**

- **Applications in Sheet Metal Using Pro/SHEETMETAL & Pro/ENGINEER**

Dedication

A special acknowledgment goes to our loving daughter, Stephanie Planchard, who supported us during this intense and lengthy project. Stephanie continues to support us with her patience, love and understanding.

Contact the Authors

This is the 8th edition of this book. We realize that keeping software application books current is imperative to our customers. We value the hundreds of professors, students, designers, and engineers that have provided us input to enhance our book. We value your suggestions and comments. Please visit our website at **www.dmeducation.net** or contact us directly with any comments, questions, or suggestions on this book or any of our other SolidWorks books at dplanchard@msn.com.

Note to Instructors

SolidWorks 2009 Tutorial with Multi-media CD is target toward a two year college or four year university instructor/student or industry professional that is a beginner or intermediate user who is looking for a step-by-step project based approach with an enclosed 1.5 hour Multi-media CD with SolidWorks model files. The physical components and corresponding Science, Technology, Engineering, and Math (STEM) curriculum are available from Gears Educational Systems **www.gearseds.com**. Please contact the publisher **www.schroff.com** for additional materials and the Instructor's Guide that support the usage of this text in the classroom or visit **www.dmeducation.net** for additional book information.

Trademarks, Disclaimer, and Copyrighted Material

SolidWorks® Corp. is a Dassault Systèmes S.A. (Nasdaq: DASTY) company that develops and markets software for design, analysis, and product data management applications Microsoft Windows®, Microsoft Office® and its family of products are registered trademarks of the Microsoft Corporation. Other software applications and parts described in this book are trademarks or registered trademarks of their respective owners.

Dimensions of parts are modified for illustration purposes. Every effort is made to provide an accurate text. The authors and the manufacturers shall not be held liable for any parts or drawings developed or designed with this book or any responsibility for inaccuracies that appear in the book. Web and company information was valid at the time of this printing.

The Y14 ASME Engineering Drawing and Related Documentation Publications utilized in this text are as follows: ASME Y14.1 1995, ASME Y14.2M-1992 (R1998), ASME Y14.3M-1994 (R1999), ASME Y14.41-2003, ASME Y14.5-1982, ASME Y14.5M-1994, and ASME B4.2. Note: By permission of The American Society of Mechanical Engineers, Codes and Standards, New York, NY, USA. All rights reserved.

References

- SolidWorks Users Guide, SolidWorks Corporation, 2009.
- ASME Y14 Engineering Drawing and Related Documentation Practices.
- Beers & Johnson, Vector Mechanics for Engineers, 6th ed. McGraw Hill, Boston, MA.
- Betoline, Wiebe, Miller, Fundamentals of Graphics Communication, Irwin, 1995.
- Earle, James, Engineering Design Graphics, Addison Wesley, 1999.
- Hibbler, R.C, Engineering Mechanics Statics and Dynamics, 8th ed, Prentice Hall, Saddle River, NJ.
- Hoelscher, Springer, Dobrovolny, Graphics for Engineers, John Wiley, 1968.
- Jensen, Cecil, Interpreting Engineering Drawings, Glencoe, 2002.
- Jensen & Helsel, Engineering Drawing and Design, Glencoe, 1990.
- Olivo C., Payne, Olivo, T, Basic Blueprint Reading and Sketching, Delmar, 1988.
- Planchard & Planchard, Drawing and Detailing with SolidWorks, SDC Pub., Mission, KS 2008.
- Walker, James, Machining Fundamentals, Goodheart Wilcox, 1999.
- 80/20 Product Manual, 80/20, Inc., Columbia City, IN, 2008.
- Reid Tool Supply Product Manual, Reid Tool Supply Co., Muskegon, MI, 2008.
- Simpson Strong Tie Product Manual, Simpson Strong Tie, CA, 2008.
- Ticona Designing with Plastics – The Fundamentals, Summit, NJ, 2008.
- SMC Corporation of America, Product Manuals, Indiana, 2008.
- Gears Educational Design Systems, Product Manual, Hanover, MA, 2008.
- Emhart – A Black and Decker Company, On-line catalog, Hartford, CT, 2008.

TABLE OF CONTENTS

What is SolidWorks?

SolidWorks is a design automation software package used to produce parts, assemblies and drawings. SolidWorks is a Windows native 3D solid modeling CAD program. SolidWorks provides easy to use, highest quality design software for engineers and designers who create 3D models and 2D drawings ranging from individual parts to assemblies with thousands of parts.

The SolidWorks Corporation, headquartered in Concord, Massachusetts, USA develops and markets innovative design solutions for the Microsoft Windows platform. Additional information on SolidWorks and its family of products can be obtained at their URL, www.SolidWorks.com.

In SolidWorks, you create 3D parts, 3D assemblies, and 2D drawings. The part, assembly and drawing documents are related.

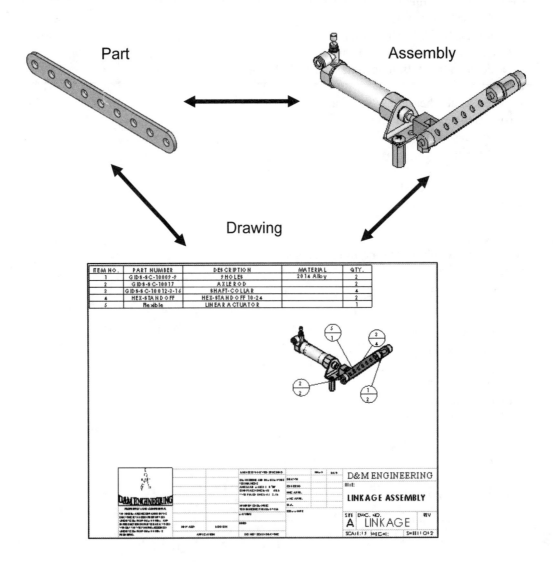

Features are the building blocks of parts. Use features to create parts, such as: Extruded Boss/Base and Extruded Cut. Extruded features begin with a 2D sketch created on a Sketch plane.

The 2D sketch is a profile or cross section. Sketch tools such as: lines, arcs, and circles are used to create the 2D sketch. Sketch the general shape of the profile. Add Geometric relationships and dimensions to control the exact size of the geometry.

Create features by selecting edges or faces of existing features, such as a Fillet. The Fillet feature rounds sharp corners.

Dimensions drive features. Change a dimension, and you change the size of the part.

Apply Geometric relationships: Vertical, Horizontal, Parallel, etc. to maintain Design intent.

Create a hole that penetrates through a part. SolidWorks maintains relationships through the change.

The step-by-step approach used in this text allows you to create parts, assemblies, and drawings.

The book provides the knowledge to modify all parts and components in a document. Change is an integral part of design.

Design Intent

The SolidWorks definition of design intent is the process in which the model is developed to accept future changes.

Models behave differently when design changes occur. Design for change.

Utilize geometry for symmetry, reuse common features and reuse common parts.

Build change into the following areas:

1. Sketch

2. Feature

3. Part

4. Assembly

5. Drawing

1. **Design Intent in the Sketch**

Build design intent in the sketch.

A profile is determined from your selected Sketch tool: Example: Corner Rectangle, Line, Circle, Arc etc.

Build symmetry into the profile through a sketch Centerline, Mirror entity and position about a Reference plane and Origin.

Build design intent as you sketch with automatic relationships.

Horizontal		**Vertical**
Coincident		**Midpoint**
Perpendicular		**Tangent**

A rectangle contains Horizontal, Vertical, and Perpendicular automatic Geometric relations.

Apply design intent using added Geometric relations: Example: Horizontal, Vertical, Collinear, Perpendicular, Parallel, etc.

Example A: Apply design intent to create a Square profile. Sketch a rectangle.

Apply the Center Rectangle tool. Note: No Construction reference centerlines or Midpoint relation is required with the Center Rectangle Sketch tool.

Fully define the sketch, insert dimensions.

Example B: Develop a Rectangular profile.

Apply the Corner Rectangle Sketch tool. The bottom horizontal Midpoint of the rectangular profile is located at the Origin.

Origin

Insert a Midpoint relation between the horizontal edge of the rectangle and the Origin.

Insert dimensions to define the width and height of the rectangle as illustrated. The sketch is fully defined.

2. Design Intent in the Feature

Build design intent into a feature by addressing symmetry, feature selection and the order of feature creations.

Example A: The Extruded feature as illustrated remains symmetric about the Front Plane.

Utilize the Mid Plane End Condition option. Modify the depth and the Extruded feature remains symmetric about the Front Plane.

Example B: Create six holes for a pattern.

Do you create six separate holes? No. Create a single hole using the Hole Wizard tool from the Feature toolbar.

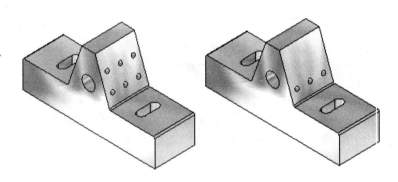

Insert a Linear Pattern feature. Note: The first hole is called the seed feature.

Modify the number of holes from six to three using the LPattern folder in the FeatureManager.

3. Design Intent in the Part

Utilize symmetry, feature order and reusing common features to build design intent into the part.

Example A: Feature order.

Is the entire part symmetric?

Feature order affects the part. Apply the Shell feature before the Fillet feature and the inside corners remain perpendicular.

4. Design Intent in the Assembly

Utilizing symmetry, reusing common parts and using the Mate relationship between parts builds design intent into an assembly.

Example A: Reuse Geometry in an assembly.

The PNEUMATIC-TEST-MODULE Assembly contains a Linear Pattern of holes. Insert one SCREW into the first hole. Utilize the Component Pattern tool to copy the original SCREW to the other holes. Note: The original SCREW is known as the seed feature.

5. Design Intent in the Drawing

Utilize dimensions, tolerance and notes in parts and assemblies to build the design intent into a Drawing.

Example A: Tolerance and material in the drawing.

Insert an outside diameter tolerance +.000/-.002 into the TUBE part. The tolerance propagates to the drawing.

Define the Custom Property MATERIAL in the Part. The MATERIAL Custom Property propagates to the drawing.

Additional information on design process and design intent is available in SolidWorks Help.

Overview of Projects

Project 1: Linkage Assembly

Project 1 introduces the basic concepts behind SolidWorks and the SolidWorks 2009 User Interface.

Create a file folder to manage projects. Create three parts: AXLE, SHAFT-COLLAR, and FLATBAR. Utilize the following features: *Extruded Base, Extruded Boss, Extruded Cut, and Linear Pattern*.

Create the LINKAGE assembly. The LINKAGE assembly utilizes the SMC AirCylinder component located on the enclosed CD in the book. Note: Copy all SolidWorks files from the CD to your hard drive. Work from the hard drive folder: SW-TUTORIAL 2009.

Project 2: Front Support Assembly

Project 2 introduces various Sketch planes to create parts. The Front, Top, and Right Planes each contain the Extruded Base feature for the TRIANGLE, HEX-STANDOFF, and ANGLE-13HOLE parts. Utilize Geometric relationships in your sketch.

Create the SCREW part using the following features: *Revolved Base, Extruded Cut, Fillet, and Circular Pattern*.

Create the FRONT-SUPPORT assembly. Utilize additional parts from the Web or the enclosed CD to create the RESERVOIR SUPPORT assembly in the Project exercises.

Project 3: Fundamentals of Drawing

Project 3 covers the development of a customized Sheet format and Drawing template.

Review the differences between the Sheet and the Sheet format. Develop a company logo from a bitmap or picture file.

Create a FLATBAR drawing. Insert dimensions created from the part features. Create the LINKAGE assembly drawing with multiple views and assemblies.

ITEM NO.	PART NUMBER	DESCRIPTION	MATERIAL	QTY.
1	Flexible	LINEAR ACTUATOR		1
2	GIDS-SC-10017	AXLE ROD		2
3	GIDS-SC-10009-9	9HOLES	2014 Alloy	2
4	GIDS-SC-10012-3-16	SHAFT-COLLAR		4
5	HEX-STANDOFF	HEX-STANDOFF		2

Develop and incorporate a Bill of Materials into the drawing Custom Properties in the parts and assemblies. Add information to the Bill of Materials in the drawing. Insert a Design Table to create multiple configurations of parts and assemblies.

Project 4: Advanced Features

Project 4 focuses on creating six parts for the PNEUMATIC-TEST-MODULE Assembly: WEIGHT, HOOK, WHEEL, HEX-ADAPTER, AXLE-3000, and SHAFTCOLLAR-500.

Apply the following Advanced model features: *Plane, Lofted Base, Extruded Cut, Swept Base, Dome, Helix and Spiral, Swept Cut, Extruded Base, Revolved Cut, Extruded Cut, Circular Pattern, Axis, and Hole Wizard.*

Reuse existing geometry and modify existing parts to create new parts with the Save as copy command.

Project 5: PNEUMATIC-TEST-MODULE Assembly and Final ROBOT Assembly

Project 5 focuses on the PNEUMATIC-TEST-MODULE Assembly and the final ROBOT Assembly.

Create the WHEEL-AND-AXLE assembly. First, create the 3HOLE-SHAFTCOLLAR assembly and the 5HOLE-SHAFTCOLLAR assembly.

Insert the WHEEL part, AXLE 3000 part, HEX-ADAPTER part, and SHAFTCOLLAR-500 part.

Insert the FLAT-PLATE part that was create in the Project 2 exercises. Insert the LINKAGE assembly and add components: HEX-STANDOFF, AXLE, and SHAFT-COLLAR.

Insert the AIR-RESERVOIR-SUPPORT assembly. Insert the SCREW part. Utilize the Feature Driven Component Pattern tool and the Linear Component Pattern tool.

Insert the FRONT-SUPPORT assembly and apply the Mirror Components tool to complete the Pneumatic Test Module Assembly.

Create the final ROBOT Assembly as illustrated with the Robot-platform sub-assembly, PNEUMATIC-TEST-MODULE sub-assembly, basic_integration sub-assembly and the HEX-ADAPTER component. Add additional components in the Project exercises.

You learn the process to work with multiple documents between parts and assemblies and to apply the following Assembly tools: Insert Component, Standard Mates: Concentric, Coincident, and Parallel, Linear Component Pattern, Feature Driven Component Pattern, Circular Component Pattern, Mirror Components and Replace Components. ***Note: All assemblies and components for the final ROBOT assembly are located in the CD under the Chapter 5 models folder.***

Project 6: Introduction to the Certified SolidWorks Associate Exam

Project 6 provides a basic introduction into the curriculum and exam categories for the Certified SolidWorks Associated CSWA Certification program. Review the exam procedure, process and required model knowledge needed to take and pass the exam.

Review the five exam categories: *Basic Theory and Drawing Theory, Part Modeling, Advanced Part Modeling, Assembly Modeling, and Advanced Modeling Theory and Analysis.*

Given:
A = 63, B = 50, C = 100
Material: Copper
Units: MMGS
Density: .0089 g/mm^3
All HOLES THROUGH ALL

Origin

All model files for the solutions in this project are located in the Chapter 6 models folder on the CD.

View the Certified SolidWorks Associate CSWA exam pdf file on the enclosed CD for a sample exam!

About the Book

The following conventions are used throughout this book:

- The term document is used to refer to a SolidWorks part, drawing, or assembly file.

- The list of items across the top of the SolidWorks interface is the Menu bar menu or the Menu bar toolbar. Each item in the Menu bar has a pull-down menu. When you need to select a series of commands from these menus, the following format is used: Click **Insert**, **Reference Geometry**, **Plane** from the Menu bar. The Plane PropertyManager is displayed.

- The book is organized into six Projects. Each Project is focused on a specific subject or feature. Use the enclosed Multi-media CD to obtain parts and models that are used in this book, and to view the features created in each Project.

- Copy all folders and files from the CD to your hard drive. Work from the hard drive. All assemblies and components for the final ROBOT assembly are located on the CD under the Chapter 5 models folder.

The following command syntax is used throughout the text. Commands that require you to perform an action are displayed in **Bold** text.

Format:	Convention:	Example:
Bold	• All commands actions. • Selected icon button. • Selected icon button. • Selected geometry: line, circle. • Value entries.	• Click **Options** from the Menu bar toolbar. • Click **Corner Rectangle** ☐ from the Sketch toolbar. • Click **Sketch** ✓ from the Context toolbar. • Select the **centerpoint**. • Enter **3.0** for Radius.
Capitalized	• Filenames. • First letter in a feature name.	• Save the **FLATBAR** assembly. • Click the **Fillet** feature.

Windows Terminology in SolidWorks

The mouse buttons provide an integral role in executing SolidWorks commands. The mouse buttons execute commands, select geometry, display Shortcut menus and provide information feedback.

A summary of mouse button terminology is displayed below:

Item:	Description:
Click	Press and release the left mouse button.
Double-click	Double press and release the left mouse button.
Click inside	Press the left mouse button. Wait a second, and then press the left mouse button inside the text box. Use this technique to modify Feature names in the FeatureManager design tree.
Drag	Point to an object, press and hold the left mouse button down. Move the mouse pointer to a new location. Release the left mouse button.
Right-click	Press and release the right mouse button. A Shortcut menu is displayed. Use the left mouse button to select a menu command.
ToolTip	Position the mouse pointer over an Icon (button). The tool name is displayed below the mouse pointer.
Large ToolTip	Position the mouse pointer over an Icon (button). The tool name and a description of its functionality are displayed below the mouse pointer.
Mouse pointer feedback	Position the mouse pointer over various areas of the sketch, part, assembly or drawing. The cursor provides feedback depending on the geometry.

A mouse with a center wheel provides additional functionality in SolidWorks. Roll the center wheel downward to enlarge the model in the Graphics window. Hold the center wheel down. Drag the mouse in the Graphics window to rotate the model.

SolidWorks System requirements for Microsoft Windows Operating Systems and hardware are as illustrated.

Requirements for Data Management products (PDMWorks Workgroup and Enterprise).				
Microsoft® Windows® Supported Operating Systems (9)				
	SolidWorks 2006	SolidWorks 2007	SolidWorks 2008	SolidWorks 2009
Vista (64-bit) (12)(11)	✗	✗	✓	✓
Vista (32-bit) (11)	✗	✗	✓	✓
XP Professional (32-bit) (1)	✓	✓	✓	✓
XP Professional (64-bit)	✓ (4)	✓	✓	✓
2000 Professional (2)	✓	✗	✗	✗

Your default system document templates may be different if you are a new user of SolidWorks 2009 vs. an existing user who has upgraded from a previous version.

Notes:

Project 1

LINKAGE Assembly

LINKAGE Assembly
Courtesy of
Gears Educational Systems &
SMC Corporation of America

Below are the desired outcomes and usage competencies based on the completion of Project 1.

Desired Outcomes:	Usage Competencies:

• Create three parts:
 	
  o AXLE
 	
  o SHAFT-COLLAR
 	
  o FLATBAR
	• Understand the SolidWorks default User Interface. Establish a SolidWorks session.
	
	• Create 2D sketch profiles on the correct Sketch plane.
	
	• Apply the following 3D features: Extruded Base, Extruded Cut, and Linear Pattern.

• Create an assembly: o LINKAGE assembly	• Understand the Assembly toolbar. • Insert components into an assembly. • Insert the following Standard mates: Concentric, Coincident, and Parallel.

Notes:

Project 1 – LINKAGE Assembly

Project Objective

SolidWorks is a design software application used to model and create 2D and 3D sketches, 3D parts, assemblies, and 2D drawings. The Project objective is to provide a comprehensive understanding of the SolidWorks default User Interface and CommandManager: *Menu bar toolbar, Menu bar menu, Drop-down menu, Context toolbar / menus, Flyout FeatureManager, System feedback, Confirmation Corner, Heads-up View toolbar and an understanding of Document Properties.*

Obtain the working familiarity of the following SolidWorks sketch and feature tools: Line, Circle, Centerpoint Straight Slot, Smart Dimension, Extruded Base, Extruded Cut, and Linear Pattern.

Create three individual parts: AXLE, SHAFT-COLLAR, and FLATBAR.

Create an assembly using the three created parts and a downloaded sub-assembly from the CD in the book:

- LINKAGE assembly.

On the completion of this project, you will be able to:

- Start a SolidWorks session and navigate through the SolidWorks (UI) and CommandManager.

- Set units and dimensioning standards for a SolidWorks document.

- Generate a 2D sketch and identify the correct Sketch plane.

- Add and modify sketch dimensions.

- Create a 3D model.

- Understand and apply the following SolidWorks features:

  o Extruded Base, Extruded Cut, and Linear Pattern

- Insert the following Geometric relations: MidPoint and Equal.

- Download an assembly into SolidWorks and create an assembly.

- Understand the Assembly toolbar.

- Apply the following Standard mates: Coincident, Concentric and Parallel.

Project Overview

SolidWorks is a 3D solid modeling CAD software package used to produce and model parts, assemblies, and drawings.

SolidWorks provides design software to create 3D models and 2D drawings.

Create three parts in this project:

- AXLE

- SHAFT-COLLAR

- FLATBAR

Download the AirCylinder assembly from the enclosed CD.

☼ The AirCylinder assembly is also available to download from the internet.

AirCylinder assembly

Combine the created parts and the downloaded AirCylinder assembly to create the LINKAGE assembly.

☼ Screen shots and illustrations in the book display the SolidWorks user default setup and interface for SP1.0.

LINKAGE assembly

AXLE Part

The AXLE is a cylindrical rod. The AXLE
supports the two FLATBAR parts.

AXLE

FLATBAR

The AXLE rotates about its axis. The
dimensions for the AXLE are determined from the other
components in the LINKAGE assembly.

Axis

Start a new SolidWorks session. Create the AXLE part.

Use features to create parts. Features are the building
blocks that add or remove material.

Utilize the Extruded Base tool from the Features
toolbar. The Extruded Base feature adds material. The
Base feature is the first feature of the part. The Base feature
is the foundation of the part. Keep the Base feature simple!

The Base feature geometry for the AXLE is a simple extrusion.
How do you create a solid Extruded Base feature for the
AXLE?

Origin

- Select the Front Plane as the Sketch plane.

- Sketch a circular 2D profile on the Front Plane, centered at
  the Origin as illustrated.

- Apply the Extruded Base Feature. Extend the
  profile perpendicular (⊥) to the Front Plane.

Utilize symmetry. Extrude the sketch with the Mid
Plane End Condition in Direction 1. The Extruded Base
feature is centered on both sides of the Front Plane.

Start a SolidWorks session. The SolidWorks
application is located in the Programs folder.

Origin

SolidWorks displays the Tip of the Day box. Read the Tip of the Day to obtain additional knowledge on SolidWorks.

Create a new part. Select File, New from the Menu bar toolbar or click New □ from the Menu bar menu. There are two options for new documents: Novice and Advanced. Select the Advanced option. Select the default Part document.

Activity: Start a SolidWorks Session

Start a SolidWorks 2009 session.

1)   Click **Start** from the Windows Taskbar.

2)   Click **All Programs** All Programs ▷.

3)   Click the **SolidWorks 2009** folder.

4)   Click the **SolidWorks 2009** application. The SolidWorks program window opens. Note: Do not open a document at this time.

⌖ If available, double-click the SolidWorks 2009 icon on the Windows Desktop to start a SolidWorks session.

⌖ The book was written using SolidWorks Office 2003 on Windows XP Professional SP3.0 with a Windows Classic desktop theme.

Read the Tip of the Day dialog box.

5)   If you do not see this screen, click the SolidWorks **Resources** 🏠 tab on the right side of the Graphics window located in the Task Pane as illustrated.

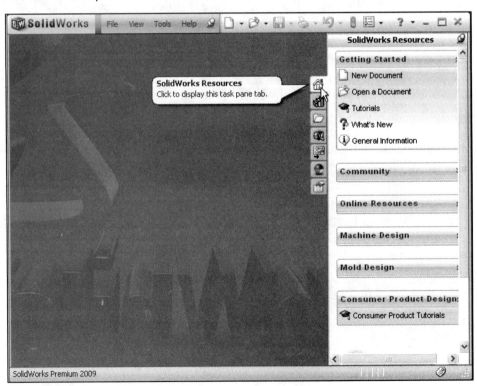

Activity: Understand the SolidWorks User Interface and CommandManager

Menu bar toolbar

SolidWorks 2009 (UI) is design to make maximum use of the Graphics window area. The default Menu bar toolbar contains a set of the most frequently used tool buttons from the Standard toolbar. The available tools are: **New** ⬜ – Creates a new document, **Open** 🗁 – Opens an existing document, **Save** 🖫 – Saves an active document, **Print** 🖶 – Prints an active document, **Undo** 🔙 – Reverses the last action, **Rebuild** 🔴 – Rebuilds the active part, assembly or drawing, **Options** 🔲 – Changes system options and Add-Ins for SolidWorks.

Menu bar menu

Click SolidWorks in the Menu bar toolbar to display the Menu bar menu. SolidWorks provides a Context-sensitive menu structure. The menu titles remain the same for all three types of documents, but the menu items change depending on which type of document is active.

Example: The Insert menu includes features in part documents, mates in assembly documents, and drawing views in drawing documents. The display of the menu is also dependent on the work flow customization that you have selected. The default menu items for an active document are: *File*, *Edit*, *View*, *Insert*, *Tools*, *Window*, *Help*, and *Pin*.

🔆 The Pin 📌 option displays the Menu bar toolbar and the Menu bar menu as illustrated. Throughout the book, the Menu bar menu and the Menu bar toolbar is referred to as the Menu bar.

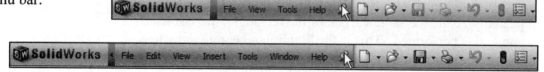

🔆 Until a file is converted to the current version of SolidWorks and saved, a warning icon is displayed on the Save tool as illustrated.

🔆 Expand the drop-down menu to display additional options and tools.

Drop-down menu

SolidWorks takes advantage of the familiar Microsoft®
Windows® user interface. Communicate with SolidWorks
either through the Drop-down menu, Pop-up menu, Shortcut
toolbar, Flyout toolbar or the CommandManager. A command
is an instruction that informs SolidWorks to perform a task.

To close a SolidWorks drop-down menu, press the Esc key.
You can also click any other part of the SolidWorks Graphics
window, or click another drop-down menu.

Right-click Pop-up menus

Right-click in the Graphics window on a model, or in the
FeatureManager on a feature or sketch to display a Context-
sensitive toolbar. If you are in the middle of a command, this
toolbar displays a list of options specifically related to that
command

Consolidated toolbar

Similar commands are grouped together in the
CommandManager. Example: Variations of the Rectangle
sketch tool are grouped in a single fly-out button as illustrated.

If you select the Consolidated toolbar button without
expanding:

- For some commands such as Sketch, the most commonly used
  command is performed. This command is the first listed and
  the command shown on the button.

For commands such as rectangle, where you may want to
repeatedly create the same variant of the rectangle, the last used
command is performed. This is the highlighted command when
the Consolidated toolbar is expanded.

System feedback

SolidWorks provides system feedback by attaching
a symbol to the mouse pointer cursor. The system
feedback symbol indicates what you are selecting or
what the system is expecting you to select.

As you move the mouse pointer across your model, system feedback is provided to you in the form of symbols, riding next to the cursor arrow as illustrated.

Confirmation Corner

When numerous SolidWorks commands are active, a symbol or a set of symbols are displayed in the upper right corner of the Graphics window. This area is called the Confirmation Corner.

When a sketch is active, the confirmation corner box displays two symbols. The first symbol is the sketch tool icon. The second symbol is a large red X. These three symbols supply a visual reminder that you are in an active sketch. Click the sketch symbol icon to exit the sketch and to saves any changes that you made.

When other commands are active, the confirmation corner box provides a green check mark and a large red X. Click the green check mark to execute the current command. Click the large red X to cancel the command.

Heads-up View toolbar

SolidWorks provides the user with numerous view options from the Standard Views, View, and Heads-up View toolbar.

The Heads-up View toolbar is a transparent toolbar that is displayed in the Graphics window when a document is active. You can't hide nor move the Heads-up View toolbar. The following views are available:

Views are document dependent.

For an active Part or assembly document

For an active drawing document

- *Zoom to Fit* : Zooms the model to fit the Graphics window.

- *Zoom to Area* : Zooms to the areas you select with a bounding box.

- *Previous View* : Displays the previous view.

- *Section View* : Displays a cutaway of a part or assembly, using one or more cross section planes.

- *View Orientation* : Provides the ability to select a view orientation or the number of viewports. The available options are: *Top, Isometric, Trimetric, Dimetric, Left, Front, Right, Back, Bottom, Single view, Two view - Horizontal, Two view - Vertical, Four view.*

- *Display Style* : Provides the ability to display the style for the active view. The available options are: *Wireframe, Hidden Lines Visible, Hidden Lines Removed, Shaded, Shaded With Edges.*

- *Hide/Show Items* : Provides the ability to select items to hide or show in the Graphics window. Note: The available items are document dependent.

- *Edit Appearance* : Provides the ability to apply appearances from the Appearances PropertyManager.

- *Apply Scene* : Provides the ability to apply a scene to an active part or assembly document. View the available options.

- *View Setting* : Provides the ability to select the following: *RealView Graphics, Shadows in Shaded Mode,* and *Perspective.*

- *Rotate* : Provides the ability to rotate a drawing view.

- *3D Drawing View* : Provides the ability to dynamically manipulate the drawing view to make a selection.

To deactivate the reference planes for an active document, click **View**, uncheck **Planes** from the Menu bar. To deactivate the grid, click **Options** , **Document Properties** tab. Click **Grid/Snaps**, uncheck the **Display grid** box.

To deactivate a single reference plane in an active document, right-click the **selected plane**, click **Hide**.

Modify the Heads-up View toolbar. Press the **space** key. The Orientation dialog box is display.

Click the **New View** tool. The Name View dialog box is displayed. Enter a new **named** view. Click **OK**. The new view is displayed in the Heads-up View toolbar

CommandManager

The CommandManager is document dependent. Drop-down tabs are located on the bottom left side of the CommandManager and display the available toolbars and features for each corresponding tab.

The default Part tabs are: *Features*, *Sketch*, *Evaluate*, *DimXpert*, and *Office Products*. Below is an illustrated CommandManager for a default Part document.

 The Office Products toolbar display is dependent on the activated Add-Ins during a SolidWorks session.

If you have SolidWorks, SolidWorks Professional, or SolidWorks Premium, the Office Products tab is displayed in the CommandManager.

Instant3D and Rapid Sketch are activated by default.

The CommandManager tabs that are displayed are document dependent and can be work flow customize. To customize the CommandManager tabs, **right-click** on a tab, and select the required **custom** option or select **Customize CommandManager** to access the Customize dialog box.

DimXpert provides the ability to graphically check if the model is fully dimensioned and toleranced. DimXpert automatically recognize manufacturing features. Manufacturing features are *not SolidWorks features*. Manufacturing features are defined in 1.1.12 of the ASME Y14.5M-1994 Dimensioning and Tolerancing standard. See SolidWorks Help for additional information.

FeatureManager Design Tree

The FeatureManager design tree is located on the left side of the SolidWorks Graphics window. The design tree provides a summarize view of the active part, assembly, or drawing document. The tree displays the details on how the part, assembly, or drawing document is created.

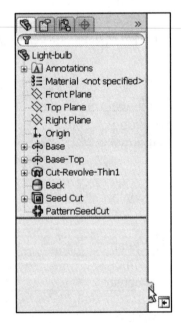

Understand the FeatureManager design tree to troubleshoot your model. The FeatureManager is use extensively throughout this book.

The FeatureManager consist of four default tabs:

- *FeatureManager design tree*
- *PropertyManager*
- *ConfigurationManager*
- *DimXertManager*

Select the Hide FeatureManager Tree Area arrows tab

from the FeatureManager to enlarge the Graphics window for modeling.

The Sensors tool ⬛ Sensors located in the FeatureManager monitors selected properties in a part or assembly and alerts you when values deviate from the specified limits. There are four sensor types: *Mass properties*, *Measurement*, *Interference Detection*, and *Simulation data*.

Various commands provide the ability to control what is
displayed in the FeatureManager design tree. They are:

1. Show or Hide
FeatureManager items.

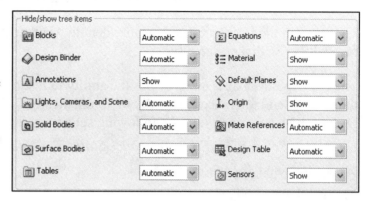

Click **Options** from the
Menu bar. Click
FeatureManager from the
System Options tab. **Customize**
your FeatureManager from the
Hide/Show Tree Items dialog
box.

2. Filter the FeatureManager design tree. Enter information in
the filter field. You can filter by: *Type of features, Feature
names, Sketches, Folders, Mates, User-defined tags*, and
Custom properties.

Tags are keywords you can add to a SolidWorks
document to make them easier to filter and to search. The Tags
icon is located in the bottom right corner of the Graphics
window.

To collapse all items in the FeatureManager, **right-click**
and select **Collapse items**, or press the **Shift +C** keys.

The FeatureManager design tree and the Graphics window are
dynamically linked. Select sketches, features, drawing views,
and construction geometry in either pane.

Split the FeatureManager design tree and either
display two FeatureManager instances, or
combine the FeatureManager design tree with
the ConfigurationManager or PropertyManager.

Rollback
bar

Move between the FeatureManager design tree,
PropertyManager, ConfigurationManager, and
DimXpertManager by selecting the tabs at the
top of the menu.

Press the **s** key to view/access previous command tools in
the Graphics window.

Split the ConfigurationManager and either display two ConfigurationManager instances, or combine the ConfigurationManager with the FeatureManager design tree, PropertyManager, or a third party application that uses the panel.

The icons in the ConfigurationManager denote whether the configuration was created manually or with a design table.

The DimXpertManager tab provides the ability to insert dimensions and tolerances manually or automatically. The DimXpertManager provides the following selections: *Auto Dimension Scheme* , *Show Tolerance Status* , *Copy Scheme* , and *TolAnalyst Study* .

Fly-out FeatureManager

The fly-out FeatureManager design tree provides the ability to view and select items in the PropertyManager and the FeatureManager design tree at the same time.

Throughout the book, you will select commands and command options from the drop-down menu, fly-out FeatureManager, Context toolbar, or from a SolidWorks toolbar.

Another method for accessing a command is to use the accelerator key. Accelerator keys are special keystrokes which activates the drop-down menu options. Some commands in the menu bar and items in the drop-down menus have an underlined character. Press the Alt key followed by the corresponding key to the underlined character activates that command or option.

Press the **g** key to activate the Magnifying glass tool. Use the Magnifying glass tool to inspect a model and make selections without changing the overall view.

Illustrations may vary slightly depending on your SolidWorks version.

Task Pane

The Task Pane is displayed when a SolidWorks session starts. The Task Pane contains the following default tabs: *SolidWorks Resources* 🏠, *Design Library* 🏛️, *File Explorer* 🗁, *SolidWorks Search* 🔍, *View Palette* ⬚, *Appearances/Scenes* 🔵, and *Custom Properties* 📄.

💡 The Document Recovery tab 🗂️ is displayed in the Task Pane if your system terminates unexpectedly with an active document and if auto-recovery is enabled in the System Options section.

SolidWorks Resources

The basic SolidWorks Resources 🏠 menu displays the following default selections: *Getting Started*, *Community*, *Online Resources*, and *Tip of the Day*.

Other user interfaces are available during the initial software installation selection: *Machine Design*, *Mold Design*, or *Consumer Products Design*.

Design Library

The Design Library 🏛️ contains reusable parts, assemblies, and other elements, including library features.

The Design Library tab contains four default selections. Each default selection contains additional sub categories. The default selections are: *Design Library*, *Toolbox*, *3D ContentCentral*, and *SolidWorks Content*.

💡 Click **Tools**, **Add-Ins...**, **SolidWorks Toolbox** and **SolidWorks Toolbox Browser** to active the SolidWorks Toolbox.

💡 To access the Design Library folders in a non network environment for an new installation, click **Add File Location** 🏛️, enter: **C:\Documents and Settings\All Users\Application Data\SolidWorks\SolidWorks 2009\design library**. Click **OK**. In a network environment, contact your IT department for system details.

File Explorer

File Explorer 📂 duplicates Windows Explorer from your local computer and displays *Resent Documents*, *directories*, and the *Open in SolidWorks* and *Desktop* folders

Search

SolidWorks Search 🔍 is installed with Microsoft Windows Search and indexes the resources once before searching begins, either after installation, or when you initiate the first search.

The SolidWorks Search box is display in the upper right corner of the SolidWorks Graphics window. Enter the text or key words to search. Click the drop-down arrow to view the last 10 recent searches.

The Search tool 🔍 in the Task Pane searches the following default locations: *All Locations*, *Local Files*, *Design Library*, *SolidWorks Toolbox*, and *3D ContentCentral*.

💡 Select any or all of the above locations. If you do not select a file location, all locations are searched.

View Palette

The View Palette 📑 tool located in the Task Pane provides the ability to insert drawing views of an active document, or click the Browse button to locate the desired document.

Click and drag the view from the View Palette into an active drawing sheet to create a drawing view.

Appearances/Scenes

Appearances/Scenes 🌐 provide a simplified way to
display models in a photo-realistic setting using a
library of Appearances and Scenes. Note:
Appearances/Scenes require graphics card support.

💡 Appearances/Scenes graphics is only available
with supported graphics cards. For the latest
information on graphics cards that support
Appearances/Scenes Graphics display, visit:
www.solidworks.com/pages/services/videocardtesting.html.

Custom Properties

New in 2009 is the Custom Properties tab located in
the Task Pane. The Custom Properties 🔖 tool
provides the ability to enter custom and configuration
specific properties directly into SolidWorks files.

Document Recovery

If auto recovery is initiated in the System Options section and the system terminates
unexpectedly with an active document, the saved information files are available on the
Task Pane Document Recovery tab the next time you start a SolidWorks session.

Motion Study tab

Motion Studies are graphical simulations of motion for an assembly. Access
MotionManager from the Motion Study tab. The Motion Study tab is located in the
bottom left corner of the Graphics window.

Incorporate visual properties such as lighting and camera perspective. Click the Motion
Study tab to view the MotionManager. Click the Model tab to return to the
FeatureManager design tree.

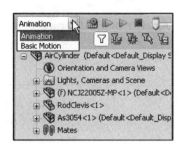

The MotionManager display a timeline-based interface, and provide the following selections from the drop-down menu as illustrated:

Animation: Apply Animation to animate the motion of an assembly. Add a motor and insert positions of assembly components at various times using set key points. Use the Animation option to create animations for motion that does not require accounting for mass or gravity.

Basic Motion. Apply Basic Motion for approximating the effects of motors, springs, collisions, and gravity on assemblies. Basic Motion takes mass into account in calculating motion. Basic Motion computation is relatively fast, so you can use this for creating presentation animations using physics-based simulations. Use the Basic Motion option to create simulations of motion that account for mass, collisions, or gravity.

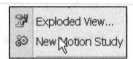

To create a new Motion Study, click **Insert, New Motion Study** from the Menu bar.

There are two modes in the New SolidWorks Document dialog box: Novice and Advanced. The Novice option is the default option with three templates. The Advanced option contains access to more templates.

Activity: Create a new Part

A part is a 3D model which consists of features. What are features?

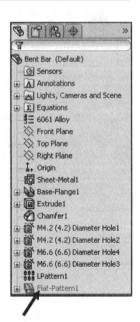

- Features are geometry building blocks.

- Features add or remove material.

- Features are created from 2D or 3D sketched profiles or from edges and faces of existing geometry.

- Features are an individual shape that combined with other features, makes up a part or assembly. Some features, such as bosses and cuts, originate as sketches. Other features, such as shells and fillets, modify a feature's geometry.

- Features are displayed in the FeatureManager as illustrated.

You can suppress a feature, as is *Flat-Pattern1* in the Bent Bar FeatureManager. A suppress feature is display in light gray.

The first sketch of a part is the Base sketch. The Base sketch is the foundation for the 3D model.

Create a new part.

6) Click **New** from the Menu bar. The New SolidWorks Document dialog box is displayed.

Select Advanced Mode.

7) Click the **Advanced** button to display the New SolidWorks Document dialog box in Advance mode.

8) The Templates tab is the default tab. Part is the default template from the New SolidWorks Document dialog box. Click **OK**.

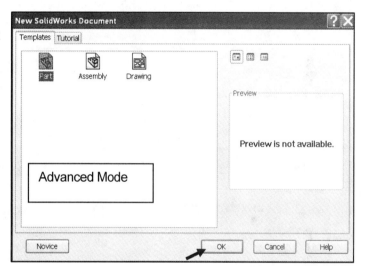

The Advanced mode remains selected for all new documents in the current SolidWorks session. When you exit SolidWorks, the Advanced mode setting is saved.

The default SolidWorks installation contains two tabs in the New SolidWorks Document dialog box: Templates and Tutorial.

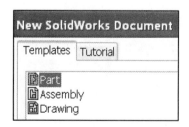

The Templates tab corresponds to the default SolidWorks templates.

The Tutorial tab corresponds to the templates utilized in the SolidWorks Online Tutorials.

Part1 is displayed in the FeatureManager and is the name of the document. Part1 is the default part window name. The Menu bar, CommandManager, FeatureManager, Heads-up View toolbar, SolidWorks Resources, SolidWorks Search, Task Pane, and the Origin are displayed in the Graphics window.

The Origin ⊥ is displayed in blue in the center of the Graphics window. The Origin represents the intersection of the three default reference planes: *Front Plane*, *Top Plane*, and *Right Plane*. The positive X-axis is horizontal and points to the right of the Origin in the Front view. The positive Y-axis is vertical and point upward in the Front view. The FeatureManager contains a list of features, reference geometry, and settings utilized in the part.

The Tags icon is displayed in the bottom right corner of the Graphics window. Tags are keywords you add to SolidWorks documents and features to make them easier to filter and search for.

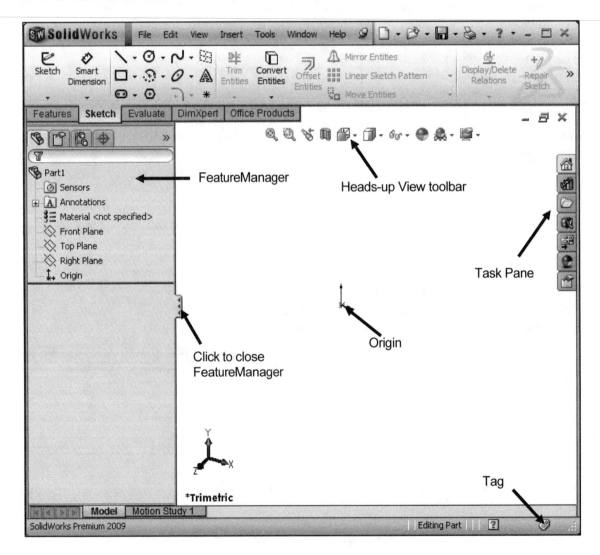

🔅 In the book, Reference planes and Grid/Snaps are deactivated in the Graphics window to improve model clarity.

The CommandManager is document dependent. The tabs are located on the bottom left side of the CommandManager and display the available toolbars and features for each corresponding tab. The default tabs for a Part are: *Features*, *Sketch*, *Evaluate*, *DimXpert*, and *Office Products*.

🔅 The Features icon and Features toolbar should be selected by default in Part mode.

The CommandManager is utilized in this text. Control the CommandManager display.

Right-click in the gray area to the right of the Options 🔲 ⁻ icon in the Menu bar toolbar. A complete list of toolbars is displayed. Check CommandManager if required.

🔅 Another way to display a toolbar, click **View, Toolbars** from the Menu bar menu. Select the required toolbar.

Select individual toolbars from the View, Toolbars list to display in the Graphics window. Reposition toolbars by clicking and dragging.

🔅 Click **View**, **Origins** from the Menu bar menu to display the Origin in the Graphics window.

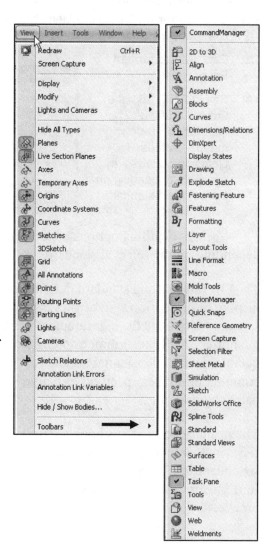

Activity: Create the AXLE Part

Set the Menu bar toolbar and Menu bar menu.
9)   Click **SolidWorks** to expand the Menu bar menu.

10)   Pin the Menu bar as illustrated. Use both the Menu bar menu and the Menu bar toolbar in this book.

🔆 The SolidWorks Help Topics contains step-by-step instructions for various commands. The Help 💡 icon is displayed in the dialog box or in the PropertyManager for each feature.

Set the Document Properties.
11)   Click **Options** 📧 from the Menu bar. The System Options General dialog box is displayed

12)   Click the **Document Properties** tab.

13)   Select **ANSI** from the Overall drafting standard drop-down menu. Various Detailing options are available depending on the selected standard.

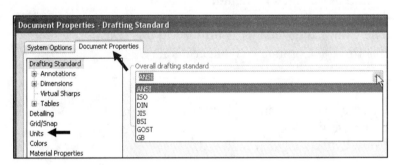

🔆 Various detailing options are available depending on the selected standard.

The Overall drafting standard determines the display of dimension text, arrows, symbols, and spacing. Units are the measurement of physical quantities. Millimeter dimensioning and decimal inch dimensioning are the two most common unit types specified for engineering parts and drawings.

The primary units in this book are provided in IPS, (inch, pound, seconds). The optional secondary units are provided in MMGS, (millimeters, grams, second) and are indicated in brackets [ ].

Illustrations are provided in both inches and millimeters.

Set the document units.

14) Click **Units**.

15) Click **IPS** (inch, pound, second) **[MMGS]** for Unit system.

16) Select **.123**, **[.12]** (three decimal places) for Length basic units.

17) Select **None** for Angle decimal places.

18) Click **OK** from the Document Properties - Units dialog box. The Part FeatureManager is displayed.

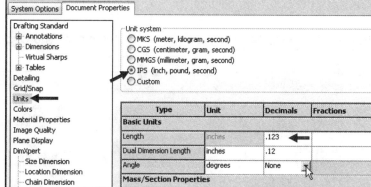

Activity: AXLE Part-Extruded Base Feature

Insert a new sketch for the Extruded Base feature.

19) Right-click **Front Plane** from the FeatureManager. This is your Sketch plane. The Context toolbar is displayed.

20) Click **Sketch** 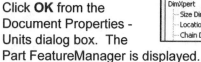 from the Context toolbar as illustrated.

The Sketch toolbar is displayed. Front Plane is your Sketch plane. Note: the grid is deactivated for picture clarity.

💡 You can also click the Front Plane from the FeatureManager and click the Sketch tab from the CommandManager.

21)   Click the **Circle** ⊘ tool from the Sketch toolbar. The Circle PropertyManager is displayed.

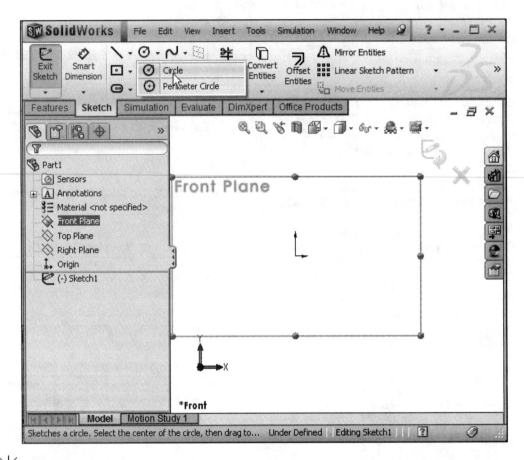

💡 The Circle-based tool uses a Consolidated Circle PropertyManager. The SolidWorks application defaults to the last used tool type.

22)   Drag the **mouse pointer** into the Graphics window. The cursor displays the Circle icon symbol ⊘ .

23)   Click the **Origin** ↳ of the circle. The cursor displays the Coincident to point feedback symbol.

24)   Drag the **mouse pointer** to the right of the Origin to create the circle as illustrated. The center point of the circle is positioned at the Origin.

25)   Click a **position** to create the circle. The activated circle is
displayed in blue.

Add a dimension.

26)   Click **Smart Dimension** ✧ from the Sketch
toolbar. The cursor displays the Smart

Dimension icon ✎.

27)   Click the **circumference** of the circle.

28)   Click a **position** diagonally above the circle in the Graphics
window.

29)   Enter **.188**in, **[4.78]** in the Modify dialog box.

30)   Click the **Green Check mark** ✓
in the Modify dialog box. The
diameter of the circle is .188
inches.

💡 If required, click the blue arrow
head dots to toggle the direction of the dimension arrow.

The circular sketch is centered at the Origin. The dimension
indicates the diameter of the circle.

💡 If your sketch is not correct, select the Undo ↺ tool.

💡 To fit your sketch to the Graphics window, press the f
key.

Extrude the sketch to create the Extruded Base Feature.
31)   Click the **Features** tab from the CommandManager.

32)   Click the **Extruded Boss/Base** 🗔 Features tool. The Extrude
PropertyManager is displayed. Blind is the default End Condition
in Direction 1.

33)   Select **Mid Plane** for End Condition in Direction 1.

34)   Enter **1.375**in, **[34.93]** for Depth in Direction 1. Accept the default
conditions.

35)   Click **OK** ✓ from the Extrude PropertyManager. Exturde1 is
displayed in the FeatureManager.

Fit the model to the Graphics window.
36) Press the **f** key. Note the location
of the Origin in the model.

Origin

The Extrude PropertyManager displays the parameters utilized to
define the feature. The Mid Plane End Condition in the
Direction 1 box extrudes the sketch equally on both sides of the
Sketch plane. The depth defines the extrude distance.

The Extrude1 feature name is displayed in the FeatureManager.
The FeatureManager lists the features, planes, and other geometry
that construct the part. Extrude features add material. Extrude
features require the following: *Sketch plane*, *Sketch*, and *depth*.

The Sketch plane is the Front Plane. The Sketch is a circle with
the diameter of .188in, [4.76]. The Depth is 1.375in, [34.93].

Activity: AXLE Part-Save

Save the part.
37) Click **Save As** from the Menu bar.

38) Double-click the **MY-DOCUMENTS** file folder.

39) Click the **Create New Folder** icon.

40) Enter **SW-TUTORIAL-2009** for the file
folder name.

41) Double-click the **SW-TUTORIAL-2009**
file folder. SW-TUTORIAL-2009 is the
Save in file folder name.

42) Enter **AXLE** for the File name.

43) Enter **AXLE ROD** for the Description.

44) Click **Save**. The AXLE FeatureManager is displayed.

 Organize parts into file folders. The file folder for this project is named: SW-TUTORIAL-2009. Save all documents in the SW-TUTORIAL-2009 file folder.

 Copy all files from the CD in the book to the SW-TUTORIAL-2009 folder.

Activity: AXLE Part-Edit Color

Modify the color of the part.

45) Right-click the **AXLE** AXLE icon at the top of the FeatureManager.

46) Click the **Appearances** drop down arrow.

47) Click the **Appearance** box as illustrated. The Appearances PropertyManager is displayed. AXLE is displayed in the Selection box.

48) Select a **light blue** color from the Color box.

49) Click **OK** from the Color And Optics PropertyManager. View the AXLE in the Graphics window.

The SolidWorks FeatureManager design tree provides an indicator informing you on the status of your sketch. The sketch can either be:

1.) *(+) Over defined.* The sketch is displayed in red.

2.) *(-) Under defined.* The sketch is displayed in blue.

3.) *(?) Cannot be solved.*

4.) *No prefix.* The sketch is fully defined. This is the ideal state. A fully defined sketch has complete information and is displayed in black.

☀ The SketchXpert PropertyManager provides the ability to diagnose an over defined sketch to create a fully defined sketch.

If you have an over defined sketch, click Over Defined at the bottom of the Graphics window toolbar. The SketchXpert PropertyManager is displayed. Click the Diagnose button.

Select the desired solution and click the Accept button from the Results box.

Activity: AXLE Part-View Modes

Orthographic projection is the process of projecting views onto Parallel planes with ⊥ projectors.

The default reference planes are the Front, Top and Right Planes.

The Isometric view displays the part in 3D with two equal projection angles.

☀ The Heads-up View toolbar illustration may vary depending on your SolidWorks release version.

Origin

Display the various view modes using the Heads-up View toolbar.

50) Click **Front view** 🔲 from the Heads-up View toolbar.

51) Click **Top view** 🔲 from the Heads-up View toolbar.

52) Click **Right view** 🔲 from the Heads-up View toolbar.

53)   Click **Isometric view** from the Heads-up View toolbar.

💡 View modes manipulate the model in the Graphics window.

Display the various View modes.
54)   Press the lower case **z** key to zoom out.

55)   Press the upper case **Z** key to zoom in.

56)   Click **Zoom to Fit** 🔍 to display the full size of the part in the current window.

57)   **Right-click** in the Graphics window. View the available view tools.

58)   Click **inside** the Graphics window.

Rotate the model.
59)   Click the **middle mouse** button and move your mouse. The model rotates. The Rotate icon 🔄 is displayed.

60)   Press the **up arrow** on your key board. The arrow keys rotate the model in 15 degree increments.

💡 View modes remain active until deactivated from the View toolbar or unchecked from the pop-up menu.

💡 Utilize the center wheel of the mouse to Zoom In/Zoom Out and Rotate the model in the Graphics window.

View the various Display Styles.
61)   Click **Isometric view** from the Heads-up View toolbar.

62)   Click the **drop down arrow** from the Display Styles box from the Heads-up Views toolbar as illustrated. SolidWorks provides five key Display Styles:

- *Shaded* 🔲. Displays a shaded view of the model with no edges.

- *Shaded With Edges* 🔲. Displays a shaded view of the model, with edges.

- *Hidden Lines Removed* . Displays only those model edges that can be seen from the current view orientation.

- *Hidden Lines Visible* . Displays all edges of the model. Edges that are hidden from the current view are displayed in a different color or font.

- *Wireframe* . Displays all edges of the model.

Save the AXLE part.

63) Click **Save** . The AXLE part is complete.

     Review the AXLE Part

The AXLE part utilized an Extruded Base feature. The Extruded Base feature adds material. The Extruded feature required a Sketch plane, sketch, and depth. The AXLE Sketch plane was the Front Plane. The 2D circle was sketched centered at the Origin. A dimension defined the overall size of the sketch based on the dimensions of mating parts in the LINKAGE assembly.

The name of the feature is Extrude1. Extrude1 utilized the Mid Plane End Condition. The Extrude1 feature is symmetrical about the Front plane.

The Edit Color option modified the part color. Select the Part icon in the FeatureManager to modify the color of the part. Color and a prefix defines the sketch status. A blue sketch is under defined. A black sketch is fully defined. A red sketch is over defined.

The default Reference planes are the Front, Top, and Right Planes. Utilize the Heads-up View toolbar to display the principle views of a part. The View Orientation and Display Style tools manipulate the model in the Graphics windows.

Instant3D provides the ability to click and drag geometry and dimension manipulator points to resize features in the Graphics window, and to use on-screen rulers to measure modifications. In this book, you will primarily use the PropertyManager and dialog boxes to create and modify model dimensions.

SHAFT-COLLAR Part

The SHAFT-COLLAR part is a hardened steel ring
fastened to the AXLE part.

Two SHAFT-COLLAR parts are used to position the two
FLATBAR parts on the AXLE.

Create the SHAFT-COLLAR part.

Utilize the Extruded Base 🗗 feature. The Extruded Base
feature requires a 2D circular profile.

Utilize symmetry. Sketch a circle on the Front Plane centered at
the Origin.

Extrude the sketch with the Mid Plane End Condition. The
Extruded Base feature is centered on both sides of the Front
Plane.

[11.11]
Ø.438

The Extruded Cut 🖽 feature removes material. Utilize an
Extruded Cut feature to create a hole. The Extruded Cut feature
requires a 2D circular profile. Sketch a circle on the front face
centered at the Origin.

SHAFT-COLLAR

The Through All End Condition extends the Extruded Cut
feature from the front face through all existing geometry.

Activity: SHAFT-COLLAR Part-Extruded Base Feature

Create a new part.

64) Click **New** ⬜ from the Menu bar. The New SolidWorks
Document dialog box is displayed. The Templates tab is the
default tab. Part is the default template from the New
SolidWorks Document dialog box.

65) Double-click **Part**. The Part FeatureManager is displayed.

Save the part.

66) Click **Save As** from the Menu bar.

67) Enter **SHAFT-COLLAR** for File name in the SW-TUTORIAL-2009 folder.

68) Enter **SHAFT-COLLAR** for Description.

69) Click **Save**. The SHAFT-COLLAR FeatureManager is displayed.

Set the Dimension standard and part units.

70) Click **Options** 🖺 , **Document Properties** tab from the Menu bar.

71) Select **ANSI** from the Overall drafting standard drop-down menu.

72) Click **Units**.

73) Click **IPS** (inch, pound, second), [**MMGS**] for Unit system.

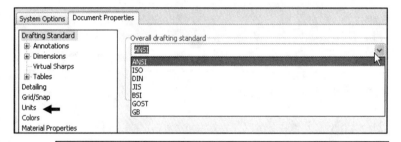

74) Select **.123**, [**.12**] (three decimal places) for Length units Decimal places.

75) Select **None** for Angular units Decimal places.

76) Click **OK** from the Document Properties - Units dialog box.

🔆 To view the Origin, click **View**, **Origins** from the Menu bar menu.

🔆 Press the **g** key to activate the Magnifying glass tool. Use the Magnifying glass tool to inspect a model and make selections without changing the overall view.

Insert a new sketch for the Extruded Base feature.

77) Right-click **Front Plane** from the FeatureManager. This is the Sketch plane. The Context toolbar is displayed.

78) Click **Sketch** ✏ from the Context toolbar as illustrated. The Sketch toolbar is displayed.

79) Click the **Circle** ⊘ tool from the Sketch toolbar. The Circle PropertyManager is displayed. The cursor displays the Circle icon symbol ⊘ .

80) Click the **Origin** ↳. The cursor displays the Coincident to point feedback symbol.

81) Drag the **mouse pointer** to the right of the Origin as illustrated.

82) Click a **position** to create the circle.

Add a dimension.

83) Click **Smart Dimension** ⟨ from the Sketch toolbar. Click the **circumference** of the circle. The cursor displays the diameter feedback symbol.

84) Click a **position** diagonally above the circle in the Graphics window.

85) Enter **.4375**in, [**11.11**] in the Modify dialog box.

86) Click the **Green Check mark** ✔ in the Modify dialog box. The black sketch is fully defined.

Note: Three decimal places are displayed. The diameter value .4375 rounds to .438.

Extrude the sketch to create the Base feature.

87) Click the **Features** tab from the CommandManager.

88) Click the **Extruded Boss/Base** 🔲 features tool. The Extrude PropertyManager is displayed.

89) Select **Mid Plane** for End Condition in Direction 1. Enter **.250**in, [**6.35**] for Depth. Accept the default conditions. Note the location of the Origin.

90) Click **OK** ✔ from the Extrude PropertyManager. Extrude1 is displayed in the FeatureManager.

Fit the model to the Graphics window.

91) Press the **f** key.

92) Click **Isometric view** from the Heads-Up View toolbar.

Save the model.

93) Click **Save** .

Activity: SHAFT-COLLAR Part-Extruded Cut Feature

Insert a new sketch for the Extruded Cut feature.

94) Right-click the **front circular face** of the Extrude1 feature for the Sketch plane. The mouse pointer displays the face feedback icon.

🔆 View the mouse pointer feedback icon for the correct geometry: line, face, point, or vertex.

95) Click **Sketch** from the Context toolbar as illustrated. The Sketch toolbar is displayed.

96) Click **Hidden Lines Removed** from the Heads-up View toolbar.

97) Click the **Circle** tool from the Sketch toolbar. The Circle PropertyManager is displayed. The cursor displays the Circle icon symbol .

98) Click the red **Origin** . The cursor displays the Coincident to point feedback symbol. Drag the **mouse pointer** to the right of the Origin.

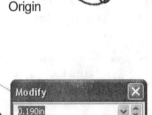

99) Click a **position** to create the circle as illustrated.

Origin

Add a dimension.

100) Click the **Smart Dimension** Sketch tool.

101) Click the **circumference** of the circle.

102) Click a **position** diagonally above the circle in the Graphics window.

103) Enter **.190**in, **[4.83]** in the Modify dialog box.

104) Click the **Green Check mark** in the Modify dialog box.

Insert an Extruded Cut feature.
105) Click the **Features** tab from the CommandManager.

106) Click **Extruded Cut** 🔲 from the Features toolbar. The Extrude PropertyManager is displayed.

107) Select **Through All** for End Condition in Direction 1. The direction arrow points to the right. Accept the default conditions.

108) Click **OK** ✔ from the Extrude PropertyManager. Extrude2 is displayed in the FeatureManager,

🔆 The Extruded Cut feature is named Extrude2. The Through All End Condition removes material from the Front Plane through the Extrude1 geometry.

Activity: SHAFT-COLLAR-Modify Dimensions and Edit Color

Modify the dimensions.

109) Click **Trimetric view** 🔲 from the Heads-up View toolbar.

110) Click the **z** key a few times to Zoom in.

111) Click the **outside cylindrical face** of the SHAFT-COLLAR. The Extrude1 dimensions are displayed. Sketch dimensions are displayed in black. The Extrude depth dimensions are displayed in blue.

112) Click the **.250**in, **[6.35]** depth dimension.

113) Enter **.500**in, **[12.70]**.

The Extrude1 and Extrude2 are modified.

Return to the original dimensions.
114) Click the **Undo** 🔄 tool from the Menu bar.

115) Click **Shaded With Edges** 🔲 from the Heads-up View toolbar.

Modify the part color.

116) Right-click the **SHAFT-COLLAR Part**
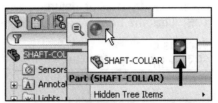
SHAFT-COLLAR icon at the top of the FeatureManager.

117) Click the **Appearances** drop-down arrow.

118) Click the **Appearance** box as illustrated. The Appearances PropertyManager is displayed. AXLE is displayed in the Selection box.

119) Select a **light green** color from the Color box.

120) Click **OK** ✔ from the Appearances PropertyManager. View the SHAFT-COLLAR in the Graphics window.

Save the SHAFT-COLLAR part.

121) Click **Save** 🖫 . The SHAFT-COLLAR part is complete.

Review the SHAFT-COLLAR Part

The SHAFT-COLLAR utilized an Extruded Base 🗗 feature. The Extruded Base feature adds material. An Extruded feature required a Sketch plane, sketch, and depth.

The Sketch plane was the Front Plane. The 2D circle was sketched centered at the Origin. A dimension defined the overall size of the sketch.

The name of the feature was Extrude1. Extrude1 utilized the Mid Plane End Condition. The Extrude1 feature was symmetric about the Front Plane.

The Extruded Cut 🗖 feature removed material to create the hole. The Extruded Cut feature default named is Extrude2. The Through All End Condition option created the Extrude2 feature. Feature dimensions were modified. The Edit Color option was utilized to modify the part color.

🔆 Click **Options**, **Document Properties** tab, **Dimension** and click the **Smart box** to have the dimension leader arrow head point inwards for ANSI.

The SolidWorks Help contains step-by-step instructions for various commands. The Help 💡 icon is displayed in the dialog box or in the PropertyManager for each feature.

Display Help for a rectangle.

122) Click **Help** from the Menu bar.

123) Click **SolidWorks Help**.

124) Click the **Index** tab.

125) Enter **rectangles**. The description is displayed in the right window.

126) Close ⊠ the Help window.

The Help option contains tools to assist the user.
SolidWorks Help contains the following tabs:

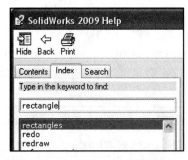

- **Contents**: Contains the SolidWorks Online User's Guide documents.

- **Index**: Contains additional information on key words.

- **Search**: To locate information.

Display the SolidWorks Tutorials.

127) Click **Help** from the Menu bar.

128) Click **SolidWorks Tutorials**. The SolidWorks Tutorials categories are displayed.

129) Click the **Getting Started** category. Review Lesson 1. This is a great location for additional information.

130) Close ☒ the SolidWorks Tutorial dialog box. Return to the Graphics window.

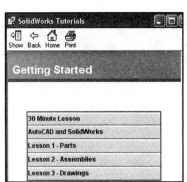

FLATBAR Part

The FLATBAR part fastens to the AXLE.
The FLATBAR contains nine, ∅.190in holes
spaced 0.5in apart.

The FLATBAR part is manufactured from
.090inch 6061 alloy.

Create the FLATBAR part. Utilize the new
Straight Slot Sketch ⬚ tool with an Extruded
Base 🗔 feature.

The Extruded feature requires a 2D profile
sketched on the Front Plane.

The Straight Slot Sketch tool automatically
applies design symmetry, (Midpoint and Equal
geometric relations). Create the 2D profile
centered about the Origin.

First Point   Second Point

Relations control the size and
position of entities with
constraints.

Utilize an Extruded Cut 🔲 feature to create
the first hole. This is the seed feature for the
Linear Pattern.

Utilize a Linear Pattern 🔳 feature to create the remaining holes. A Linear Pattern
creates an array of features in a specified direction.

Activity: FLATBAR Part-Extruded Base Feature

Create a new part.

131) Click **New** ⬚ from the Menu bar. The New SolidWorks
Document dialog box is displayed. The Templates tab is the
default tab. Part is the default template from the New SolidWorks
Document dialog box.

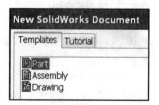

132) Double-click **Part**. The Part FeatureManager is displayed.

Save the part.
133) Click **Save As** from the Menu bar.

134) Enter **FLATBAR** for File name in the SW-TUTORIAL-2009 folder

135) Enter **FLAT BAR 9 HOLES** for Description.

136) Click **Save**. The FLATBAR FeatureManager is displayed.

Set the Dimension standard and part units.

137) Click **Options**, **Document Properties** tab from the Menu bar.

138) Select **ANSI** from the Overall drafting standard drop-down menu.

139) Click **Units**.

140) Click **IPS**, [**MMGS**] for Unit system.

141) Select **.123**, [**.12**] for Length units Decimal places.

142) Select **None** for Angular units Decimal places.

143) Click **OK** to set the document units.

Insert a new sketch for the Extruded Base feature.

144) Right-click **Front Plane** from the FeatureManager. This is the Sketch plane.

145) Click **Sketch** from the Context toolbar as illustrated. The Sketch toolbar is displayed.

Utilize the new Consolidated Slot Sketch toolbar. Apply the Centerpoint Straight Slot Sketch tool. The Straight Slot Sketch tool provides the ability to sketch a straight slot from a centerpoint. In this example, use the Origin as your centerpoint.

146) Click the **Centerpoint Straight Slot** tool from the Sketch toolbar. The Slot PropertyManager is displayed.

Create the Straight Slot with three points.
147) Click the **Origin**. This is your first point.

148) Click a **point** directly to the right of the Origin. This is your second point.

149) Click a **point** directly above the second point. This is your third point. The Straight Slot is displayed.

First Point   Second Point

150) Click **OK** ✔ from the Slot PropertyManager

View the Sketch relations.
151) Click **View**, **Sketch Relations** from the Menu bar menu. View the sketch relations in the Graphics window.

Deactivate the Sketch relations.
152) Click **View**, uncheck **Sketch Relations** from the Menu bar. The Straight Slot Sketch tool provides a midpoint relation with the Origin and Equal relations between the other sketch entities.

Add a dimension.
153) Click the **Smart Dimension** ✎ tool from the Sketch toolbar.

154) Click the **horizontal centerline**.

155) Click a **position** above the top horizontal line in the Graphics window.

156) Enter **4.000**in, **[101.60]** in the Modify dialog box.

157) Click the **Green Check mark** ✔ in the Modify dialog box.

158) Click the **right arc** of the FLATBAR.

159) Click a **position** diagonally to the right in the Graphics window.

160) Enter **.250**in, **[6.35]** in the Modify dialog box.

161) Click the **Green Check mark** ✔ in the Modify dialog box. The black sketch is fully defined.

Extrude the sketch to create the Base feature.

162) Click **Extruded Boss/Base** from the Features toolbar. The Extrude PropertyManager is displayed.

163) Enter .090in, [**2.29**] for Depth. Accept the default conditions.

164) Click **OK** ✓ from the Extrude PropertyManager. Extrude1 is displayed in the FeatureManager.

Fit the model to the Graphics window.
165) Press the **f** key.

Save the FLATBAR part.
166) Click **Save** 💾.

💡 Click **View, Origins** from the Menu bar menu to display the Origin in the Graphics window.

Activity: FLATBAR Part-Extruded Cut Feature

Insert a new sketch for the Extruded Cut Feature.
167) Right-click the **front face** of the Extrude1 feature in the Graphics window. This is the Sketch plane. Extrude1 is highlighted in the FeatureManager.

168) Click **Sketch** from the Context toolbar as illustrated. The Sketch toolbar is displayed.

Display the Front view.
169) Click **Front view** from the Heads-up View toolbar.

170) Click **Hidden Lines Removed** from the Heads-up View toolbar.

The process of placing the mouse pointer over an existing arc to locate its centerpoint is called "wake up".

Wake up the center point.

171) Click the **Circle** ⊘ Sketch tool from the Sketch toolbar. The Circle PropertyManager is displayed.

Center point of the arc

172) Place the **mouse pointer** on the left arc. Do not click. The center point of the slot arc is displayed.

173) Click the **centerpoint** of the arc.

174) Click a **position** to the right of the center point to create the circle as illustrated.

Add a dimension.

175) Click the **Smart Dimension** ✦ Sketch tool.

176) Click the **circumference** of the circle.

177) Click a **position** diagonally above and to the left of the circle in the Graphics window.

178) Enter **.190**in, **[4.83]** in the Modify box.

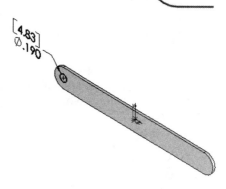

[4.83]
⌀.190

179) Click the **Green Check mark** ✓ in the Modify dialog box.

180) Click **Isometric view** ⬚ from the Heads-up View toolbar.

181) Click **Shaded With Edges** ▱ from the Heads-up View toolbar.

Insert an Extruded Cut feature.

182) Click the **Features** tab from the CommandManager.

183) Click **Extruded Cut** ▣ from the Features toolbar. The Extrude PropertyManager is displayed.

[4.83]
⌀.190

184) Select **Through All** for End Condition in Direction 1. The direction arrow points to the back. Accept the default conditions.

185) Click **OK** ✓ from the Extrude PropertyManager. The Extrude2 feature is displayed in the FeatureManager.

Save the FLATBAR part.

186) Click **Save** 💾.

Direction 1
Through All

The blue Extrude2 icon indicates that the feature is selected.

Select features by clicking their icons in the FeatureManager or by selecting their geometry in the Graphics window.

Activity: FLATBAR Part-Linear Pattern Feature

Create a Linear Pattern feature.

187) Click the **Linear Pattern** tool from the Features toolbar. The Linear Pattern PropertyManager is displayed. Extrude2 is displayed in the Features to Pattern box. Note: If Extrude2 is not displayed, click inside the Features to Pattern box. Click Extrude2 from the fly-out FeatureManager.

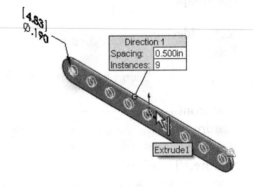

188) Click the **top edge** of the Extrude1 feature for Direction1 in the Graphics window. Edge<1> is displayed in the Pattern Direction box.

189) Enter **0.5**in, [**12.70**] for Spacing.

190) Enter **9** for Number of Instances. Instances are the number of occurrences of a feature.

191) The Direction arrow points to the right.

Click the **Reverse Direction** button if required.

192) Geometry Pattern is check by default. Click **OK** from the Linear Pattern PropertyManager. The LPattern1 feature is displayed in the FeatureManager.

Save the FLATBAR part.

193) Click **Save** . The FLATBAR part is complete.

Close all documents.
194) Click **Windows, Close All** from the Menu bar.

 Review the FLATBAR Part

The FLATBAR part utilized an Extruded Base 🔲 feature as the first feature. The Sketch plane was the Front Plane. The 2D sketch utilized the Straight Slot Sketch tool to create the slot profile.

You added linear and radial dimensions to define your sketch. You applied the Extruded Base feature with a Blind End Condition in Direction 1. Extrude1 is created.

You created a circle sketch for the Extruded Cut feature on the front face of Extrude1.

The front face was your Sketch plane for the Extruded Cut feature. The Extruded Cut 🔲 feature removed material to create the hole. The Extruded Cut feature default name is Extrude2. The Through All End Condition option in Direction 1 created the Extrude2 feature. The Extrude2 feature is the seed feature for the Linear Pattern of holes.

The Linear Pattern ⣿ feature created an array of 9 holes, equally spaced along the length of the FLATBAR part.

LINKAGE Assembly

An assembly is a document that contains two or more parts. An assembly inserted into another assembly is called a sub-assembly. A part or sub-assembly inserted into an assembly is called a component. The LINKAGE assembly consists of the following components: AXLE, SHAFT-COLLAR, FLATBAR, and AirCylinder sub-assembly.

Establishing the correct component relationship in an assembly requires forethought on component interaction. Mates are geometric relationships that align and fit components in an assembly. Mates remove degrees of freedom from a component.

Mate Types

Mates reflect the physical behavior of a component in an
assembly. The components in the LINKAGE assembly utilize
Standard mate types. Review the Standard, Advanced, and
Mechanical mate types.

Standard Mates:

Components are assembled with various mate types. The
Standard mate types are:

Coincident Mate: Locates the selected faces, edges, or planes
so they use the same infinite line. A Coincident mate positions
two vertices for contact

Parallel Mate: Locates the selected items to lie in the same
direction and to remain a constant distance apart.

Perpendicular Mate: Locates the selected items at a 90 degree
angle to each other.

Tangent Mate: Locates the selected items in a tangent mate. At
least one selected item must be either a conical, cylindrical,
spherical face.

Concentric Mate: Locates the selected items so they can share the
same center point.

Lock Mate: Maintains the position and orientation between two
components.

Distance Mate: Locates the selected items with a specified distance
between them. Use the drop-down arrow box or enter the distance
value directly.

Angle Mate: Locates the selected items at the specified angle to each
other. Use the drop-down arrow box or enter the angle value directly.

There are two Mate Alignment options. The Aligned option
positions the components so that the normal vectors from the selected
faces point in the same direction. The Anti-Aligned option positions the
components so that the normal vectors from the selected faces point in
opposite directions.

Mates reflect the physical behavior of a component in an assembly. In this project, the two most common mate types are Concentric and Coincident.

Advanced Mates:

The Advanced mate types are:

Symmetric Mate: Positions two selected entities to be symmetric about a plane or planar face. A Symmetric Mate does not create a Mirrored Component.

Width Mate: Centers a tab within the width of a groove.

Path Mate: Constrains a selected point on a component to a path.

Linear/Linear Coupler Mate: Establishes a relationship between the translation of one component and the translation of another component.

Distance Mate: Locates the selected items with a specified distance between them. Use the drop-down arrow box or enter the distance value directly.

Angle Mate: Locates the selected items at the specified angle to each other. Use the drop-down arrow box or enter the angle value directly.

Mechanical Mates:

The Mechanical mate types are:

Cam Mate: Forces a plane, cylinder, or point to be tangent or coincident to a series of tangent extruded faces.

Hinge Mate: Limits the movement between two components to one rotational degree of freedom.

Gear Mate: Forces two components to rotate relative to one another around selected axes.

Rack Pinion Mate: Provides the ability to have Linear translation of a part, rack causes circular rotation in another part, pinion, and vice versa.

Screw Mate: Constrains two components to be concentric, and also adds a pitch relationship between the rotation of one component and the translation of the other.

Universal Joint Mate: The rotation of one component (the output shaft) about its axis is driven by the rotation of another component (the input shaft) about its axis.

Example: Utilize a Concentric mate between the AXLE cylindrical face and the FLATBAR Extruded Cut feature, (hole). Utilize a Coincident mate between the SHAFT-COLLAR back face and the FLATBAR front flat face.

The LINKAGE assembly requires the AirCylinder assembly. The AirCylinder assembly is located on the SolidWorks Tutorial Multimedia CD in the Pneumatic Components folder.

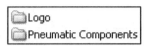

Activity: AirCylinder Assembly-Open and Save As option

Copy the folders and files from the CD in the book.
195) Minimize the SolidWorks Graphics window.

196) Insert the CD from the book into your computer. If required, **exit** out of AutoPlay for the Multi-media movies.

197) Right-click your CD drive icon.

198) Click **Explore**. View the available folders.

199) Copy the folders and files from the CD to your SW-TUTORIAL-2009 folder on the hard drive.

Return to SolidWorks. Create a new assembly.
200) Maximize the SolidWorks Graphics window.

201) Click **New** ⬚ from the Menu bar. The New SolidWorks Document dialog box is displayed. The Templates tab is the default tab.

202) Double-click **Assembly** from the New SolidWorks Document dialog box. The Begin Assembly PropertyManager is displayed.

203) Click the **Browse** button.

204) Double-click the **AirCylinder** assembly from the SW-TUTORIAL-2009/Pneumatic Components folder. The AirCylinder assembly is displayed in the Graphics window.

🔅 If an assembly or component is loaded in a Lightweight 🪶 state, right-click the **assembly name** or **component name** from the FeatureManager. Click **Set Lightweight to Resolved**.

205) Click **OK** ✓ from the Begin Assembly PropertyManager to fix the AirCylinder assembly in the Graphics window. The (f) symbol is placed in front of the AirCylinder name in the FeatureManager.

206) If required, click **Yes** to Rebuild.

207) Click **Save As** from the Menu bar.

208) Select **SW-TUTORIAL-2009** for Save in folder.

209) Enter **LINKAGE** for file name.

210) Click the **References** button.

211) Click the **Browse** button from the Specify folder for selected items.

212) Select the **SW-TUTORIAL-2009** folder.

213) Click **OK** from the Browse For Folder dialog box.

214) Click **Save All**. The LINKAGE assembly FeatureManager is displayed.

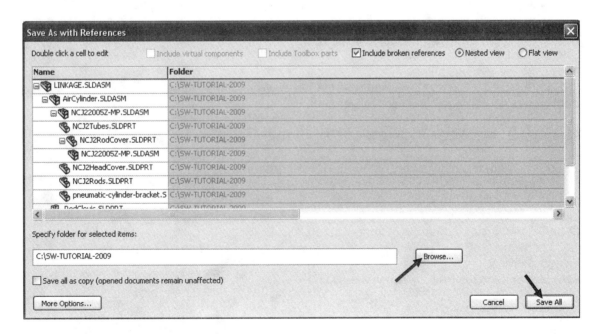

The AirCylinder assembly and its references are copied to the SW-TUTORIAL-2009 folder. Assemble the AXLE to the holes in the RodClevis.

Display the RodClevis component in the FeatureManager.

215) **Expand** the AirCylinder assembly in the FeatureManager.

216) Click **RodClevis<1>** from the FeatureManager. Note: The RodClevis is displayed in blue in the Graphics window.

If required hide the Origins.
217) Click **View**, uncheck **Origins** from the Menu bar.

The AirCylinder is the first component in the LINKAGE assembly and is fixed (f) to the LINKAGE assembly Origin.

Display an Isometric view.
218) Click **Isometric view** from the Heads-up View toolbar.

Insert the AXLE part.
219) Click the **Assembly** tab in the CommandManager.

220) Click the **Insert Components** Assembly tool. The Insert Component PropertyManager is displayed.

221) Click the **Browse** button.

222) Select **All Files** from the Files of type box.

223) Double-click **AXLE** from the SW-TUTORIAL-2009 folder.

224) Click a **position** to the front of the AirCylinder assembly as illustrated.

Move the AXLE component.
225) Click and drag a **position** in front of the RODCLEVIS.

Enlarge the view.
226) **Zoom in** on the RodClevis and the AXLE.

Insert a Concentric mate.
227) Click the **Mate** tool from the Assembly toolbar. The Mate PropertyManager is displayed.

228) Click the inside **front hole face** of the RodClevis. The cursor displays the face feedback symbol.

229) Click the **long cylindrical face** of the AXLE. The cursor displays the face feedback symbol. The selected faces are displayed in the Mate Selections box. Concentric mate is selected by default. The AXLE is positioned concentric to the RodClevis hole.

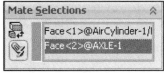

230) Click the **Green Check mark** ✔ as illustrated.

Move the AXLE.
231) Click and drag the **AXLE** left to right. The AXLE translates in and out of the RodClevis holes.

The Mate Pop-up toolbar is displayed after selecting the two cylindrical faces. The Mate Pop-up toolbar minimizes the time required to create a mate.

Lock   Flip Mate Alignment

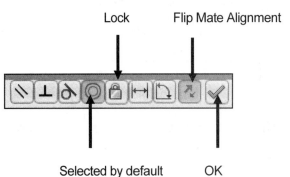

Selected by default   OK

Position the mouse pointer in the middle of the face to select the entire face. Do not position the mouse pointer near the edge of the face. If the wrong face or edge is selected, perform one of the following actions:

- Click the face or edge again to remove it from the Mate Selections box.

- Right-click in the Graphics window. Click Clear Selections to remove all geometry from the Items Selected text box.

- Right-click in the Mate Selections box to either select Clear Selections or to delete a single selection.

- Utilize the Undo button to begin the Mate command again.

Display the Top view.
232) Click **Top view** ⬚ from the Heads-up View toolbar.

Expand the LINKAGE assembly and components in the fly-out FeatureManager.
233) Expand the LINKAGE assembly from the fly-out FeatureManager.

234) Expand the AirCylinder assembly from the fly-out FeatureManager.

235) Expand the AXLE part from the fly-out FeatureManager.

236) Expand the Features folder.

Clear all sections from the Mate Selections box.
237) Right-click **Clear Selections** inside the Mate Selections box.

Insert a Coincident mate.
238) Click the **Front Plane** of the AirCylinder assembly from the fly-out FeatureManager.

239) Click the **Front Plane** of the AXLE part from the fly-out FeatureManager. The selected planes are displayed in the Mate Selections box. Coincident mate is selected by default.

240) Click the **Green Check mark** ✓.

241) Click **OK** ✓ from the Mate PropertyManager.

The AirCylinder Front Plane and the AXLE Front Plane are Coincident. The AXLE is centered in the RodClevis.

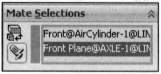

💡 Display the Mates in the FeatureManager to check that the components and the Mate types correspond to the design intent. Note: If you delete a Mate and then recreate it, the Mate numbers will be in a different order.

Display an Isometric view.
242) Click **Isometric view** 🔲 from the Heads-up View toolbar.

Display the Mates in the folder.
243) Expand the Mates folder in the FeatureManager. View the created mates.

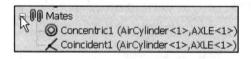

Save the LINKAGE assembly.
244) Click **Save** 💾.

Activity: LINKAGE Assembly-Insert FLATBAR Part

Insert the FLATBAR part.

245) Click the **Insert Components** 🖪 Assembly tool. The Insert Component PropertyManager is displayed. Click the **Browse** button.

246) Select **Part** for Files of type from the SW-TUTORIAL-2009 folder.

247) Double-click **FLATBAR**.

Place the component in the assembly.
248) Click a **position** in the Graphics window as illustrated. Note: Use the z key to Zoom out if required.

Enlarge the view.
249) Zoom in on the AXLE and the left side of the FLATBAR to enlarge the view.

Insert a Concentric mate.

250) Click the **Mate** 🔖 tool from the Assembly toolbar. The Mate PropertyManager is displayed. If required, right-click **Clear Selections** inside the Mate Selections box.

251) Click the inside **left hole face** of the FLATBAR.

252) Click the **long cylindrical face** of the AXLE. The selected faces are displayed in the Mate Selections box. Concentric is selected by default.

253) Click the **Green Check mark** ✅ .

Fit the model to the Graphics window.
254) Press the **f** key.

Move the FLATBAR.
255) Click and drag the **FLATBAR**. The FLATBAR translates and rotates along the AXLE.

Insert a Coincident mate.
256) Click the **front face** of the FLATBAR.

257) Press the **left arrow key** approximately 5 times to rotate the model and to view the back face of the RodClevis.

258) Click the **back face** of the RodClevis as illustrated. The selected faces are displayed in the Mate Selections box. Coincident is selected by default.

259) Click the **Green Check mark** ✔ .

260) Click **OK** ✔ from the Mate
PropertyManager.

Display the Isometric view.

261) Click **Isometric view** 🔲 from the
Heads-up View toolbar.

Insert the second FLATBAR component.

262) Click the **Insert Components** 🖐
Assembly tool. The Insert Component
PropertyManager is displayed.

263) Click the **Browse** button.

264) Select **Part** for Files of type from the
SW-TUTORIAL-2009 folder.

265) Double-click **FLATBAR**.

266) Click a **position** to the front of the
AirCylinder in the Graphics window as
illustrated.

Enlarge the view.

267) **Zoom in** on the second FLATBAR and
the AXLE.

Insert a Concentric mate.

268) Click the **Mate** 🖉 tool from the
Assembly tool. The Mate
PropertyManager is displayed.

269) Click the **left inside hole face** of the
second FLATBAR.

270) Click the **long cylindrical face** of the
AXLE. The selected faces are
displayed in the Mate Selections box.
Concentric is selected by default.

271) Click the **Green Check mark** ✔ .

272) Click and drag the **second FLATBAR** to the front.

Fit the model to the Graphics window.

273) Press the **f** key.

Insert a Coincident mate.

274) Press the **left arrow key** approximately 5 times to rotate the model to view the back face of the second FLATBAR.

275) Click the **back face** of the second FLATBAR.

276) Press the **right arrow key** approximately 5 times to rotate the model to view the front face of the RodClevis.

277) Click the **front face** of the RodClevis. The selected faces are displayed in the Mate Selections box. Coincident is selected by default.

278) Click the **Green Check mark** ✔.

Insert a Parallel mate.

279) Press the **Shift-z** keys to Zoom in on the model.

280) Click the **top narrow face** of the first FLATBAR.

281) Click the **top narrow face** of the second FLATBAR. The selected faces are displayed in the Mate Selections box.

282) Click **Parallel** ╲.

283) Click the **Green Check mark** ✔.

284) Click **OK** ✔ from the Mate PropertyManager.

285) Click **Isometric view** 🧊 from the Heads-up View toolbar.

Move the two FLATBAR parts.

286) Click and drag the **second FLATBAR**. Both FLATBAR parts move together.

View the Mates folder.

287) **Expand** the Mates folder from the FeatureManager. View the created mates.

Activity: LINKAGE Assembly-Insert SHAFT-COLLAR Part

Insert the first SHAFT-COLLAR.

288) Click the **Insert Components** 🖱 Assembly tool. The Insert Component PropertyManager is displayed.

289) Click the **Browse** button.

290) Select **Part** for Files of type from the SW-TUTORIAL-2009 folder.

291) Double-click **SHAFT-COLLAR**.

292) Click a **position** to the back of the AXLE as illustrated.

Enlarge the view.

293) Click the **Zoom to Area** 🔍 tool.

294) Zoom-in on the SHAFT-COLLAR and the AXLE component.

Deactivate the tool.

295) Click the **Zoom to Area** 🔍 tool.

Insert a Concentric mate.

296) Click the **Mate** 🖇 tool from the Assembly toolbar. The Mate PropertyManager is displayed.

297) Click the inside **hole face** of the SHAFT-COLLAR.

298) Click the **long cylindrical face** of the AXLE. The selected faces are displayed in the Mate Selections box. Concentric is selected by default.

299) Click the **Green Check mark** ✔.

Insert a Coincident mate.
300) Press the **Shift-z** keys to Zoom in on the model.

301) Click the **front face** of the SHAFT-COLLAR as illustrated.

302) Press the **left arrow key** approximately 5 times to rotate the model to view the back face of the first FLATBAR.

303) Click the **back face** of the first FLATBAR. The selected faces are displayed in the Mate Selections box. Coincident is selected by default.

304) Click the **Green Check mark** ✔.

305) Click **OK** ✔ from the Mate PropertyManager.

Display the Isometric view.

306) Click **Isometric view** from the Heads-up View toolbar.

Insert the second SHAFT-COLLAR.

307) Click the **Insert Components** Assembly tool. The Insert Component PropertyManager is displayed.

308) Click the **Browse** button.

309) Select **Part** for Files of type from the SW-TUTORIAL-2009 folder.

310) Double-click **SHAFT-COLLAR**.

311) Click a **position** near the AXLE as illustrated.

Enlarge the view.

312) Click the **Zoom to Area** tool.

313) **Zoom-in** on the second SHAFT-COLLAR and the AXLE to enlarge the view.

314) Click the **Zoom to Area** tool to deactivate the tool.

Insert a Concentric mate.

315) Click **Mate** from the Assembly toolbar. The Mate PropertyManager is displayed.

316) Click the **inside hole face** of the second SHAFT-COLLAR.

317) Click the **long cylindrical face** of the AXLE. Concentric is selected by default. The selected faces are displayed in the Mate Selections box.

318) Click the **Green Check mark** ✔.

Insert a Coincident mate.

319) Click the **back face** of the second SHAFT-COLLAR.

320) Click the **front face** of the second FLATBAR. The selected faces are displayed in the Mate Selections box. Coincident is selected by default.

321) Click the **Green Check mark** ✔.

322) Click **OK** ✔ from the Mate PropertyManager.

323) **Expand** the Mates folder. View the created mates.

Display an Isometric view.

324) Click **Isometric view** 🔲 from the Heads-up View toolbar.

Fit the model to the Graphics window.

325) Press the **f** key.

Save the LINKAGE assembly.

326) Click **Save** 💾. The LINKAGE assembly is complete.

  Review the LINKAGE Assembly

An assembly is a document that contains two or more parts. A part or sub-assembly inserted into an assembly is called a component. You created the LINKAGE assembly.

The AirCylinder sub-assembly was the first component inserted into the LINKAGE assembly. The AirCylinder assembly was obtained from the CD in the book and copied to the SW-TUTORIAL-2009 folder.

The AirCylinder assembly was fixed to the Origin. The Concentric and Coincident mates added Geometric relationships between the inserted components in the LINKAGE assembly.

The AXLE part was the second component inserted into the LINKAGE assembly. The AXLE required a Concentric mate between the two cylindrical faces and a Coincident mate between two the Front Planes.

The FLATBAR part was the third component inserted into the LINKAGE assembly. The FLATBAR required a Concentric mate between the two cylindrical faces and a Coincident mate between the two flat faces.

A second FLATBAR was inserted into the LINKAGE assembly. A Parallel mate was added between the two FLATBARs.

Two SHAFT-COLLAR parts were inserted into the LINKAGE assembly. Each SHAFT-COLLAR required a Concentric mate between the two cylindrical faces and a Coincident mate between the two flat faces.

Motion Study – Basic Motion Tool

Motion Studies are graphical simulations of motion for assembly models. You can incorporate visual properties such as lighting and camera perspective into a motion study. Motion studies do not change an assembly model or its properties. They simulate and animate the motion you prescribe for your model. Use SolidWorks mates to restrict the motion of components in an assembly when you model motion.

Create a Motion Study. Select the Basic Motion option from the MotionManager. The Basic Motion option provides the ability to approximate the effects of motors, springs, collisions and gravity on your assembly. Basic Motion takes mass into account in calculating motion. Note: The Animation option does not!

Activity: LINKAGE Assembly-Basic Motion

Insert a Rotary Motor using the Motion Study tab.

327) Click the **Motion Study 1** tab located in the bottom left corner of the Graphics window. The MotionManager is displayed.

328) Select **Basic Motion** for Type of study from the MotionManager drop-down menu as illustrated.

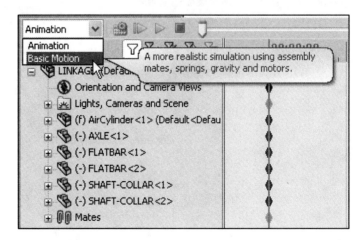

329) Click **Motor** from the MotionManager. The Motor PropertyManager is displayed.

330) Click the **Rotary Motor** box.

331) Click the **FLATBAR front face** as illustrated. A red Rotary Motor icon is displayed. The red direction arrow points counterclockwise.

332) Enter **150 RPM** for speed in the Motion box.

333) Click **OK** from the Motor PropertyManager.

Record the Simulation.

334) Click **Calculate** . The FLATBAR rotates in a counterclockwise direction for a set period of time.

335) Click **Play** . View the simulation.

Linear Assembly Basic Simulation

Save the simulation in an AVI file to the SW-
TUTORIAL-2009 folder.
336) Click **Save Animation**.

337) Click **Save** from the Save Animation to File dialog
box. View your options.

338) Click **OK** from the Video Compression box.

Close the Motion Study and return to SolidWorks.
339) Click the **Model** tab location in the bottom left corner
of the Graphics window.

Fit the assembly to the Graphics window.
340) Press the **f** key.

Save the LINKAGE assembly.
341) Click **Save** 💾 .

Exit SolidWorks.
342) Click **Windows**, **Close All** from the Menu bar.

The LINKAGE assembly project is complete.

 Review the Motion Study

The Rotary Motor Basic Motion tool combined Mates and Physical Dynamics to rotate
the FLATBAR components in the LINKAGE assembly. The Rotary Motor was applied
to the front face of the FLATBAR. You utilized the Calculate option to play the
simulation. You saved the simulation in an .AVI file.

🔍 Additional details on Motion Study, Assembly, mates, and Simulation are available
in SolidWorks Help. Keywords: Motion Study and Basic Motion.

Project Summary

In this project you created three parts, copied the AirCylinder assembly from the CD in the book, and created the LINKAGE assembly.

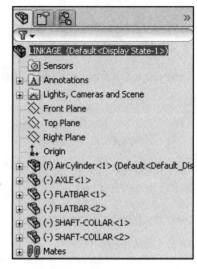

You developed an understanding of the SolidWorks User Interface: Menus, Toolbars, Task Pane, CommandManager, FeatureManager, System feedback icons, Document Properties, Parts, and Assemblies.

You created 2D sketches and addressed the three key states of a sketch: *Fully Defined*, *Over Defined*, and *Under Defined*. Note: Always review your FeatureManager for the proper Sketch state.

You obtained the knowledge of the following SolidWorks features: Extruded Base, Extruded Cut, and Linear Pattern. Features are the building blocks of parts. The Extruded Boss/Base feature required a Sketch plane, sketch, and depth.

The Extruded Boss/Base feature added material to a part. The Extruded Base feature was utilized in the AXLE, SHAFT-COLLAR, and FLATBAR parts.

The Extruded Cut feature removed material from the part. The Extruded Cut feature was utilized to create a hole in the SHAFT-COLLAR, and FLATBAR parts.

The Linear Pattern feature was utilized to create an array of holes in the FLATBAR part.

When parts are inserted into an assembly, they are called components. You created the LINKAGE assembly by inserting the AirCylinder assembly, AXLE, SHAFT-COLLAR, and FLATBAR parts.

Mates are geometric relationships that align and fit components in an assembly. Concentric, Coincident, and Parallel mates were utilized to assemble the components.

You created a Motion Study. The Rotary Motor Basic Motion tool combined Mates and Physical Dynamics to rotate the FLATBAR components in the LINKAGE assembly.

 If an assembly or component is loaded in a Lightweight state, right-click the **assembly name** or **component name** from the FeatureManager. Click **Set Lightweight to Resolved**.

Project Terminology

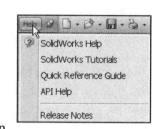

Utilize SolidWorks Help for additional information on the terms utilized in this project.

Assembly: An assembly is a document which contains parts, features, and other sub-assemblies. When a part is inserted into an assembly it is called a component. Components are mated together. The filename extension for a SolidWorks assembly file name is .SLDASM.

Component: A part or sub-assembly within an assembly.

Cursor Feedback: Feedback is provided by a symbol attached to the cursor arrow indicating your selection. As the cursor floats across the model, feedback is provided in the form of symbols, riding next to the cursor.

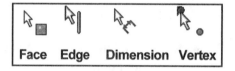

Dimension: A value indicating the size of feature geometry.

Drafting Standard: A set of drawing and detailing options developed by national and international organizations. The Dimensioning standard options are: ANSI, ISO, DIN, JIS, BSI, GOST and GB.

Features: Features are geometry building blocks. Features add or remove material. Features are created from sketched profiles or from edges and faces of existing geometry.

Instance Number: The instance number increments every time you insert the same component or mate. If you delete a component or mate and then reinsert the component or mate in the same SolidWorks session, the instance number increments by one.

Mates: A mate is a geometric relationship between components in an assembly.

Mouse Buttons: The left and right mouse buttons have distinct meanings in SolidWorks. Left mouse button is utilized to select geometry. Right-mouse button is utilized to invoke commands.

Part: A part is a single 3D object made up of features. The filename extension for a SolidWorks part file name is .SLDPRT.

Plane: To create a sketch, select a plane. Planes are flat and infinite. They are represented on the screen with visible edges. The reference plane for this project is the Front Plane.

Relation: A relation is a geometric constraint between sketch entities or between a sketch entity and a plane, axis, edge, or vertex.

Sketch: The name to describe a 2D profile is called a sketch. 2D Sketches are created on flat faces and planes within the model. Typical geometry types are lines, arcs, rectangles, circles, polygons and ellipses.

Status of a Sketch: Three states are utilized in this Project:

- *Fully Defined*: Has complete information, (Black), *Over Defined*: Has duplicate dimensions, (Red), or *Under Defined*: There is inadequate definition of the sketch, (Blue).

Toolbars: The toolbar menus provide shortcuts enabling you to quickly access the most frequently used commands.

Trim Entities: Deletes selected sketched geometry. Extends a sketch segment unit it is coincident with another entity.

Units: Used in the measurement of physical quantities. Millimeter dimensioning and decimal inch dimensioning are the two types of common units specified for engineering parts and drawings.

Project Features

Extruded Boss/Base: An Extruded Base feature is the first feature in a part. The Extruded Boss/Base feature starts with either a 2D or 3D sketch. An Extruded Boss feature occurs after the Extruded Base feature. The Extruded Boss/Base feature adds material by extrusion. Steps to create an Extruded Boss/Base Feature:

- Select the Sketch plane; Sketch the profile; Add needed dimensions and Geometric relations; Select Extruded Boss/Base from the Features toolbar; Select an End Condition and/or options; Enter a depth; Click OK from the Extrude PropertyManager.

Extruded Cut: The Extruded Cut feature removes material from a solid. The Extruded Cut feature performs the opposite function of the Extruded Boss/Base feature. The Extruded Cut feature starts with either a 2D or 3D sketch and removes material by extrusion. Steps to create an Extruded Cut Feature:

- Select the Sketch plane; Sketch the profile, Add Dimensions and Relations; Select Extruded Cut from the Features toolbar; Select an End Condition and/or options; Enter a depth; Click OK from the Extrude PropertyManager.

Linear Pattern: A Linear Pattern repeats features or geometry in an array. A Linear Patten requires the number of instances and the spacing between instances. Steps to create a Linear Pattern Feature:

- Select the features to repeat; Select Linear Pattern from the Feature toolbar; Enter Direction of the pattern; Enter Number of pattern instances in each direction; Enter Distance between pattern instances; Optional: Pattern instances to skip; Click OK from the Linear Pattern PropertyManager.

Engineering Journal

Engineers and designers utilize mathematics, science, economics and history to calculate additional information about a project. Answers to questions are written in an engineering journal.

1. Volume of a cylinder is provided by the formula, $V = \pi r^2 h$. Where:

- V is volume.

- r is the radius.

- h is the height.

a) Determine the radius of the AXLE in mm.

b) Determine the height of the AXLE in mm.

c) Calculate the Volume of the AXLE in mm^3.

2. Density of a material is provided by the formula: $\rho = m/V$. Where:

    - ρ is density.

    - m is mass.

    - V is volume.

a) Determine the mass of the AXLE in grams if the AXLE is manufactured from hardened steel. The density of hardened steel is .007842 g/mm^3.

```
_____

_____
```

3. The material supplier catalog lists Harden Steel Rod in foot lengths.

Harden Steel Rod (Ø 3/16):		
Part Number:	Length:	Cost:
23-123-1	1 ft	$10.00
23-123-2	2 ft	$18.00
23-123-3	3 ft	$24.00

Utilize the table above to determine the following questions:

How many 1-3/8 inch AXLES can be cut from each steel rod?

Twenty AXLE parts are required for a new assembly. What length of Harden Steel Rod should be purchased?

```
_____

_____

_____

_____

_____
```

4. Air is a gas. Boyle's Law states that with constant temperature, the pressure, P of a given mass of a gas is inversely proportional to its volume, V.

    * $P_1 / P_2 = V_2 / V_1$

    * $P_1 \times V_1 = P_2 \times V_2$

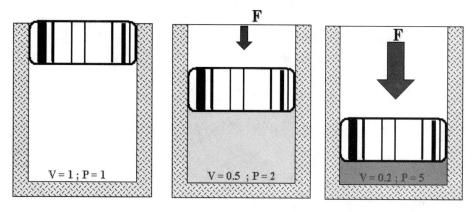

Illustration of Boyle's Law
Courtesy of SMC Corporation of America

The pressure in a closed container is doubled. How will the volume of air inside the container be modified?

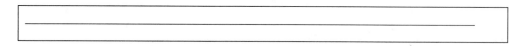

Robert Boyle (1627-1691) was an Irish born, English scientist, natural philosopher and a founder of modern chemistry. Boyle utilized experiments and the scientific method to test his theories. Along with his student, Robert Hooke (1635-1703), Boyle developed the air pump.

Research other contributions made by Robert Boyle and Robert Hooke that are utilized today.

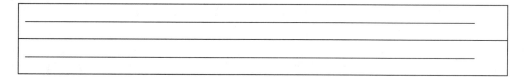

Questions

1. Explain the steps in starting a SolidWorks session.

2. Describe the procedure to begin a new 2D sketch.

3. Explain the steps required to modify part unit dimensions from inches to millimeters.

4. Describe the procedure to create a simple 3D part with an Extruded Base feature.

5. Identify the three default Reference planes.

6. Describe a Base feature? Provide two examples from this Project.

7. Describe the differences between an Extruded Base feature and an Extruded Cut feature.

8. The sketch color black indicates a sketch is _____ defined.

9. The sketch color blue indicates a sketch is _____ defined.

10. The sketch color red indicates a sketch is _____ defined.

11. Describe the procedure to "wake up" a centerpoint.

12. Define a Geometric relation. Provide an example.

13. Describe the procedure to create a Linear Pattern feature.

14. Describe an assembly or sub-assembly.

15. What are mates and why are they important in assembling components?

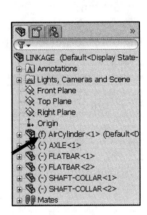

16. In an assembly, each component has_____# degrees of freedom? Name them.

17. True or False. A fixed component cannot move in an assembly.

18. Review the Design Intent section in the book. Identify how you incorporated design intent into the parts and assembly.

Exercises

Exercise 1.1: Identify the Sketch plane for the **Extrude1 (Base) feature as illustrated**.

A: Top Plane

B: Front Plane

C: Right Plane

D: Left Plane

Correct answer _____.

Create the part. Dimensions are arbitrary.

Origin

Exercise 1.2: Identify the Sketch plane for the Extrude1 (Base) feature as illustrated.

A: Top Plane

B: Front Plane

C: Right Plane

D: Left Plane

Correct answer _____.

Create the part. Dimensions are arbitrary.

Origin

Exercise 1.3: Identify the Sketch plane for the Extrude1 (Base) feature as illustrated.

A: Top Plane

B: Front Plane

C: Right Plane

D: Left Plane

Correct answer _____.

Create the part. Dimensions are arbitrary.

Origin

Exercise 1.4: FLATBAR-3HOLE.

Create the FLATBAR-3HOLE part.

- Utilize the Front Plane for the Sketch plane. Insert an Extruded Base feature.

- Create an Extruded Cut feature. This is your seed feature. Apply the Linear Pattern feature. The FLATBAR–3HOLE part is manufactured from 0.060in, [1.5mm] 6061 Alloy.

FLATBAR-3HOLE

Exercise 1.5: FLATBAR-5HOLE.

Create the FLATBAR-5HOLE part as illustrated.

- Utilize the Front Plane for the Sketch plane. Insert an Extruded Base feature.

- Create an Extruded Cut feature. This is your seed feature. Apply the Linear Pattern feature. The FLATBAR–5HOLE part is manufactured from 0.060in, [1.5mm] 6061 Alloy.

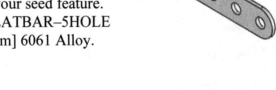

- Calculate the required dimensions for the FLATBAR-5HOLE part. Use the following information: Holes are .500in on center, Radius is .250in, and Hole diameter is .190in.

FLATBAR-5HOLE

Exercise 1.6

Create the illustrated part. Note the location of the Origin in the illustration.

- Calculate the overall mass of the illustrated model.

- Apply the Mass Properties tool.

- Think about the steps that you would take to build the model.

- Review the provided information carefully.

- Units are represented in the IPS, (inch, pound, second) system.

- A = 3.50in, B = .70in

Given:
A = 3.50
B = .70
Material: 1060 Alloy
Density = 0.0975 lb/in^3
Units: IPS
Decimal places = 2

Exercise 1.7

Create the illustrated part. Note the location of the Origin in the illustration.

- Calculate the overall mass of the illustrated model.

- Apply the Mass Properties tool.

- Think about the steps that you would take to build the model.

- Review the provided information carefully. Units are represented in the IPS, (inch, pound, second) system.

- A = 3.00in, B = .75in

- Note: The part is symmetrical.

Given:
A = 3.00
B = .75
Material: Copper
Density = 0.321 lb/in^3
Units: IPS
Decimal places = 2

Exercise 1.8

Create the illustrated part. Note the location of the Origin in the illustration.

- Calculate the volume of the part and locate the Center of mass with the provided information.

- Apply the Mass Properties tool.

- Think about the steps that you would take to build the model.

- Review the provided information carefully.

Given:
A = 3.30
B = 2.00
Material: 2014 Alloy
Density = .101 lb/in^3
Units: IPS
Decimal places = 2

Exercise 1.9

Create the part from the illustrated drawing: Front, Top, Right, and Isometric views. Note: The location of the Origin in the illustration.

- Apply 1060 Alloy for material.

- Calculate the Volume of the part and locate the Center of mass.

- Think about the steps that you would take to build the model. The part is symmetric about the Front Plane.

Exercise 1.10

Create the part from the illustrated drawing: Front, Top, Right, and Isometric views.

- Apply 1060 Alloy for material.

- The part is symmetric about the Front Plane.

- Calculate the Volume of the part and locate the Center of mass.

- Think about the steps that you would take to build the model.

Exercise 1.11:
LINKAGE-2 Assembly.

Create the LINKAGE-2 assembly.

- Open the LINKAGE assembly. If required, set the LINKAGE assembly to (**Set Lightweight to Resolved**).

- Select Save As from the Menu bar.

- Check the Save as copy check box.

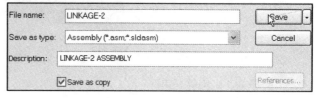

- Enter LINKAGE-2 for file name. LINKAGE-2 ASSEMBLY for description.

The FLATBAR-3HOLE part was created in
Exercise 1.1. Utilize two AXLE parts, four SHAFT
COLLAR parts, and two FLATBAR-3HOLE parts
to create the LINKAGE-2 assembly as illustrated.

- Insert the first AXLE part.

- Insert a Concentric mate.

- Insert a Coincident mate.

- Insert the first FLATBAR-3HOLE part.

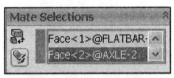

- Insert a Concentric
  mate.

- Insert a Coincident
  mate.

- Perform the same
  procedure for the
  second FLATBAR-
  3HOLE part.

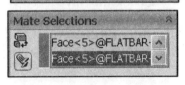

- Insert a Parallel mate
  between the 2
  FLATBAR-3HOLE parts. Note: The 2 FLATBAR-
  3HOLE parts move together.

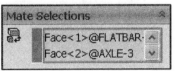

- Insert the second AXLE part.

- Insert a Concentric mate.

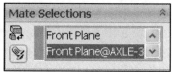

- Insert a Coincident mate.

- Insert the first SHAFT-COLLAR part.

- Insert a Concentric mate.

- Insert a Coincident mate.

- Perform the same tasks to insert the other three required SHAFT-COLLAR parts as illustrated.

Exercise 1.12: LINKAGE-2 Assembly Motion Study.

Create a Motion Study using the LINKAGE-2 Assembly that was created in the previous exercise.

- Create a Basic Motion Study.

- Apply a Rotary Motor to the front FLATBAR-3HOLE as illustrated.

- Play and Save the Simulation.

Exercise 1.13: **ROCKER Assembly**.

Create a ROCKER assembly. The ROCKER assembly
consists of two AXLE parts, two FLATBAR-5HOLE
parts, and two FLATBAR-3HOLE parts.

The FLATBAR-3HOLE parts are linked together with
the FLATBAR-5HOLE.

The three parts rotate clockwise and counterclockwise,
above the Top Plane. Create the ROCKER assembly.

- Insert the first FLATBAR-5HOLE part. The
  FLATBAR-5HOLE is fixed to the Origin of the
  ROCKER assembly.

- Insert the first AXLE part.

- Insert a Concentric mate.

- Insert a Coincident mate.

- Insert the second AXLE part.

- Insert a Concentric mate.

- Insert a Coincident mate.

- Insert the first FLATBAR-3HOLE part.

- Insert a Concentric mate.

- Insert a Coincident mate.

- Insert the second FLATBAR-
  3HOLE part.

- Insert a Concentric mate.

- Insert a Coincident mate.

- Insert the second FLATBAR-5HOLE part.

- Insert the required mates.

Note: The end holes of the second FLATBAR-5HOLE are concentric with the end holes of the FLATBAR-3HOLE parts.

Note: In mechanical design, the ROCKER assembly is classified as a mechanism. A Four-Bar Linkage is a common mechanism comprised of four links.

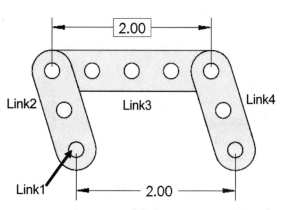

Link1 is called the Frame.

The AXLE part is Link1.

Link2 and Link4 are called the Cranks.

The FLATBAR-3HOLE parts are Link2 and Link4. Link3 is called the Coupler. The FLATBAR-5HOLE part is Link3.

If an assembly or component is loaded in a Lightweight state, right-click the **assembly name** or **component name** from the FeatureManager. Click **Set Lightweight to Resolved**.

Exercise 1.14: Industry Application.

Engineers and designers develop a
variety of products utilizing
SolidWorks.

Model information is utilized to
create plastic molds for products
from toys to toothbrushes.

- Utilize the World Wide Web
  and review the following web
  sites: mikejwilson.com and
  zxys.com.

The models obtained from these
web sites are for educational
purposes only.

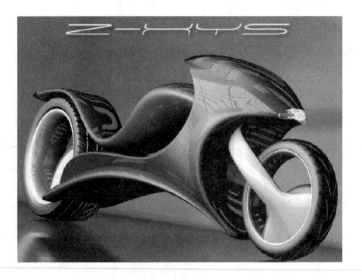

Model Courtesy of
Mike J. Wilson,
CSWP

Learn modeling techniques from
others; create your own designs. A
common manufacturing procedure for
plastic parts is named the Injection
Molding Process. Today's automobiles
utilize over 50% plastic components.

Engineers and designers work with mold
makers to produce plastic parts. Cost
reduction drives plastic part production.

Project 2

FRONT-SUPPORT Assembly

Below are the desired outcomes and usage competencies based on the completion of Project 2.

Desired Outcomes:	Usage Competencies:

• Create four parts:
 	
    o HEX-STANDOFF
 	
    o ANGLE-13HOLE
 	
    o TRIANGLE
 	
    o SCREW
	• Apply the following model features: Extruded Boss/Base, Extruded Thin, Extruded Cut, Revolved Boss/Base, Hole Wizard, Linear Pattern, Circular Pattern, Mirror, Fillet, and Chamfer.
	
	• Apply sketch techniques with various sketch tools and Construction geometry.

• Create an assembly: o FRONT-SUPPORT assembly	• Comprehend the assembly process and insert the following Standard mate types: Concentric, Coincident, Parallel, and Distance.

Notes:

Project 2 – FRONT-SUPPORT Assembly

Project Objective

Create four new parts utilizing the Top, Front, and Right Planes. Determine the Sketch plane for each feature. Obtain the knowledge of the following SolidWorks features: *Extruded Boss/Base, Extruded Thin, Extruded Cut, Revolved Boss/Base, Hole Wizard, Linear Pattern, Circular Pattern, Fillet, and Chamfer.*

Apply sketch techniques with various Sketch tools: *Line, Circle, Corner Rectangle, Centerline, Dynamic Mirror, Straight Slot, Trim Entities, Polygon, Tangent Arc, Sketch Fillet, Offset Entities, and Convert Entities.* Utilize centerlines as construction geometry to reference dimensions and relationships.

Create four new parts:

1. HEX-STANDOFF
2. ANGLE-13HOLE
3. TRIANGLE
4. SCREW

Create the FRONT-SUPPORT assembly.

On the completion of this project, you will be able to:

- Select the correct Sketch plane.
- Generate a 2D sketch.
- Insert the required dimensions and Geometric relations.
- Apply the following SolidWorks features:
  - Extruded Base
  - Extruded Boss
  - Extruded Cut
  - Extruded Thin
  - Revolved Base
  - Linear and Circular Pattern
  - Mirror
  - Fillet
  - Hole Wizard
  - Chamfer

Project Overview

The FRONT-SUPPORT assembly supports various pneumatic components and is incorporated into the final PNEUMATIC-TEST-MODULE in Project 5.

Create four new parts in this Project:

1. HEX-STANDOFF

2. ANGLE-13HOLE

3. TRIANGLE

4. SCREW

HEX-STANDOFF

ANGLE-13HOLE

Create the FRONT-SUPPORT assembly using the four new created parts.

The FRONT-SUPPORT assembly is used in the exercises at the end of this Project and in a later Project of the book.

To display the Origin, click **View**, **Origins** from the Menu bar menu.

TRIANGLE

SCREW

FRONT-SUPPORT

Reference Planes and Orthographic Projection

The three default ⊥ Reference planes represent infinite 2D planes in 3D space:

- Front
- Top
- Right

Planes have no thickness or mass.

Orthographic projection is the process of projecting views onto parallel planes with ⊥ projectors.

The default ⊥ datum planes are:

- Primary
- Secondary
- Tertiary

These are the planes used in manufacturing:

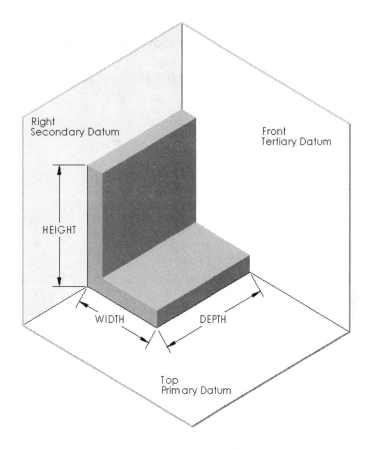

- Primary datum plane contacts the part at a minimum of three points.
- Secondary datum plane contacts the part at a minimum of two points.
- Tertiary datum plane contacts the part at a minimum of one point.

The part view orientation depends on the Base feature Sketch plane.

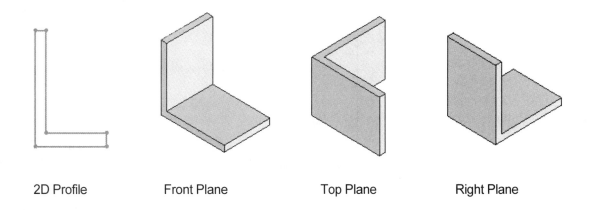

2D Profile   Front Plane   Top Plane   Right Plane

The part view orientation is dependent on the Base feature Sketch plane. Compare the available default Sketch planes in the FeatureManager: *Front Plane*, *Top Plane*, *and Right Plane*.

Each Extruded Base feature above was created with and L-shaped 2D Sketch profile. The six principle views of Orthographic projection listed in the ASME Y14.3M standard are:

- Top

- Front

- Right side

- Bottom

- Rear

- Left side

SolidWorks Standard view names correspond to these Orthographic projection view names.

ASME Y14.3M Principle View Name:	SolidWorks Standard View:
Front	Front
Top	Top
Right side	Right
Bottom	Bottom
Rear	Back
Left side	Left

The standard drawing views in third angle Orthographic projection are:

- Front

- Top

- Right

- Isometric

There are two Orthographic projection drawing systems. The first Orthographic projection system is called the third angle projection. The second Orthographic projection system is called the first angle projection. The systems are derived from positioning a 3D object in the third or first quadrant.

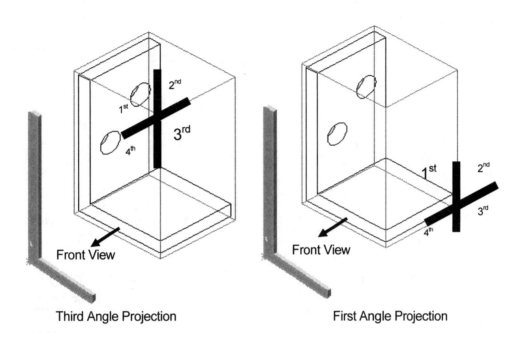

Third Angle Projection   First Angle Projection

Third Angle Projection

The part is positioned in the third quadrant in third angle projection. The 2D projection planes are located between the viewer and the part. The projected views are placed on a drawing.

First Angle Projection

The part is positioned in the first quadrant in first angle projection. Views are projected onto the planes located behind the part. The projected views are placed on a drawing. First angle projection is primarily used in Europe and Asia.

Third angle projection is primarily used in the U.S. & Canada and is based on the ASME Y14.3M Multi and Sectional View Drawings standard. Designers should have knowledge and understanding of both systems.

There are numerous multi-national companies. Example: A part is designed in the U.S., manufactured in Japan and destined for a European market.

Third angle projection is used in this text. A truncated cone symbol, appears on the drawing to indicate the Projection System:

Select the Sketch plane based on symmetry and orientation of the part in the FRONT-SUPPORT assembly. Utilize the standard views: Front, Back, Right, Left, Top, Bottom, and Isometric to orient the part. Create the 2D drawings for the parts in Project 3.

HEX-STANDOFF Part

The HEX-STANDOFF part is a hexagonal shaped part utilized to elevate components in the FRONT-SUPPORT assembly. Machine screws are utilized to fasten components to the HEX-STANDOFF.

Create the HEX-STANDOFF part with the Extruded Base feature 🔲 tool. The Sketch plane for the HEX-STANDOFF Extruded Base feature is the Top Plane.

Origin

Create the HEX-STANDOFF in the orientation utilized by the FRONT-SUPPORT assembly. The Front and Right Plane creates the Extruded Base and Boss feature.

Origin   Origin   Origin

💡 Note the location of the Origin in the models.

The Extruded Base feature sketch consists of two profiles. The first sketch is a circle centered at the Origin on the Top Plane.

The second sketch is a polygon with 6 sides centered at the Origin. The polygon utilizes an inscribed circle to construct the geometry.

Geometric relations are constraints that control the size and position of the sketch entities. Apply a Horizontal relation in the polygon sketch.

Extrude the sketch perpendicular to the Top Plane. Utilize the Edit Sketch tool to modify the sketch.

Origin

The Hole Wizard feature creates complex and simple Hole features. Utilize the Hole Wizard feature to create a Tapped Hole.

The Tapped Hole depth and diameter are based on drill size and screw type parameters. Apply a Coincident relation to position the Tapped Hole aligned with the Origin.

Activity: HEX-STANDOFF Part-Extruded Base Feature

Create a new part.

1) Click **New** ⬜ from the Menu bar. The Templates tab is the default tab. Part is the default template from the New SolidWorks Document dialog box.

2) Double-click **Part**. The Part FeatureManager is displayed.

Set the dimensioning standard and part units.

3) Click **Options** ▤, **Document Properties** tab from the Menu bar.

4) Select **ANSI** from the Overall drafting standard box.

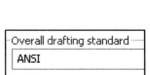

Set units and decimal places.
5) Click **Units**.

6) Select **IPS**, [**MMGS**] for Unit system.

7) Select **.123**, [**.12**] for Length units Decimal places.

8) Select **None** for Angular units Decimal places.

9) Click **OK**. The Part FeatureManager is displayed.

The primary units are provided in IPS, (inch, pound, seconds). The optional secondary units are provided in MMGS, (millimeter, gram, second) and are indicated in brackets [ ]. Illustrations are provided in inches and millimeters.

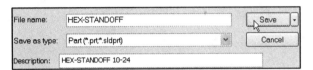

Save the part.

10) Click **Save As** from the Menu bar.

11) Select the **SW-TUTORIAL-2009** folder. Enter **HEX-STANDOFF** for File name.

12) Enter **HEX-STANDOFF 10-24** for Description.

13) Click **Save**. The HEX-STANDOFF FeatureManager is displayed.

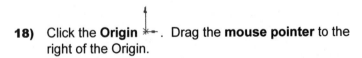

Select the Sketch plane.

14) Right-click **Top Plane** from the FeatureManager. This is the Sketch plane.

Insert an Extruded Base feature sketched on the Top Plane. Note: A plane is an infinite 2D area. The blue boundary is for visual reference.

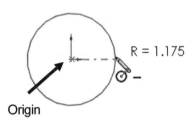

Insert a new sketch.

15) Click **Sketch** ✎ from the Context toolbar. The Sketch toolbar is displayed.

16) Click the **Circle** ⊘ Sketch tool. The Circle PropertyManager is displayed.

17) Drag the **mouse pointer** into the Graphics window. The cursor displays the Circle icon ⊘.

R = 1.175

Origin

18) Click the **Origin** ↳. Drag the **mouse pointer** to the right of the Origin.

19) Click a **position** to create the circle as illustrated.

Insert a Polygon.

20) Click the **Polygon** ⊕ Sketch tool. The Polygon PropertyManager is displayed. The cursor displays the Polygon icon ⊕.

21) Click the **Origin** ↳ as illustrated.

22) Drag the **mouse pointer** horizontally to the right.

23) Click a **position** to the right of the circle to create the hexagon as illustrated.

Add a dimension.

24) Click the **Smart Dimension** ✧ Sketch tool.

25) Click the **circumference** of the first circle.

26) Click a **position** diagonally above the hexagon to locate the dimension.

27) Enter **.150**in, [**3.81**] in the Modify box.

28) Click the **Green Check mark** ✔ in the Modify dialog box.

29) Click the **circumference** of the inscribed circle.

30) Click a **position** diagonally below the hexagon to locate the dimension. Enter **.313**in, [**7.94**] in the Modify box.

31) Click the **Green Check mark** ✔ in the Modify dialog box. The black sketch is fully defined.

32) Press the **f** key to fit the model to the Graphics window.

☀ If required, click the arrow head dot to toggle the direction of the dimension arrow.

33) Click **OK** ✔ from the Dimension PropertyManager.

Add a Horizontal relation.

34) Click the **Origin** ⊥. Hold the **Ctrl** key down.

35) Click the right most **point** of the hexagon. The Properties PropertyManager is displayed.

36) Release the **Ctrl** key. Click **Horizontal** — from the Add Relations box.

37) Click **OK** ✔ from the Properties PropertyManager.

☀ You can also right-click and click **Make Horizontal** from the Context toolbar.

Extrude the sketch.
38) Click the **Features** tab in the CommandManager.

39) Click **Extruded Boss/Base** 🗔 from the Features toolbar. The Extrude PropertyManager is displayed. Blind is the default End Condition in Direction1. The direction arrow points upward.

40) Enter **.735**in, **[18.67]** for Depth.

41) Click **OK** ✔ from the Extrude PropertyManager. Extrude1 is displayed in the FeatureManager.

Fit the model to the Graphics window.
42) Press the **f** key.

The Extruded Base feature was sketched on the Top Plane. Changes occur in the design process. Edit the sketch of Extrude1. Delete the circle and close the sketch. Apply the Hole Wizard feature to create a Tapped Hole.

Edit Sketch1
43) **Expand** Extrude1 in the FeatureManager.

44) Right-click **Sketch1** in the FeatureManager.

45) Click **Edit Sketch** 🖉 from the Context toolbar.

Delete the inside circle.
46) Click the **circumference** of the inside circle as illustrated. The Circle PropertyManager is displayed.

47) Press the **Delete** key.

48) Click **Yes** to the Sketcher Confirm Delete message. Both the circle geometry and its dimension are deleted.

Save and close the sketch.
49) Click **Save** 🖫.

50) Click **OK** to Rebuild. The Extrude1 feature is updated.

Fit the model to the Graphics window.
51) Press the **f** key.

Activity: HEX-STANDOFF Part-Hole Wizard Feature

Insert a Tapped Hole with the Hole Wizard feature tool.
52) Click the **top face** of Extrude1 in the Graphics window as illustrated.

53) Click **Hidden Lines Visible** from the Heads-up View toolbar.

54) Click **Hole Wizard** from the Features toolbar. The Hole Specification PropertyManager is displayed.

Note: For metric, utilize ANSI Metric and M5x0.8 for size.

55) Click **Tap** for Hole Specification.

56) Select **Ansi Inch**, [**Ansi Metric**] for Standard.

57) Select **Bottoming Tapped Hole** for Type.

58) Select **#10-24**, [**Ø5**] for Size.

59) Select **Through All** for End Condition. Accept the default conditions.

60) Click the **Positions** tab.

The Tapped Hole is displayed in yellow. Yellow is a preview color.

The Tap Hole center point is displayed in blue. The Point Sketch tool is automatically selected. No other holes are required.

Utilize a Coincident relation to locate the center point of the Tapped Hole in the Top view. Note: the selected center point will vary depending on your original selection location on the face.

Add a Coincident relation.
61) Right-click **Select** to deselect the Point Sketch tool.

62) Click the **Origin** as illustrated.

63) Hold the **Ctrl** key down. Click the **blue center point** of the Tapped Hole. Note: This is the initial location were you clicked the top face of Extrude1. The Properties PropertyManager is displayed.

64) Release the **Ctrl** key. Click **Coincident** from the Add Relations box.

65) Click **OK** from the Properties PropertyManager.

66) Click **OK** from the Hole Position PropertyManager.

Origin

The #10-24 Tapped Hole1 feature is displayed in the FeatureManager. Sketch3 determines the center point location of the Tapped Hole. Sketch2 is the profile of the Tapped Hole.

Save the HEX-STANDOFF part.

67) Click **Shaded With Edges** from the Heads-up View toolbar.

68) Click **inside** the Graphics window.

69) Click **Save**. The HEX-STANDOFF is complete.

Origin

 Review the HEX-STANDOFF Part

The HEX-STANDOFF part utilized an Extruded Base feature. The Extruded Base feature required a sketch on the Top Plane. The first profile was a circle centered at the Origin on the Top Plane. The second profile used the Polygon Sketch tool. You utilized the Edit Sketch tool to modify the Sketch profile and to delete the circle.

The Hole Wizard feature created a Tapped Hole. The Hole Wizard feature required the Extruded Base top face as the Sketch plane.

A Coincident relation located the center point of the Tapped Hole aligned with respect to the Origin.

Additional details on Hexagon, Add Relations, Centerline, Delete, Hole Wizard, and Extruded Base are available in SolidWorks Help. Keywords: Polygon, Relations, Delete, Sketch Entities, Sketch Tools, Hole Wizard, and Extruded Boss/Base.

ANGLE-13HOLE Part

The ANGLE-13HOLE part is an L-shaped support bracket. The ANGLE-13HOLE part is manufactured from 0.090in, [2.3] aluminum.

There ANGLE-13HOLE part contains fillets, holes, and slot cuts.

Simplify the overall design into seven features. Utilize symmetry and Linear Patterns.

The open L-Shaped profile is sketched on the Right Plane.

Utilize an Extruded Thin feature with the Mid Plane option to locate the part symmetrical to the Right Plane.

Insert the first Extruded Cut feature for the first hole. This is the seed feature for the Linear Pattern. The hole sketch is located on the top face of the Extruded Thin feature.

Insert a Linear Pattern feature to create an array of 13 holes along the bottom horizontal edge.

Insert a Fillet feature to round the four corners.

Insert the second Extruded Cut feature on the front
face of the Extruded Thin feature. This is the seed
feature for the second Linear Pattern.

Insert a Linear Pattern feature to create an array
of 3 holes along the top horizontal edge.

Utilize the Sketch Mirror tool to create the slot
profile. Use the Slot Sketch tool.

Insert the third Extruded Cut feature to
create the two slots.

Select the Sketch plane for the Base feature
that corresponds to the parts orientation in the
assembly.

Activity: ANGLE-13HOLE Part-Documents Properties

Create a new part.

70) Click **New** ⬜ from the Menu bar. Part is the default template from the New SolidWorks
Document dialog box.

71) Double-click **Part**. The Part FeatureManager is displayed.

Set the dimensioning standard and part units.

72) Click **Options** 🗒, **Document Properties**
tab from the Menu bar.

73) Select **ANSI** from the Overall drafting
standard drop-down menu.

74) Click **Units**.

75) Select **IPS**, **[MMGS]** for Unit system.

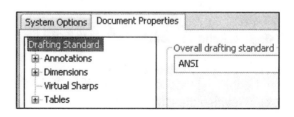

76) Select **.123**, [**.12**] for Length units Decimal places.

77) Select **None** for Angular units Decimal places. Click **OK**.

Save the part.
78) Click **Save As** from the Menu bar.

79) Select the **SW-TUTORIAL-2009** file folder.

80) Enter **ANGLE-13 HOLE** for File name.

81) Enter **ANGLE BRACKET-13 HOLE** for Description.

82) Click **Save**. The ANGLE-13 Hole FeatureManager is displayed.

Unit system
○ MKS (meter, kilogram, second)
○ CGS (centimeter, gram, second)
○ MMGS (millimeter, gram, second)
● IPS (inch, pound, second)
○ Custom

Type	Unit	Decimals
Basic Units		
Length	inches	.123
Dual Dimension Length	millimeters ▾	.12
Angle	degrees	None

Activity: ANGLE-13HOLE Part-Extruded Thin Feature

Insert an Extruded Thin feature sketched on the Right Plane.

Select the Sketch plane.
83) Right-click **Right Plane** from the FeatureManager.

Sketch a horizontal line.
84) Click **Sketch** from the Context toolbar. The Sketch toolbar is displayed.

85) Click the **Line** Sketch tool from the Sketch toolbar.

86) Click the **Origin** as illustrated.

87) Click a **position** to the right of the Origin.

Sketch a vertical line.
88) Click a **position** directly above the right end point.

Deselect the Line Sketch tool
89) Right-click **Select** in the Graphics window.

Add an Equal relation.
90) Click the **vertical** line. Hold the **Ctrl** key down.

91) Click the **horizontal line**.

92) Release the **Ctrl** key.

93) Right-click **Make Equal** = from the Context toolbar.

94) Click **OK** from the Properties PropertyManager.

Origin

Add a dimension.

95) Click the **Smart Dimension** ✧ Sketch tool.

96) Click the **horizontal** line.

97) Click a **position** below the profile.

98) Enter **.700**in, [**17.78**] in the Modify box.

99) Click the **Green Check mark** ✅ . The black sketch is fully defined.

☀ Save rebuild time. Add relations and dimensions to fully define a sketch. Fully defined sketches are displayed in black.

Extrude the sketch.

100) Click **Extruded Boss/Base** 🔲 from the Features toolbar. The Extrude PropertyManager is displayed.

101) Select **Mid Plane** for End Condition in Direction 1.

102) Enter **7.000**in, [**177.80**] for Depth. Note: Thin Feature is checked.

103) Click the **Reverse Direction Arrow** button for One-Direction. Material thickness is created above the Origin.

104) Enter **.090**in, [**2.3**] for Thickness.

105) Check the **Auto-fillet corners** box.

106) Enter **.090**in, [**2.3**] for Fillet Radius.

107) Click **OK** ✅ from the Extrude PropertyManager. Extrude-Thin1 is displayed in the FeatureManager.

Origin

Fit the model to the Graphics window.
108) Press the **f** key.

🔆 Clarify the Extrude-Thin1 feature direction and thickness options. Utilize multiple view orientations and Zoom In before selecting OK ✔ from the Extrude PropertyManager.

Modify feature dimensions.

109) Click **Extrude-Thin1** in the FeatureManager.

110) Click the **7.000**in, **[177.80]** dimension in the Graphics window.

111) Enter **6.500**in, **[165.10]**.

112) Click **inside** the Graphics window.

Save the model.

113) Click **Save** 💾.

Activity: ANGLE-13HOLE Part-Extruded Cut Feature

Insert a new sketch for the Extruded Cut feature.

114) Right-click the **top face** of Extrude-Thin1 as illustrated. This is the Sketch plane.

115) Click **Sketch** ✏ from the Context toolbar. The Sketch toolbar is displayed.

116) Click **Top view** 🔲 from the Heads-up View toolbar.

117) Click the **Circle** ⊙ Sketch tool.

118) Sketch a **circle** on the left side of the Origin as illustrated.

Origin

Add dimensions.

119) Click the **Smart Dimension** ✏ Sketch tool.

120) Click the **Origin** .

121) Click the **center point** of the circle.

122) Click a **position** below the horizontal profile line. Enter **3.000**in, [**76.20**].

123) Click the **Green Check mark** .

124) Click the **bottom horizontal line**.

125) Click the **center point** of the circle.

126) Click a **position** to the left of the profile.

127) Enter **.250**in, [**6.35**].

128) Click the **Green Check mark** .

129) Create a diameter dimension. Click the **circumference** of the circle.

130) Click a **position** diagonally above the profile.

131) Enter **.190**in, [**4.83**].

132) Click the **Green Check mark** .

Insert an Extruded Cut Feature.

133) Click **Extruded Cut** from the Features toolbar. The Extrude PropertyManager is displayed.

134) Select **Through All** for End Condition in Direction 1. Accept the default conditions.

135) Click **OK** from the Extrude PropertyManager. Extrude1 is displayed in the FeatureManager. Extrude1 is the seed feature for the Linear Pattern feature of holes.

136) Click **Isometric view** from the Heads-up View toolbar.

Save the model.
137) Click **Save** .

Activity: ANGLE-13HOLE Part-Linear Pattern Feature

Insert a Linear Pattern feature.

138) Click **Top View** ⊞ from the Heads-up View toolbar.

139) Click **Linear Pattern** from the Features toolbar. The Linear Pattern PropertyManager is displayed. Extrude1 is displayed in the Features to Pattern box.

140) Click the **bottom horizontal edge** of the Extrude-Thin1 feature for Direction1. Edge<1> is displayed in the Pattern Direction box. The direction arrow points to the right. If required, click the Reverse Direction button.

141) Enter **0.5**in, [**12.70**] for Spacing.

142) Enter **13** for Number of Instances.

143) Click **OK** ✔ from the Linear Pattern PropertyManager. LPattern1 is displayed in the FeatureManager.

144) Click **Isometric view** from the Heads-up View toolbar.

Save the ANGLE-13HOLE part.

145) Click **Save** 💾.

Activity: ANGLE-13HOLE Part-Fillet Feature

Insert a Fillet Feature.
146) Zoom in on the right top edge as illustrated.

147) Click the **right top edge** of the Extrude-Thin1 feature.

148) Click **Fillet** from the Features toolbar. The Fillet PropertyManager is displayed.

149) Click the **Manual** tab. Constant radius is the default Fillet Type.

150) Enter **.250 [6.35]** for Radius.

151) Click the **right bottom edge**. Edge<1> and Edge<2> are displayed in the Items To Fillet box.

152) Click **OK** from the Fillet PropertyManager. Fillet1 is displayed in the FeatureManager.

Two Fillet PropertyManager tabs are available. Use the Manual tab to control features for all Fillet types. Use the FilletXpert tab when you want SolidWorks to manage the structure of the underlying features only for a Constant radius Fillet type. Click the ? button for additional information.

Fit the model to the Graphics window.
153) Press the **f** key.

Edit the Fillet feature.
154) Zoom in on the left side of the Extrude-Thin1 feature.

155) Right-click **Fillet1** from the FeatureManager.

156) Click **Edit Feature** from the Context toolbar. The Fillet1 PropertyManager is displayed.

157) Click the **left top edge** and **left bottom edge**. Edge<3> and Edge <4> are added to the Items To Fillet box.

158) Click **OK** ✔ from the Fillet1 PropertyManager. The four edges have a Fillet feature with a .25in radius.

Display the Isometric view.

159) Click **Isometric view** ⬡ from the Heads-up View toolbar.

Save the ANGLE-13HOLE part.

160) Click **Save** 💾.

Activity: ANGLE-13HOLE Part-Second Extruded Cut / Linear Pattern

Insert a new sketch for the second Extruded Cut feature.

161) Right-click the **front face** of the Extrude-Thin1 feature in the Graphics window. The front face is the Sketch plane.

162) Click **Sketch** ⬏ from the Context toolbar. The Sketch toolbar is displayed.

163) Click **Front view** ⬜ from the Heads-up View toolbar.

164) Click **Wireframe** ⬜ from the Heads-up View toolbar to display LPattern1.

Note: Do not align the center point of the circle with the center point of the LPattern1 feature. Do not align the center point of the circle with the center point of the Fillet radius. Control the center point position with dimensions.

165) Click the **Circle** ⊙ Sketch tool. The cursor displays the Circle icon ⊙ .

166) Sketch a **circle** on the left side of the Origin between the two LPattern1 holes as illustrated.

Add dimensions.

167) Click the **Smart Dimension** ✏ Sketch tool.

168) Click the **Origin** ⁎.

169) Click the **center point** of the circle.

170) Click a **position** below the horizontal profile line. Enter **3.000**in, **[76.20]**.

171) Click the **Green Check mark** ✔.

172) Click the **top horizontal line**.

173) Click the **center point** of the circle.

174) Click a **position** to the left of the profile.

175) Enter **.250**in, **[6.35]**.

176) Click the **Green Check mark** ✔.

177) Click the **circumference** of the circle.

178) Click a **position** above the profile.

179) Enter **.190**in, **[4.83]**.

180) Click the **Green Check mark** ✔.

Insert an Extruded Cut Feature.

181) Click **Extruded Cut** 🔲 from the Features toolbar. The Extrude PropertyManager is displayed

182) Select **Through All** for End Condition in Direction1. Accept the default conditions.

183) Click **OK** ✔ from the Extrude PropertyManager. Extrude2 is displayed in the FeatureManager.

Create the second Linear Pattern Feature.

184) Click **Linear Pattern** 🔢 from the Features toolbar. The Linear Pattern FeatureManager is displayed. Extrude2 is displayed in the Features to Pattern box.

185) Click inside the **Pattern Direction** box.

186) Click the **top horizontal edge** of the Extrude-Thin1 feature for Direction1. Edge<1> is displayed in the Pattern Direction box. The Direction arrow points to the right. If required, click the **Reverse Direction** button

187) Enter **3.000**in, [76.20] for Spacing.

188) Enter **3** for Number of Instances. Note: Extude2 is displayed in the Features to Pattern box.

189) Click **OK** ✔ from the Linear Pattern PropertyManager. LPattern2 is displayed in the FeatureManager.

190) Click **Isometric view** 🎲 from the Heads-up View toolbar.

191) Click **Shaded With Edges** ▱ from the Heads-up View toolbar.

Save the ANGLE-13HOLE part.
192) Click **Save** 💾 .

Activity: ANGLE-13HOLE Part-Third Extruded Cut

Insert a new sketch for the third Extruded Cut Feature.
193) Select the Sketch plane. Right-click the **front face** of Extrude-Thin1.

194) Click **Sketch** ✎ from the Context toolbar. The Sketch toolbar is displayed.

195) Click **Front view** 🔲 from the Heads-up View toolbar.

196) Click **Hidden Lines Removed** ▱ from the Heads-up View toolbar.

Sketch a vertical centerline.
197) Click the **Centerline** ⦙ Sketch tool. The Insert Line PropertyManager is displayed.

198) Click the **Origin** ⤶ .

199) Click a vertical **position** above the top horizontal line as illustrated.

200) Click **Tools, Sketch Tools, Dynamic Mirror** from the Menu bar.

201) Click the **centerline** in the Graphics window.

Sketch a rectangle.

202) Click **Wireframe** from the Heads-up View toolbar.

Apply the Straight Slot Sketch tool. Sketch a straight slot using two end points and a point for height.

203) Click the **Straight Slot** ▣ Sketch tool from the Consolidated Slot toolbar. Do not align the rectangle first point and second point to the center points of Lpattern1.

204) Click the **first point** of the rectangle to the left of the Origin as illustrated.

205) Click the **second point** directly to the right.

206) Click the **third point** to create the slot as illustrated. View the two slots on the model.

207) Click **OK** ✔ from the Slot PropertyManager.

Deactivate the Dynamic Mirror tool.
208) Click **Tools**, **Sketch Tools**, **Dynamic
      Mirror** from the Menu bar.

Add a Concentric relation.
209) Zoom in on the centerline.

210) Click the **top endpoint** of the
      centerline.

211) Hold the **Ctrl** key down.

212) Click the **circumference** of the circle.

213) Release the **Ctrl** key.

214) Click **Concentric** from the Add Relations box.

The endpoint of the centerline is positioned in the center of the circle.
Note: Right-click Clear Selections to remove selected entities from the
Add Relations box.

Add an Equal relation.
215) Click the circumference of the **circle**.

216) Hold the **Ctrl** key down.

217) Click the **left arc** of the first rectangle.

218) Release the **Ctrl** key.

219) Click **Equal** ═ from the Add Relations box.
      The arc radius is equal to the circle radius.

Add a Horizontal relation.
220) Click the **top endpoint** of the centerline as
      illustrated.

221) Hold the **Ctrl** key down.

222) Click the **center point** of the left arc of the first
      rectangle.

223) Release the **Ctrl** key.

224) Click **Horizontal** ▬ from the Add Relations box.

225) Click **OK** ✔ from the Properties PropertyManager.

The right arc is horizontally aligned to the left arc due to symmetry from the Sketch Mirror tool.

Add dimensions. Dimension the distance between the two slots.

226) Click the **Smart Dimension** ✏ Sketch tool.

227) Click the **right arc centerpoint** of the left slot.

228) Click the **left arc centerpoint** of the right slot.

229) Click a **position** above the top horizontal line.

230) Enter **1.000**in, [**25.40**] in the Modify dialog box.

231) Click the **Green Check mark** ✅ .

232) Click the **left center point** of the left arc.

233) Click the **right center point** of the left arc.

234) Click a **position** above the top horizontal line.

235) Enter **2.000**in, [**50.80**] in the Modify dialog box.

236) Click the **Green Check mark** ✅ . The black sketch is fully defined.

237) Click **Isometric view** 🔲 from the Heads-up View toolbar.

Insert an Extruded Cut Feature.

238) Click **Extruded Cut** from the Features toolbar. The Extrude PropertyManager is displayed.

239) Select **Through All** for End Condition in Direction1. The direction arrow points to the back.

240) Click **OK** ✔ from the Extrude PropertyManager. Extrude3 is displayed in the FeatureManager.

241) Click **Shaded With Edges** ⬛ from the Heads-up View toolbar.

Save the ANGLE-13HOLE part.

242) Click **Save** 💾. The ANGLE-13HOLE is complete. All sketches in the FeatureManager should be Fully Defined.

💡 The dimension between the two slots is over-defined if the arc center points are aligned to the center points of the LPattern1 feature. An over-defined sketch is displayed in red, in the FeatureManager.

💡 The mouse pointer displays a blue dashed line when horizontal and vertical sketch references are inferred.

Review the ANGLE-13HOLE Part

The ANGLE-13HOLE part utilized an open L-Shaped profile sketched on the Right Plane. The Extruded Thin feature with the Mid Plane option located the part symmetrical to the Right Plane. The first Extruded Cut feature created the first hole sketched on the top face of the Extruded Thin feature.

The first Linear Pattern feature created an array of 13 holes along the bottom horizontal edge. The Fillet feature rounded the four corners. The second Extruded Cut feature created a hole on the Front face. The second Linear Pattern feature created an array of 3 holes along the top horizontal edge. The third Extruded Cut feature created two slot cuts using the Straight Slot Sketch tool.

Additional details on Extruded Base/Thin, Extruded Cut, Linear Pattern, Fillet, Mirror Entities, Add Relations, Slot, Straight Slot, Centerline, Line, Rectangle, and Smart Dimensions are available in Help. Keywords: Extruded Boss/Base - Thin, Extruded Cut, Patterns, Fillet, Sketch Entities, Sketch tools, and dimensions.

TRAINGLE Part

The TRIANGLE part is a multipurpose supporting plane.

The TRIANGLE is manufactured from .090in, [2.3] aluminum. The TRIANGLE contains numerous features.

Utilize symmetry and Sketch tools to simplify the geometry creation.

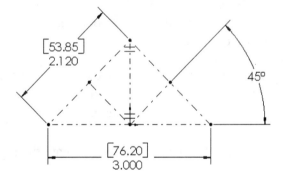

The center points of the slots and holes locate key geometry for the TRIANGLE.

Utilize sketched construction geometry to locate the center points.

🔅 Construction geometry is not
calculated in the extruded profile.

Utilize the Sketch Offset tool and
Sketch Fillet to create the sketch profile
for the Extruded Base 🔲 feature.

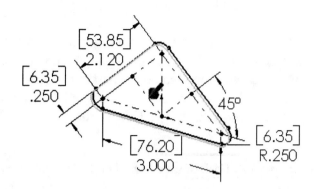

Utilize the Dynamic Mirror Sketch tool and the Circle
Sketch tool to create the first Extruded Cut 🔲 feature.

Utilize the Corner Rectangle, Trim, and the Tangent Arc
Sketch tools to create the second Extruded Cut 🔲 feature
left bottom slot.

Note: The purpose of this book is to teach you different
tools and methods. You can also apply the Straight Slot
Sketch tool and eliminate steps.

Utilize the Mirror 🔲 feature to create the right bottom
slot.

Utilize the Straight Slot Sketch tool to create the third
Extruded Cut 🔲 feature.

Utilize the Circular Pattern feature to create the three radial slot cuts.

Activity: TRIANGLE Part-Mirror, Offset, and Fillet Sketch Tools

Create a new part.

243) Click **New** ⬜ from the Menu bar. The Templates tab is the default tab.

244) Double-click **Part**. The Part FeatureManager is displayed.

Save the part.

245) Click **Save As** from the Menu bar.

246) Select **SW-TUTORIAL-2009** for the Save in file folder.

247) Enter **TRIANGLE** for File name.

248) Enter **TRIANGLE** for Description.

249) Click **Save**. The TRIANGLE FeatureManager is displayed.

Set the dimensioning standard and part units.

250) Click **Options** 📧, **Document Properties** tab from the Menu bar.

251) Select **ANSI** from the Overall drafting standard box.

252) Click **Units**.

253) Click **IPS**, **[MMGS]** for Unit system.

254) Select **.123**, **[.12]** for Length units Decimal places.

255) Select **None** for Angular units Decimal places.

256) Click **OK** to set the document units.

Insert a new sketch for the Extruded Base feature.
257) Right-click **Front Plane** from the FeatureManager.

258) Click **Sketch** ✏ from the
Context toolbar. The Sketch
toolbar is displayed.

Sketch a vertical centerline.
259) Click the **Centerline** ⁞ Sketch
tool.

260) Click the **Origin** ↧. Click a vertical **position** above the Origin
as illustrated.

Deselect the Centerline Sketch tool.
261) Right-click **Select**.

Sketch a Mirrored profile.
262) Click **Tools, Sketch Tools, Dynamic Mirror** from the Menu
bar.

263) Click the **centerline** in the Graphics window.

264) Click the **Centerline** ⁞ Sketch tool.

265) Click the **Origin** ↧.

266) Click a **position** to the left of the Origin to
create a horizontal line.

267) Click the **top end point** of the vertical
centerline to complete the triangle as
illustrated.

268) Right-click **End Chain** to end the line segment.
The Centerline tool is still active.

269) Click the **Origin** ↧.

270) Click a **position** coincident with the right-angled
centerline. Do not select the Midpoint as
illustrated.

271) Right-click **End Chain** to end the line segment.

Deactivate the Dynamic Mirror Sketch tool.
272) Click **Tools, Sketch Tools, Dynamic Mirror**
from the Menu bar.

Add a dimension.

273) Click **Smart Dimension** ✏ from the Sketch toolbar.

274) Click the **right horizontal** centerline.

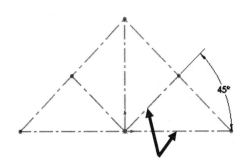

275) Click the **inside right** centerline.

276) Click a **position** between the two lines.

277) Enter **45**deg in the Modify dialog box for the angular dimension.

278) Click the **Green Check mark** ✔ in the Modify dialog box.

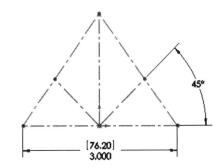

279) Click the **horizontal centerline**.

280) Click a position **below** the centerline.

281) Enter **3.000**in, **[76.20]**.

282) Click the **Green Check mark** ✔ in the Modify dialog box.

283) Click the **left angled** centerline.

284) Click **position** aligned to the left angled centerline.

285) Enter **2.120**in, **[53.85]**.

286) Click the **Green Check mark** ✔ in the Modify dialog box.

Offset the sketch
287) Right-click **Select** in the Graphics window.

288) Hold the **Ctrl** key down.

289) Click the **three outside centerlines**; Line2, Line4, and Line5 are displayed in the Selected Entities box.

290) Release the **Ctrl** key.

291) Click the **Offset Entities** ⫽ Sketch tool.

292) Enter **.250**in, **[6.35]** for Offset Distance. The yellow Offset direction is outward.

293) Click **OK** ✔ from the Offset Entities PropertyManager.

Three profile lines are displayed. The centerlines are on the inside.

Insert the Sketch Fillet.

294) Click **Sketch Fillet** ⌐ from the Sketch toolbar. The Sketch Fillet PropertyManager is displayed.

295) Enter **.250**in, [**6.35**] for Radius.

296) Click the **three outside corner points**.

297) Click **OK** ✔ from the Sketch Fillet PropertyManager.

Activity: TRIANGLE Part-Extruded Base Feature

Extrude the sketch.

298) Click **Extruded Boss/Base** 🖺 from the Features toolbar. Blind is the default End Condition in Direction1.

299) Enter **.090**in, [**2.3**] for Depth in Direction 1. The direction arrow points to the front.

300) Click **OK** ✔ from the Extrude PropertyManager. Extrude1 is displayed in the FeatureManager.

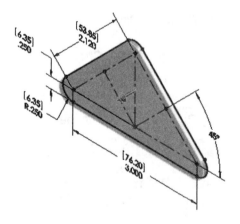

Save the TRIANGLE part.

301) Click **Isometric view** 🔲 from the Heads-up View toolbar.

302) Click **Save** 💾.

🔆 Insert centerlines and add relations to build sketches that will be referenced by multiple features.

Display Sketch1.
303) **Expand** Extrude1 in the FeatureManager.

304) Right-click **Sketch1**.

305) Click **Show**.

Activity: TRIANGLE Part-First Extruded Cut Feature

Insert a new sketch for the first Extruded Cut.
306) Right-click the **front face** of Extrude1. This is your
Sketch plane.

307) Click **Sketch** ✎ from the Context toolbar. The Sketch
toolbar is displayed.

308) Click **Front view** ⬚ from the Heads-up View toolbar.

309) Click the **Circle** ⊘ Sketch tool. The Circle
PropertyManager is displayed.

310) Sketch a **circle** centered at the Origin.

311) Sketch a **circle** centered at the endpoint of the
vertical centerline as illustrated.

Sketch a vertical centerline.
312) Click the **Centerline** ⋮ Sketch tool.

313) Click the **Origin** ↳.

314) Click the **centerpoint** of the top circle.

Deselect the Centerline Sketch tool.
315) Right-click **Select**.

Sketch a Mirrored profile.
316) Click **Tools**, **Sketch Tools**, **Dynamic Mirror** from
the Menu bar.

317) Click the **centerline** in the Graphics window.

318) Click the **Circle** ⊘ Sketch tool. The Circle
PropertyManager is displayed.

319) Sketch a **circle** on the left side of the centerline, coincident with the left centerline, in the lower half of the triangle.

320) Sketch a **circle** on the left side of the centerline, coincident with the left centerline, in the upper half of the triangle. Right-click **Select.**

321) Deactivate the Dynamic Mirror tool. Click **Tools, Sketch Tools, Dynamic Mirror** from the Menu bar.

Add an Equal relation.
322) Click a **circle**. Hold the **Ctrl** key down. Click the five other **circles**. Release the **Ctrl** key.

323) Click **Equal** = from the Add Relations box.

Add a dimension.
324) Click the **Smart Dimension** ✧ Sketch tool.

325) Click the circumference of the **top circle.**

326) Click a **position** off the TRIANGLE.

327) Enter .190in, [4.83].

328) Click the **Green Check mark** ✔ in the Modify dialog box.

Create the aligned dimensions.
329) Click the bottom **left point**. Click the **center point** of the bottom left circle.

330) Click a **position** aligned to the angled centerline.

331) Enter .**710**in, [**18.03**]. Click the **Green Check mark** ✔ in the Modify dialog box.

332) Click the bottom **left point.**

333) Click the **center point** of the top left circle as illustrated.

334) Click a **position** aligned to the angled centerline.

335) Enter **1.410**in, [**35.81**].

336) Click the **Green Check mark** ✔ in the Modify dialog box.

Insert an Extruded Cut Feature.

337) Click **Extruded Cut** from the Features toolbar. The Extrude PropertyManager is displayed. Select **Through All** for the End Condition in Direction1.

338) Click **OK** ✔ from the Extrude PropertyManager. Extrude2 is displayed in the FeatureManager.

339) Click **Isometric view** 🔲 from the Heads-up View toolbar.

340) Click **Save** 💾.

Activity: TRIANGLE Part-Second Extruded Cut Feature

Insert a new slot sketch for the second Extruded Cut.

341) Right-click the **front face** of Extrude1 for the Sketch plane.

342) Click **Sketch** 𝒮 from the Context toolbar. The Sketch toolbar is displayed.

343) Click **Front view** 🔲 from the Heads-up View toolbar.

344) Click the **Corner Rectangle** ▭ tool from the Consolidated Sketch toolbar. Note: The purpose of this book is to teach you different tools and methods. You can also apply the Straight Slot Sketch tool and eliminate many of the next steps.

345) Sketch a **rectangle** to the left of the Origin as illustrated.

Trim the vertical lines.

346) Click the **Trim Entities** ⊬ Sketch tool. The Trim PropertyManager is displayed.

First point

347) Click **Trim to closest** in the Options box. The Trim to closest ✂ icon is displayed.

348) Click the **left vertical** line of the rectangle.

349) Click the **right vertical** line of the rectangle.

350) Click **OK** ✔ from the Trim PropertyManager.

Sketch the Tangent Arcs.

351) Click the **Tangent Arc** Sketch tool from the Consolidated Sketch toolbar. The Arc PropertyManager is displayed.

352) Sketch a **180° arc** on the left side.

353) Sketch a **180° arc** on the right side.

354) Click **OK** from the Arc PropertyManager.

Add an Equal relation.
355) Click the **right arc**.

356) Hold the **Ctrl** key down.

357) Click the **bottom center circle**.

358) Release the **Ctrl** key.

359) Click **Equal** from the Add Relations box.

360) Click **OK** from the Properties PropertyManager.

Add a Coincident relation.
361) Press the f key to fit the model to the Graphics window.

362) Click the **center point** of the left arc.

363) Hold the **Ctrl** key down.

364) Click the **left lower point** as illustrated.

365) Release the **Ctrl** key.

366) Click **Coincident** from the Add Relations box.

Add a Tangent relation.
367) Click the **bottom horizontal** line.

368) Hold the **Ctrl** key down.

369) Click the **first arc tangent**.

370) Release the **Ctrl** key.

371) Click **Tangent** from the Add Relations box.

372) Click **OK** from the Properties PropertyManager.

Add a dimension.

373) Click the **Smart Dimension** ✐ Sketch tool.

374) Click the **left center point** of the left arc.

375) Click the **right center point** of the right arc.

376) Click a **position** below the horizontal line.

377) Enter **1.000**in, **[25.40]** in the Modify dialog box.

378) Click the **Green Check mark** ✓ .

Insert an Extruded Cut feature.

379) Click **Isometric view** 🔲 from the Heads-up View toolbar.

380) Click **Extruded Cut** 🔲 from the Features toolbar. The Extrude PropertyManager is displayed.

381) Select **Through All** for End Condition in Direction 1.

382) Click **OK** ✓ from the Extrude PropertyManager. Extrude3 is displayed in the FeatureManager.

383) Click **Save** 💾 . Extrude3 is highlighted in the FeatureManager.

Activity: TRIANGLE Part-Mirror Feature

Mirror the Extrude3 feature.

384) Click **Mirror** 🔲 from the Features toolbar. The Mirror PropertyManager is displayed. Extrude3 is displayed in the Feature to Mirror box.

385) Click **Right Plane** from the fly-out TRIANGLE FeatureManager. Right Plane is displayed in the Mirror Face/Plane box.

386) Check the **Geometry Pattern** box.

387) Click **OK** ✓ from the Mirror PropertyManager. Mirror1 is displayed in the FeatureManager.

Activity: TRIANGLE Part-Third Extruded Cut Feature

Insert a new sketch for the third Extruded Cut feature.
388) Right-click the **front face** of Extrude1 for the Sketch
plane.

389) Click **Sketch** ⌐ from the Context toolbar. The
Sketch toolbar is displayed.

390) Click **Front view** 🗗 from the Heads-up View toolbar.

Sketch a Straight Slot.
391) Click the **Straight Slot** ⊟ Sketch tool from the Consolidated

Rectangle toolbar. The Straight Slot ✎ icon is displayed.

392) Click a **position** coincident with the left angled centerline as
illustrated.

Sketch the second point.
393) Click a **position** aligned to the
centerline. A dashed blue line is
displayed.

Sketch the third point.
394) Click a **position** above the inside left
centerline. The Straight Slot sketch is
displayed.

💡 Click the Question mark in the
PropertyManager to obtain additional
information on the tool.

395) Click **OK** ✔ from the Slot PropertyManager.

Add an Equal relation.
396) Click the **left arc**.

397) Hold the **Ctrl** key down.

398) Click the **bottom circle**.

399) Release the **Ctrl** key.

400) Click **Equal** = from the Add Relations box.

Add a dimension.

401) Click the **Smart Dimension** Sketch tool.

402) Click the **left center point** of the left arc.

403) Click the **right center point** of the right arc.

404) Click a **position** below the horizontal line.

405) Enter **.560**in, [**14.22**] in the Modify dialog box.

[14.22]
.560

406) Click the **Green Check mark** ✔. The sketch is fully defined.

Insert an Extruded Cut Feature.

407) Click **Isometric view** 🔲 from the Heads-up View toolbar.

408) Click **Extruded Cut** 🔲 from the Features toolbar. The Extrude PropertyManager is displayed.

409) Select **Through All** for the End Condition in Direction 1.

410) Click **OK** ✔ from the Extrude PropertyManager. Extrude4 is displayed in the FeatureManager.

Save the model.

411) Click **Save** 💾.

Display the Temporary Axis.

412) Click **View**, check **Temporary Axes** from the Menu bar.

Activity: TRIANGLE Part-Circular Pattern Feature

Insert a Circular Pattern feature.

413) Click **Circular Pattern** from the Features Consolidated toolbar. The Circular Pattern PropertyManager is displayed. Extrude4 is displayed in the Features to Pattern box.

414) Click the **Temporary Axis** displayed through the center hole located at the Origin. The Temporary Axis is displayed as Axis <1> in the Pattern Axis box.

415) Enter **90**deg for Angle.

416) Enter **3** for Number of Instances.

417) Check the **Equal spacing** box. If required, click **Reverse Direction**.

418) Click **OK** from the Circular Pattern PropertyManager. CirPattern1 is displayed in the FeatureManager.

Hide Sketch1.
419) Expand Extrude1 from the FeatureManager.

420) Right-click **Sketch1**.

421) Click **Hide**.

Save the TRIANGLE part and deactivate the Temporary Axes.

422) Click **Isometric view** from the Heads-up View toolbar.

423) Click **View**, uncheck **Temporary Axes** from the Menu bar.

424) Click **Save** . The TRIANGLE part is complete.

Review the TRIANGLE Part

The TRIANGLE part utilized an Extruded Base feature. A triangular shape profile was sketch on the Front Plane. Symmetry and construction geometry sketch tools located centerpoints for slots and holes.

The Sketch Fillet tool created rounded corners for the profile. The Sketch Mirror and Circle Sketch tools were utilized to create the Extruded Cut features.

The Corner Rectangle, Sketch Trim, and Tangent Arc tools were utilized to create the second Extruded Cut feature, left bottom slot. The Mirror feature was utilized to create the right bottom slot.

The Parallelogram and Tangent Arc Sketch tools were utilized to create the third Extruded Cut feature. The Circular Pattern feature created the three radial slot cuts. The following Geometric relations were utilized: Equal, Parallel, Coincident, and Tangent.

Additional details on Rectangle, Circle, Tangent Arc, Parallelogram, Mirror Entities, Sketch Fillet, Offset Entities, Extruded Boss/Base, Extruded Cut, Mirror, and Circular Pattern are available in SolidWorks Help.

SCREW Part

The SCREW part is a simplified model of a 10-24 x 3/8 machine screw. Screws, nuts and washers are classified as fasteners.

An assembly contains hundreds of fasteners. Utilize simplified versions to conserve model and rebuild time.

Machine screws are described in terms of the following:
- Nominal diameter – Size 10.

- Threads per inch – 24.

- Length – 3/8.

Screw diameter, less than ¼ inch, are represented by a size number. Size 10 refers to a diameter of .190 inch. Utilize the SCREW part to fasten components in the FRONT-SUPPORT assembly.

Simplified version

The SCREW part utilizes a Revolved Base feature to add material. The Revolved Boss/Base feature requires a centerline and sketch on a Sketch plane. A Revolved feature requires an angle of revolution. The sketch is revolved around the centerline.

Sketch a centerline on the Front Sketch plane.

Sketch a Closed profile.

Centerline

Sketch

Revolve the sketch 360 degrees.

Utilize the Edit Sketch tool to modify the sketch. Utilize the Sketch Trim and Tangent Arc tool to create a new profile.

Utilize an Extruded Cut feature sketched on the Front Plane. This is the seed feature for the Circular Pattern.

Utilize the Circular Pattern feature to create four instances.

Apply the Fillet feature to round edges and faces. Utilize the Fillet feature to round the top edge.

Apply the Chamfer feature to bevel edges and faces. Utilize a Chamfer feature to bevel the bottom face.

Note: Utilize an M5 machine screw for metric units.

Activity: SCREW Part-Documents Properties

Create a new part.

425) Click **New** □ from the Menu bar. The Templates tab is the default tab. Double-click **Part**.

Save the part.

426) Click **Save As** from the Menu bar. Select **SW-TUTORIAL-2009** for the Save in file folder.

427) Enter **SCREW** for File name.

428) Enter **MACHINE SCREW 10-24x3/8** for Description.

429) Click **Save**. The SCREW FeatureManager is displayed.

Set the dimensioning standard and part units.

430) Click **Options** 📰, **Documents Properties** tab from the Menu bar.

431) Select **ANSI** from the Overall drafting standard box.

432) Click **Units**. Select **IPS**, [**MMGS**] for Unit system.

433) Select **.123**, [**.12**] for Length units Decimal places.

434) Select **None** for Angular units Decimal places.

435) Click **OK**.

Activity: SCREW Part-Revolved Feature

Insert a Revolved feature sketched on the Front Plane. The Front Plane is the default Sketch plane.

Insert a new sketch.

436) Right-click **Front Plane** from the FeatureManager.

437) Click **Sketch** ✏ from the Context toolbar. The Sketch toolbar is displayed.

438) Click the **Centerline** ┊ Sketch tool. The Insert Line PropertyManager is displayed.

Sketch a vertical centerline.

439) Click the **Origin** ↳.

440) Click a **position** directly above the Origin as illustrated.

 Press the **z** key to Zoom out in the Graphics window.

441) Right-click **End Chain** to end the centerline.

Add a dimension.
442) Click the **Smart Dimension** ⬦ Sketch tool.

443) Click the **centerline**. Click a **position** to the left.

444) Enter **.500**in, **[12.70]**. Click the **Green Check mark** ✓ .

Fit the sketch to the Graphics Window.
445) Press the **f** key.

Sketch the profile.
446) Click the **Line** ＼ Sketch tool.

Sketch the first horizontal line.

447) Click the **Origin** . Click a **position** to the right of the Origin.

Sketch the first vertical line.
448) Click a position **above** the horizontal line endpoint.

449) Sketch the second **horizontal line**.

450) Sketch the second **vertical line**. The top point of the vertical line is collinear with the top point of the centerline.

451) Sketch the third **horizontal line**. The left endpoint of the horizontal line is coincident with the top point of the centerline.

452) Right-click **Select** to deselect the Line Sketch tool.

Add a Horizontal relation.
453) Click the **top** most right point. Hold the **Ctrl** key down.

454) Click the **top** most left point. Release the **Ctrl** key.

455) Click **Horizontal** ▬ from the Add Relations box.

456) Click **OK** ✓ from the Properties PropertyManager.

Add a dimension.
457) Click the **Smart Dimension** ⬦ Sketch tool. Create the first diameter dimension.

458) Click the **centerline** in the Graphics window.

459) Click the **first vertical line**.

460) Click a **position** to the left of the Origin to create a diameter dimension.

461) Enter **.190**in, **[4.83]**.

462) Click the **Green Check mark** ✓ .

A diameter dimension for a Revolved sketch requires a centerline, profile line, and a dimension position to the left of the centerline.

A dimension position directly below the bottom horizontal line creates a radial dimension.

Create the second diameter dimension.
463) Click the **centerline** in the Graphics window.

464) Click the **second vertical line**.

465) Click a **position** to the left of the Origin to create a diameter dimension.

466) Enter **.373**in, **[9.47]**.

Create a vertical dimension.
467) Click the **first vertical line**.

468) Click a **position** to the right of the line.

469) Enter **.375**in, **[9.53]**.

Center the dimension text.
470) Click the **.190**in, **[4.83]** dimension.

471) Drag the **text** between the two extension lines.

472) Click the **.373**in, **[9.47]** dimension.

473) Drag the **text** between the two extension lines. If required, click the **blue arrow dots** to flip the arrows inside the extension lines.

474) Right-click **Select** to deselect the Smart Dimension Sketch tool.

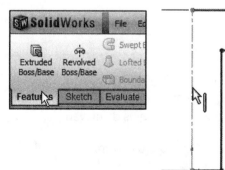

Select the Centerline for axis of revolution.
475) Click the **vertical centerline** as illustrated.

Revolve the sketch.
476) Click **Revolved Boss/Base** ⚙ from the Features toolbar.

477) Click **Yes**. The Revolve PropertyManager is displayed.

The "Yes" button causes a vertical line to be automatically sketched from the top left point to the Origin. The Graphics window displays the Isometric view and a preview of the Revolved Base feature.

The Revolve PropertyManager displays 360 degrees for the Angle of Revolution.

478) Click **OK** ✓ from the Revolve PropertyManager.

The FeatureManager displays the Revolve1 name for the first feature. The Revolved Boss/Base feature requires a centerline, sketch, and an angle of revolution. A solid Revolved Boss/Base feature requires a closed sketch. Draw the sketch on one side of the centerline.

The SCREW requires a rounded profile. Edit the Revolved Base sketch. Insert a Tangent Arc.

Edit the Revolved Base sketch.
479) Right-click **Revolve1** in the FeatureManager. Click **Edit Sketch** from the Context toolbar.

480) Click **Front view** 🔲 from the Heads-up View toolbar.

481) Click the **Tangent Arc** ⟍ Sketch tool.

482) Click the **top centerline** point as illustrated.

483) Drag the **mouse pointer** to the right and downward.

484) Click a **position** collinear with the right vertical line, below the midpoint. The arc is displayed tangent to the top horizontal line.

Deselect the Tangent Arc Sketch tool.
485) Right-click **Select**.

Delete unwanted geometry.
486) Click the **Trim Entities** ✂ Sketch tool. The Trim PropertyManager is displayed.

487) Click **Trim to closest** from the Options box. The Trim to closest icon is displayed.

Origin

488) Click the **right top vertical line** as illustrated.

489) Click the **top horizontal line** as illustrated. The two lines are removed.

490) Click **OK** ✓ from the Trim PropertyManager. Note: You may still view lines until you exit the sketch.

Add a dimension.
491) Click the **Smart Dimension** ✎ Sketch tool.

492) Click the **arc**.

493) Click a **position** above the profile.

494) Enter **.304**in, **[7.72]**.

495) Click the **Green Check mark** ✓. The sketch should be fully defined, if not add a .05 inch dimension as illustrated.

496) Click **Exit Sketch** from the Sketch toolbar.

497) Click **Save** 💾.

The SCREW requires an Extruded Cut feature on the Front Plane. Utilize the Convert Entities Sketch tool to extract the Revolved Base top arc edge for the profile of the Extruded Cut.

Activity: SCREW Part-Extruded Cut Feature

Insert a new sketch for the Extruded Cut feature.
498) Right-click **Front Plane** from the FeatureManager.

499) Click **Sketch** ✎ from the Context toolbar. The Sketch toolbar is displayed.

500) Click the **top arc** as illustrated. The mouse pointer displays the silhouette edge icon for feedback.

501) Click the **Convert Entities** 🗍 Sketch tool.

502) Click the **Line** ＼ Sketch tool.

503) Sketch a **vertical line**. The top endpoint of the line is coincident with the arc, vertically aligned to the Origin.

504) Sketch a **horizontal line**. The right end point of the line is coincident with the arc. Do not select the arc midpoint. Right-click **Select**.

505) Click **Isometric view** from the Heads-up View toolbar.

506) Click the **Trim Entities** Sketch tool. The Trim PropertyManager is displayed.

507) Click **Power trim** from the Options box.

508) Click a position to the **left** side of the arc.

509) Drag the mouse pointer to **intersect** the left arc line.

510) Click a position to the **right** side of the right arc.

511) Drag the mouse pointer to **intersect** the right arc line.

512) Click **OK** from the Trim PropertyManager.

Add a dimension.
513) Click the **Smart Dimension** Sketch tool.

514) Click the **vertical line**.

515) Click a **position** to the right of the profile.

516) Enter **.030**in, **[0.76]**.

517) Click the **Green Check mark** .

Insert an Extruded Cut Feature.
518) Click **Isometric view** from the Heads-up View toolbar.

519) Click **Extruded Cut** from the Features toolbar. The Extrude PropertyManager is displayed.

520) Select **Mid Plane** for the End Condition in Direction 1.

521) Enter **.050**in, **[1.27]** for Depth.

522) Click **OK** from the Extrude PropertyManager. Extrude1 is displayed in the FeatureManager.

Activity: SCREW Part-Circular Pattern Feature

Insert the Circular Pattern feature.

523) Click **View**, check **Temporary Axes** from the Menu bar. The Temporary Axis is required for the Circular Pattern feature.

524) Click **Circular Pattern** from the Features Consolidated toolbar. Extrude1 is displayed in the Features to Pattern box.

525) Click the **Temporary Axis** in the Graphics window. Axis<1> is displayed in the Pattern Axis box.

526) Enter **360**deg for Angle.

527) Enter **4** for Number of Instances.

528) Check the **Equal spacing** box.

529) Click **OK** ✅ from the Circular Pattern PropertyManager. CirPattern1 is displayed in the FeatureManager.

Save the model.

530) Click **Save** 💾.

Activity: SCREW Part-Fillet Feature

Insert the Fillet feature.

531) Click the **top circular edge** as illustrated.

532) Click **Fillet** 🔘 from the Features toolbar. The Fillet PropertyManager is displayed.

533) Click the **Manual** tab. Edge<1> is displayed in the Items to Fillet box.

534) Enter **.010**in, [.25] for Radius.

535) Click **OK** ✅ from the Fillet PropertyManager. Fillet1 is displayed in the FeatureManager.

Activity: SCREW Part-Chamfer Feature

Insert the Chamfer feature.
536) Click the **bottom circular edge**.

537) Click **Chamfer** 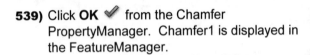 from the Features Consolidated toolbar. Edge<1> is displayed in the Items to Chamfer box.

538) Enter .050in, [**1.27**] for Distance.

539) Click **OK** ✔ from the Chamfer PropertyManager. Chamfer1 is displayed in the FeatureManager.

🔆 Simplify the part. Save rebuild time. Suppress features that are not required in the assembly.

A suppressed feature is not displayed in the Graphics window. A suppressed feature is removed from any rebuild calculations.

Suppress the Fillet and Chamfer feature.

540) Hold the **Ctrl** key down.

541) Click **Fillet1** and **Chamfer1** from the FeatureManager.

542) Release the **Ctrl** key.

543) Right-click **Suppress** ⬇ Suppress from the Context toolbar. Note: Suppressed features are displayed in light gray in the FeatureManager.

Deactivate the Temporary Axes in the Graphics window.
544) Click **View**, uncheck **Temporary Axes** from the Menu bar.

Save the SCREW part.
545) Click **Isometric view** 🔲 from the Heads-up View toolbar.

546) Click **Save** 💾.

Close all open documents.
547) Click **Window**, **Close All** from the Menu bar.

Review the SCREW Part

The Revolved Boss/Base feature was utilized to create the SCREW part. The Revolved Boss/Base feature required a centerline sketched on the Front Sketch plane and a closed profile. The sketch was revolved 360 degrees to create the Base feature for the SCREW part.

Edit Sketch was utilized to modify the sketch. The Sketch Trim and Tangent Arc tools created a new profile.

The Extruded Cut feature was sketched on the Front Plane.

The Circular Pattern feature created four instances.

The Fillet feature rounded the top edges.

The Chamfer feature beveled the bottom edge. The Fillet and Chamfer are suppressed to save rebuild time in the assembly. Note: Suppressed features are displayed in light gray in the FeatureManager.

Additional details on Convert Entities, Silhouette Edge, Revolved Boss/Base, Circular Pattern, Fillet, and Chamfer are available in SolidWorks Help. Keywords: Sketch tools, silhouette, features, Pattern, Revolve, Fillet and Chamfer.

FRONT-SUPPORT Assembly

The FRONT-SUPPORT assembly consists of the following parts:

- ANGLE-13HOLE part

- TRIANGLE part

- HEX-STANDOFF part

- SCREW part

Create the FRONT-SUPPORT assembly. Insert the ANGLE-13HOLE part. The ANGLE-13HOLE part is fixed to the FRONT-SUPPORT Origin. Insert the first HEX-STANDOFF part.

Utilize Concentric and Coincident mates to assemble the HEX-STANDOFF to the left hole of the ANGLE-13HOLE part. Insert the second HEX-STANDOFF part.

Utilize Concentric and Coincident mates to assemble the HEX-STANDOFF to the third hole from the right side. Insert the TRIANGLE part. Utilize Concentric, Distance, and Parallel mates to assemble the TRIANGLE. Utilize Concentric and Coincident SmartMates to assemble the four SCREWS.

Activity: FRONT-SUPPORT Assembly-Insert ANGLE-13HOLE

Create a new assembly.

548) Click **New** ⬚ from the Menu bar.

549) Double-click **Assembly** from the Templates tab. The Begin Assembly PropertyManager is displayed. Note: The Begin Assembly PropertyManager is displayed if the Start command when creating new assembly box is checked.

550) Click the **Browse** button.

551) Select **Part** from the Files of type in the SW-TUTORIAL-2009 folder.

552) Double-click the **ANGLE-13HOLE** part.

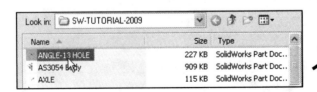

Fix the first component to the Origin.

553) Click **OK** ✓ from the Begin Assembly PropertyManager. The first component is fixed to the Origin (f).

Save the assembly.
554) Click **Save As** from the Menu bar.

555) Select **SW-TUTORIAL-2009** for the Save in file folder.

556) Enter **FRONT-SUPPORT** for File name.

557) Enter **FRONT SUPPORT ASSEMBLY** for Description.

558) Click **Save**. The FRONT-SUPPORT assembly FeatureManager is displayed.

Set the dimensioning standard and assembly units.
559) Click **Options** 📧 , **Document Properties** tab from the Menu bar.

560) Select **ANSI** from the Overall drafting standard box.

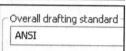

Set the units.
561) Click **Units**.

562) Select **IPS**, [**MMGS**] for Unit system.

563) Select **.123**, [**.12**] for Length units Decimal places.

564) Select **None** for Angular units Decimal places.

565) Click **OK**.

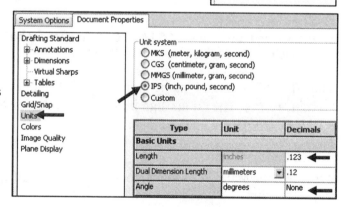

The ANGLE-13HOLE name in the FeatureManager displays an (f) symbol. The (f) symbol indicates that the ANGLE-13HOLE component is fixed to the FRONT-SUPPORT assembly Origin. The component cannot move or rotate.

🔆 To remove the fixed state, Right-click a component name in the FeatureManager. Click **Float**. The component is free to move.

Display the Isometric view.

566) Click **Isometric view** 🔲 from the Heads-up View toolbar.

Save the assembly.

567) Click **Save** 💾 .

Activity: FRONT-SUPPORT Assembly-Inset HEX-STANDOFF

Insert the HEX-STANDOFF part.

568) Click the **Insert Components** 🖱️ Assembly tool. The Insert Component PropertyManager is displayed.

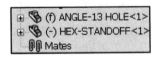

569) Click the **Browse** button.

570) Select **Part** from the Files of type box.

571) Double-click **HEX-STANDOFF** from the SW-TUTORIAL 2009 folder.

572) Click a **position** near the left top hole as illustrated.

Enlarge the view.

573) **Zoom in** on the front left side of the assembly.

Move the component.

574) Click and drag the **HEX-STANDOFF** component below the ANGLE-13HOLE left hole.

The HEX-STANDOFF name in the FeatureManager displays a (-) minus sign. The minus sign indicates that the HEX-STANDOFF part is free to move.

Insert a Concentric mate.

575) Click the **Mate** 🖇️ Assembly tool. The Mate PropertyManager is displayed.

576) Click the **left inside cylindrical hole face** of the ANGLE-13HOLE component.

577) Click inside the **cylindrical hole face** of the HEX-STANDOFF component. The selected faces are displayed in the Mate Selections box. Concentric is selected by default.

578) Click the **Green Check mark** ✔️ .

579) Click and drag the **HEX-STANDOFF** component below the ANGLE-13HOLE component until the top face is displayed.

Insert a Coincident mate.
580) Click the **HEX-STANDOFF top face**.

581) Press the **Up Arrow key** approximately 5 times to view the bottom face of the ANGLE-13HOLE component.

582) Click the **ANGLE-13HOLE bottom face**. The selected faces are displayed in the Mate Selections box. Coincident Mate is selected by default.

583) Click the **Green Check mark** ✔ .

584) Click **Isometric view** ⬛ from the Heads-up View toolbar.

585) Click and drag the **HEX-STANDOFF** component. The HEX-STANDOFF rotates about its axis.

Insert a Parallel mate.
586) Click **Front view** ⬛ from the Heads-up View toolbar.

587) Click the **HEX-STANDOFF front face**.

588) Click the **ANGLE-13HOLE front face**. The selected faces are displayed in the Mate Selections box. A Mate message is displayed.

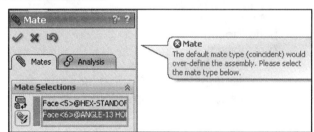

589) Click **Parallel** ⬉ .

590) Click the **Green Check mark** ✔ .

591) Click **OK** ✔ from the Mate PropertyManager.

Display the created mates.
592) **Expand** the Mates folder in the FRONT-SUPPORT FeatureManager. Three mates are displayed between the ANGLE-13HOLE component and the HEX-STANDOFF component. The HEX-STANDOFF component is fully defined.

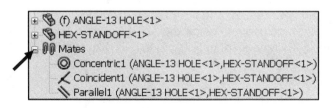

Save the FRONT-SUPPORT assembly.

593) Click **Save** 💾.

Insert the second HEX-STANDOFF part.
594) Hold the **Ctrl** key down.

595) Click and drag the **HEX-STANDOFF<1>**
⊞ ⊛ (f) ANGLE-13 HOLE<1> name from the FeatureManager into
the FRONT-SUPPORT assembly Graphics window.

596) Release the **mouse pointer** below the far right hole of the
ANGLE-13HOLE component.

597) Release the **Ctrl** key. HEX-STANDOFF<2> is displayed in the
Graphics window and listed in the FeatureManager.

💡 The number <2> indicates the second instance or copy of
the same component. The instance number increments every
time you insert the same component. If you delete a component
and then reinsert the component in the same SolidWorks session,
the instance number increments by one.

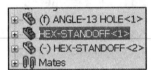

Enlarge the view.
598) Zoom in on the right
side of the assembly.

Insert a Concentric mate.
599) Click the **Mate** 📎
Assembly tool. The
Mate PropertyManager
is displayed.

600) Click the **third hole cylindrical face** from the
right ANGLE-13HOLE component.

601) Click inside the **cylindrical hole face** of the
second HEX-STANDOFF component.
Concentric is selected by default.

602) Click the **Green Check mark** ✔.

Move the second HEX-STANDOFF part.
603) Click and drag the **HEX-STANDOFF**
component below the ANGLE-13HOLE
component until its top face is displayed.

Insert a Coincident mate.

604) Click the **second HEX-STANDOFF** top face.

605) Press the **up arrow key** approximately 5 times to view the bottom face of the ANGLE-13HOLE component.

606) Click the **ANGLE-13HOLE bottom face**. The selected faces are displayed in the Mate Selections box. Coincident Mate is selected by default.

607) Click the **Green Check mark** .

Insert a Parallel mate.

608) Click **Front view** Heads-up View toolbar.

609) Click the **front face** of the second HEX-STANDOFF.

610) Click the **front face** of the ANGLE-13HOLE. A Mate message is displayed.

611) Click **Parallel** ⬂.

612) Click the **Green Check mark** ✓.

613) Click **OK** ✓ from the Mate PropertyManager.

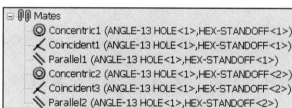

Display the created mates.

614) **Expand** the Mates folder in the FRONT-SUPPORT FeatureManager. Three mates are displayed between the ANGLE-13HOLE component and the second HEX-STANDOFF component. The second HEX-STANDOFF is fully defined.

⊟ 🎔 Mates
  ◎ Concentric1 (ANGLE-13 HOLE<1>,HEX-STANDOFF<1>)
  ⟋ Coincident1 (ANGLE-13 HOLE<1>,HEX-STANDOFF<1>)
  ⬂ Parallel1 (ANGLE-13 HOLE<1>,HEX-STANDOFF<1>)
  ◎ Concentric2 (ANGLE-13 HOLE<1>,HEX-STANDOFF<2>)
  ⟋ Coincident3 (ANGLE-13 HOLE<1>,HEX-STANDOFF<2>)
  ⬂ Parallel2 (ANGLE-13 HOLE<1>,HEX-STANDOFF<2>)

Activity: FRONT-SUPPORT Assembly-Insert the TRIANGLE

Insert the TRIANGLE part.

615) Click **Isometric view** 🗗 from the Heads-up View toolbar.

616) Click the **Insert Components** 🖽 Assembly tool. The Insert Component PropertyManager is displayed.

617) Click the **Browse** button.

618) Select **Part** from the Files of type box.

619) Double-click **TRIANGLE**.

620) Click a **position** in back of the ANGLE-13HOLE component as illustrated.

Enlarge the view.
621) **Zoom in** on the right side of the TRIANGLE and the ANGLE-13HOLE.

Insert a Concentric mate.
622) Click the **Mate** 🔗 Assembly tool. The Mate PropertyManager is displayed.

623) Click the **inside right arc face** of the TRAINGLE.

624) Click the **inside right arc face** of the ANGLE-13HOLE slot. Concentric mate is selected by default. Note: Utilize the Undo button if the mate is not correct.

625) Click the **Green Check mark** ✔ .

Fit the model to the Graphics window.
626) Press the **f** key.

Insert a Distance mate.
627) Click the **front face** of the TRIANGLE.

628) Press the **left Arrow key** approximately 5 times to view the back face of the ANGLE-13HOLE component.

629) Click the **back face** of the ANGLE-13HOLE component.

630) Click **Distance** ↦ from the Mate dialog box.

631) Enter **0**.

632) Click the **Green Check mark** ✔ .

💡 A Distance Mate of 0 provides additional flexibility compared to a Coincident mate. A

Distance mate value can be modified.

Insert a Parallel mate.

633) Click **Bottom view** ⬚ from the Heads-up View toolbar.

634) Click the **narrow bottom face** of the TRIANGLE.

635) Click the **bottom face** of the ANGLE-13HOLE. The selected faces are displayed in the Mate Selections box. A Mate message is displayed.

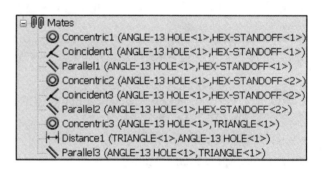

636) Click **Parallel** ⬚.

637) Click the **Green Check mark** ✔.

638) Click **OK** ✔ from the Mate PropertyManager.

Display the Isometric view.

639) Click **Isometric view** ⬚ from the Heads-up View toolbar.

View the created mates.

640) Expand the Mates folder. View the created mates.

Save the FRONT-SUPPORT assembly.

641) Click **Save** 💾.

Assemble the four SCREW parts with SmartMates.

A SmartMate is a mate that automatically occurs when a component is placed into an assembly.

The mouse pointer displays a SmartMate feedback symbol when common geometry and relationships exist between the component and the assembly.

SmartMates are Concentric, Coincident, or Concentric and Coincident.

A Concentric SmartMate assumes that the geometry on the component has the same center as the geometry on an assembled reference.

```
⊟ ◍◍ Mates
    ◎ Concentric1 (ANGLE-13 HOLE<1>,HEX-STANDOFF<1>)
    ⟨ Coincident1 (ANGLE-13 HOLE<1>,HEX-STANDOFF<1>)
    ⟍ Parallel1 (ANGLE-13 HOLE<1>,HEX-STANDOFF<1>)
    ◎ Concentric2 (ANGLE-13 HOLE<1>,HEX-STANDOFF<2>)
    ⟨ Coincident3 (ANGLE-13 HOLE<1>,HEX-STANDOFF<2>)
    ⟍ Parallel2 (ANGLE-13 HOLE<1>,HEX-STANDOFF<2>)
    ◎ Concentric3 (ANGLE-13 HOLE<1>,TRIANGLE<1>)
    ⊢⊣ Distance1 (TRIANGLE<1>,ANGLE-13 HOLE<1>)
    ⟍ Parallel3 (ANGLE-13 HOLE<1>,TRIANGLE<1>)
```

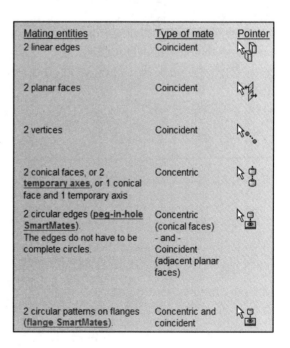

Mating entities	Type of mate	Pointer
2 linear edges	Coincident	
2 planar faces	Coincident	
2 vertices	Coincident	
2 conical faces, or 2 **temporary axes**, or 1 conical face and 1 temporary axis	Concentric	
2 circular edges (**peg-in-hole SmartMates**). The edges do not have to be complete circles.	Concentric (conical faces) - and - Coincident (adjacent planar faces)	
2 circular patterns on flanges (**flange SmartMates**).	Concentric and coincident	

As the component is dragged into place, the mouse pointer provides various feedback icons.

The SCREW utilizes a Concentric and Coincident SmartMate. Assemble the first SCREW. The circular edge of the SCREW mates Concentric and Coincident with the circular edge of the right slot of the TRIANGLE.

Activity: FRONT-SUPPORT Assembly-Inset the SCREW

Insert the SCREW part.

642) Click **Open** ⌖ from the Menu bar.

643) Double-click **SCREW** from the SW-TUTORIAL-2009 folder. The SCREW PropertyManager is displayed.

Display the SCREW part and the FRONT-SUPPORT assembly.

644) Click **Window**, **Tile Horizontally** from the Menu bar.

645) **Zoom in** on the right side of the FRONT-SUPPORT assembly. Note: Work between the two tile windows.

Insert the first SCREW.

646) Click and drag the **circular edge** of the SCREW part into the FRONT-SUPPORT assembly Graphic window.

647) Release the mouse pointer on the **top 3rd circular hole edge** of the ANGLE-13HOLE. The mouse pointer displays the 🖰 Coincident / Concentric circular edges icon.

Insert the second SCREW.
648) Zoom in on the right side of the FRONT-SUPPORT assembly.

649) Click and drag the **circular edge** of the SCREW part into the FRONT-SUPPORT assembly Graphic window.

650) Release the mouse pointer on the **right arc edge** of the ANGLE-

13HOLE. The mouse pointer displays the   Coincident/
Concentric circular edges icon.

Insert the third SCREW part.
651) Zoom in on the left side of the FRONT-SUPPORT assembly

652) Click and drag the **circular edge** of the SCREW part into the FRONT-SUPPORT Assembly Graphic window.

653) Release the mouse pointer on the **left arc edge** of the ANGLE-

13HOLE. The mouse pointer displays the   Coincident/
Concentric circular edges icon.

Insert the forth SCREW part.
654) Zoom in on the bottom circular edge of the ANGLE-13HOLE.

655) Click and drag the **circular edge** of the SCREW part into the FRONT-SUPPORT Assembly Graphic window.

656) Release the mouse pointer on the **bottom circular edge** of the

ANGLE-13HOLE. The mouse pointer displays the
Coincident/Concentric circular edges icon.

657) Close the SCREW part window.

658) Maximize the FRONT-SUPPORT assembly window.

Display the Isometric view.
659) Click **Isometric view** 🔳 from the Heads-up View toolbar.

Deactivate the Origins.
660) Click **View**, uncheck **Origins** from the Menu bar menu.

Save the FRONT-SUPPORT assembly.

661) Click **Save** 🖫 .

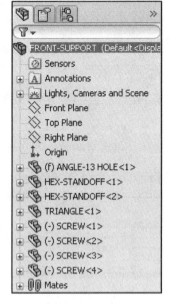

Select the Ctrl-Tab keys to quickly alternate between open SolidWorks documents.

Close all open parts and assemblies.
662) Click **Windows**, **Close All** from the Menu bar.

The FRONT-SUPPORT assembly is complete.

Display the Mates in the FeatureManager to check that the components and the mate types correspond to the design intent. Utilize the Edit Feature command to modify mate references.

If an assembly or component is loaded in a Lightweight
 state, right-click the **assembly name** or **component name** from the FeatureManager. Click **Set Lightweight to Resolved**.

Review the FRONT-SUPPORT Assembly.

The ANGLE-13HOLE part was the first part inserted into the FRONT-SUPPORT assembly. The ANGLE-13HOLE part was fixed to the FRONT-SUPPORT Origin.

Concentric, Coincident, and Parallel mates were utilized to assemble the HEX-STANDOFF to the ANGLE-13HOLE. Concentric, Distance, and Parallel mates were utilized to assemble the TRIANGLE to the ANGLE-13HOLE. The Concentric/Coincident SmartMate was utilized to mate the four SCREW parts to the FRONT-SUPPORT assembly.

Project Summary

In this project you created four parts; HEX-STANDOFF, ANGLE-13HOLE, TRIANGLE, and SCREW utilizing the Top, Front, and Right Planes and the FRONT-SUPPORT assembly.

You obtained the knowledge of the following SolidWorks features: Extruded Boss/Base, Extruded Thin, Extruded Cut, Revolved Boss/Base, Hole Wizard, Linear Pattern, Circular Pattern, Fillet, and Chamfer. You also applied sketch techniques with various Sketch tools: Line, Circle, Corner Rectangle, Centerline, Dynamic Mirror, Straight Slot, Trim Entities, Polygon, Tangent Arc, Sketch Fillet, Offset Entities, and Convert Entities.

You utilized centerlines as construction geometry to reference dimensions and relationships.

You incorporated the four new parts to create the FRONT-SUPPORT assembly. Concentric, Distance, and Parallel mates were utilized to assemble the TRIANGLE to the ANGLE-13HOLE. The Concentric/Coincident SmartMate was utilized to mate the four SCREW parts to the FRONT-SUPPORT assembly.

Project Terminology

Utilize SolidWorks Help for additional information on the terms utilized in this project.

Assembly: An assembly is a document which contains components, features, and other sub-assemblies. When a part is inserted into an assembly it is called a component. Components are mated together. The filename extension for a SolidWorks assembly file name is .SLDASM.

Component: A part or sub-assembly within an assembly.

Convert Entities: Converts model entities or sketch entities into sketch segments on the current sketch plane.

Features: Features are geometry building blocks. Features add or remove material. Features are created from sketched profiles or from edges and faces of existing geometry.

Instance Number: The instance number increments every time you insert the same component or mate. If you delete a component or mate and then reinsert the component or mate in the same SolidWorks session, the instance number increments by one.

Mates: A mate is a Geometric relation between components in an assembly.

Mirror Entities: Sketch tool that mirrors sketch geometry to the opposite side of a sketched centerline

Offset Entities: Insert sketch entities by offsetting faces, edges, curves, construction geometry by a specified distance on the current sketch plane.

Orthographic Projection: Orthographic projection is the process of projecting views onto parallel planes with ⊥ projectors. The default reference planes are the Front, Top, and Right Planes.

Part: A part is a single 3D object made up of features. The filename extension for a SolidWorks part file name is .SLDPRT.

Plane: To create a sketch, choose a plane. Planes are flat and infinite. They are represented on the screen with visible edges. The Front, Top, and Right Planes were utilized as Sketch planes for parts in this project.

Relation: A relation is a geometric constraint between sketch entities or between a sketch entity and a plane, axis, edge, or vertex.

Sketch: The name to describe a 2D or 3D profile is called a sketch. 2D Sketches are created on flat faces and planes within the model. Typical geometry types are lines, arcs, rectangles, circles, and ellipses.

SmartMates: A SmartMate is a mate that automatically occurs when a component is placed into an assembly and references geometry between that component and the assembly.

Standard Views: Front, Back, Right, Left, Top, Bottom, and Isometric are the Standard views utilized to orient the model.

Suppress features: A suppress feature is not displayed in the Graphics window. A suppress feature is removed from any rebuild calculations.

Trim Entities: Sketch tool that removes highlighted geometry.

Project Features

Chamfer: A Chamfer feature creates bevels on selected edges and faces.

Circular Pattern: A Circular Pattern feature repeats features or faces about an axis in a circular array. A Circular Pattern requires and axis, number of instances, and the angle of revolution.

Extruded Boss/Base: An Extruded Base feature is the first feature in a part. The Extruded Boss/Base feature starts with either a 2D or 3D sketch. An Extruded Boss feature occurs after the Extruded Base feature. The Extruded Boss/Base feature adds material by extrusion. Steps to create an Extruded Boss/Base Feature:

- Select the Sketch plane; Sketch the profile 2D or 3D; Add dimensions and Geometric relations; Select Extruded Boss/Base from the Features toolbar; Select an End Condition and/or options; Enter a depth; Click OK from the Extrude PropertyManager.

Extruded Cut: The Extruded Cut feature removes material from a solid. The Extruded Cut feature performs the opposite function of the Extruded Boss/Base feature. The Extruded Cut feature starts with either a 2D or 3D sketch and removes material by extrusion. Steps to create an Extruded Cut Feature:

- Select the Sketch plane; Sketch the profile, 2D or 3D; Add dimensions and Geometric relations; Select Extruded Cut from the Features toolbar; Select an End Condition and/or options; Enter a depth; Click OK from the Extrude PropertyManager.

Extruded Thin: The Extruded Thin feature adds material of constant thickness. The Extruded Thin feature requires an open profile.

Fillet: The Fillet feature creates a rounded internal or external face on a part. You can fillet all edges of a face, selected sets of faces, selected edges, or edge loops.

Hole Wizard: The Hole Wizard feature provides the ability to determine the capabilities, available selections, and graphic previews for various hole types. First select a hole type, then determine the appropriate fastener. The fastener dynamically updates the appropriate parameters.

Linear Pattern: A Linear Pattern repeats features or geometry in an array. A Linear Patten requires the number of instances and the spacing between instances. Steps to create a Linear Pattern Feature:

- Select the feature/s to repeat (seed feature); Select Linear Pattern from the Feature toolbar; Enter Direction of the pattern; Enter Number of pattern instances in each direction; Enter Distance between pattern instances; Optional: Pattern instances to skip; Click OK from the Linear Pattern PropertyManager.

Mirror: The Mirror feature mirrors features or faces about a selected plane. Select the features to copy and a plane about which to mirror them. If you select a planar face on the model, you mirror the entire model about the selected face.

Revolved Boss/Base: The Revolved Boss/Base feature adds material by revolving one or more profiles around a centerline. Create Revolved boss/bases, Revolved cuts, or Revolved surfaces. The Revolve feature can be a solid, a thin feature, or a surface.

Engineering Journal

Engineers and designers research their customer's requirements and criteria. They utilize mathematics, science, economics and history to calculate additional information about a project.

Engineers adhere to federal regulations and standards to design parts that are safe and reliable. Record the answers to the questions in an engineering journal.

1. Estimation. The volume of the golf ball is approximated with the model of a sphere. A sphere is a revolved feature. What is the volume of the sphere?

Model Courtesy of
Scott Baugh, CSWP
www.scottjbaugh.com

Volume of a sphere is provided by the formula; $V = 4/3\ \pi\ r^3$. Where:

- V is volume.

- r is the radius.

a.) Determine the radius of the sphere in mm and inches.

b.) Calculate the Volume of the sphere in mm^3 and in^3.

c.) The actual volume of the golf ball model is 1.001 in^3. Why does the volume value differ from the calculated volume of the sphere?

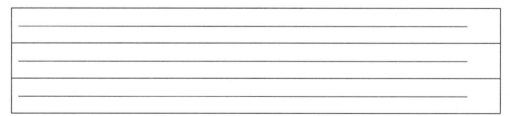

2. Sketching.

- Sketch the top view of a Flat-Plate.
  The overall dimensions of the Flat-Plate are: 8.688in x 5.688in x 0.090in.

The four corners of the Flat-Plate are rounded with a .25in Radius.

A two dimensional array of Ø.190in holes is spaced .500in apart.

The holes are .344in from all four sides.

- Determine the size of the two dimensional array of holes.
  Determine the total number of holes contained on the Flat-Plate. (Note: Sketch Not to Scale).

3. Sketching on Planes.

a) Label the Front, Top, and Right Planes. Sketch an L-shaped profile on the Front Plane.

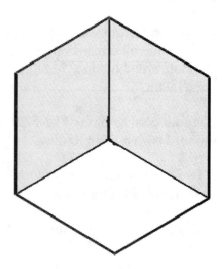

b) Sketch an L-shaped profile on the Top Plane. Label the Primary Datum plane.

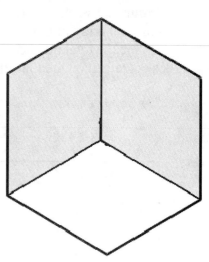

c) Sketch an L-shaped profile on the Right Plane. Label the Secondary Datum plane.

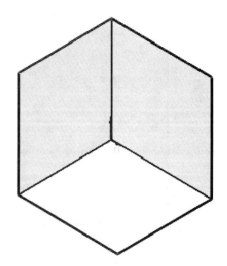

4. Industry Application

Calculating material volume is important when designing parts.

Volume = Width x Height x Depth.

The Extruded Base feature of the container is 45cm x 20cm x 30cm.

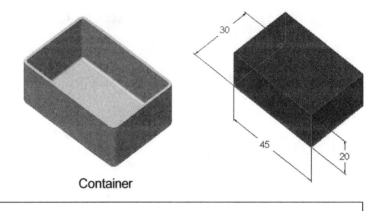

Container

- Estimate the approximate volume of the container in cm^3.

_____

Volume for food containers is commonly provided in liters or gallons.

Examples: 2-liter soda bottle or a gallon of milk.

- Calculate the volume of the container in liters and in gallons.

Given: 1 liter = 1000 cm^3

        1 gallon = 3.785 liters.

- Approximately how many liters would the container hold? How many gallons?

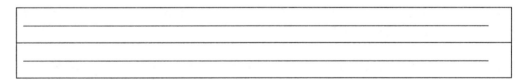

The actual volume of the Container is 23 liters. Explain why this value does not equal your first estimated volume.

_____
_____

Questions

1. Identify the three default Reference planes.

2. True or False. Sketches are created only on the Front Plane.

3. Identify the sketch tool required to create a hexagon.

4. Describe the profile required for an Extruded Thin feature.

5. Mirror Entities, Offset Entities, Sketch Fillet, and Trim Entities are located in the _____ toolbar.

6. List the six principle views in a drawing _____, _____, _____, _____, _____, _____,

7. Identify the type of Geometric relations that can be added to a sketch.

8. Describe the difference between a Circular Pattern feature and a Linear Pattern feature.

9. Describe the difference between a Fillet feature and a Chamfer feature.

10. Identify the function of the Hole Wizard feature.

11. Four 10-24X3/8 Machine Screws are required in the FRONT-SUPPORT assembly. The diameter is _____. The threads per inch are _____. The length is _____.

12. Describe the difference between a Distance mate and a Coincident mate.

13. True or False. A fixed component cannot move in an assembly.

14. Describe the procedure to remove the fix state, (f) of a component in an assembly.

15. Determine the procedure to rotate a component in an assembly.

16. Describe the procedure to resolve a Lightweight component in an assembly.

17. Describe the procedure to resolve a Lightweight assembly.

Exercises

Exercise 2.1: **HEX-NUT Part**.

Create a HEX-NUT, 6061 Alloy part
using the following dimensions:

- Depth: .125 in, [3.18].

- Inside hole diameter: .190in, [4.83].

- Outside diameter: .375in, [9.53].

Use the Top Plane as the Sketch plane.

Exercise 2.2: **FRONT-SUPPORT-2 Assembly**.

Create the FRONT-SUPPORT-2 assembly.

- Name the new assembly FRONT-SUPPORT-2.

- Insert the FRONT-SUPPORT assembly. Fix the
  FRONT-SUPPORT assembly to the Origin.

- Insert the first HEX-NUT (Exercise 2.1)
  into the FRONT-SUPPORT-2 assembly.

- Insert a Concentric mate.

- Insert a Coincident mate.

- Insert the second HEX-NUT part.

- Insert a Concentric mate.

- Insert a Coincident mate.

Note: You can also insert a Parallel mate
between the HEX-NUT parts and the FRONT-
SUPPORT assembly.

Exercise 2.3: BALL Part.

Create a Ball part. Utilize the Revolved
Base feature.

Ø1.250

- Create a new part named BALL.

- Use the Front Plane as the Sketch
  plane.

- Sketch a circle with a diameter of
  1.250in, [31.75].

- Sketch a vertical centerline Coincident with the Origin.

- Use Power Trim to trim the left half of the ball to create an
  arc.

- Utilize the Revolved Base feature to create the Revolve-Thin1
  feature as illustrated in the FeatureManager.

Exercise 2.4: Weight-Hook assembly

Create the Weight-Hook assembly. The Weight-Hook assembly
has two components: WEIGHT and HOOK.

- Create a new assembly document. Insert the WEIGHT part
  from the Chapter 2 Homework folder in the book CD.

- Fix the WEIGHT to the Origin as illustrated in the Assem1
  FeatureManager.

- Insert the HOOK part from the Chapter2 - Homework folder
  into the assembly.

- Insert a Concentric mate between the inside top
  cylindrical face of the WEIGHT and the cylindrical face
  of the thread. Concentric is the default mate.

- Insert the first Coincident mate between the top edge of
  the circular hole of the WEIGHT and the top circular
  edge of Sweep1, above the thread.

- Coincident is the default mate. The HOOK can rotate in the WEIGHT.

- Fix the position of the HOOK. Insert the second Coincident mate between the Right Plane of the WEIGHT and the Right Plane of the HOOK. Coincident is the default mate.

- Expand the Mates folder and view the created mates.

Exercise 2.5: Weight-Link assembly

Create the Weight-Link assembly. The Weight-Link assembly has two components and a sub-assembly: Axle component, FLATBAR component, and the Weight-Hook sub-assembly that you created in Exercise 2.4.

- Create a new assembly document. Insert the Axle part from the Chapter 2 Homework folder in the book CD.

- Fix the Axle component to the Origin.

- Insert the FLATBAR part from the Chapter2 - Homework folder in the book CD.

- Insert a Concentric mate between the Axle cylindrical face and the FLATBAR inside face of the top circle.

If an assembly or component is loaded in a Lightweight state, right-click the **assembly name** or **component name** from the FeatureManager. Click **Set Lightweight to Resolved**.

- Insert a Coincident mate between the Front Plane of the Axle and the Front Plane of the FLATBAR.

- Insert a Coincident mate between the Right Plane of the Axle and the Top Plane of the FLATBAR. Position the FLATBAR as illustrated.

- Insert the Weight-Hook sub-assembly that you created in exercise 2.4.

- Insert a Tangent mate between the inside bottom cylindrical face of the FLATBAR and the top circular face of the HOOK, in the Weight-Hook assembly. Tangent mate is selected by default.

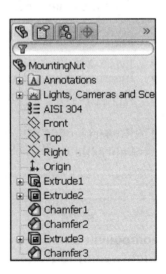

- Insert a Coincident mate between the Front Plane of the FLATBAR and the Front Plane of the Weight-Hook sub-assembly. Coincident mate is selected by default. The Weight-Hook sub-assembly is free to move in the bottom circular hole of the FLATBAR.

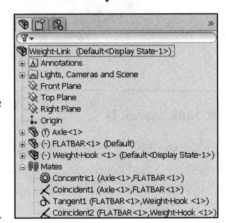

Exercise 2.6: **Mounting-Nut Part**.

Create a Mounting-Nut Part using the features displayed in the illustrated FeatureManager.

Exercise 2.7: **AIR RESERVOIR SUPPORT AND PLATE Assembly**.

The project team developed a concept sketch of the PNEUMATIC TEST MODULE assembly. Develop the AIR RESERVOIR SUPPORT AND PLATE assembly.

PNEUMATIC TEST MODULE Assembly Layout

Create three new parts:

- FLAT-PLATE.

- IM15-MOUNT.

- ANGLE-BRACKET.

The Reservoir is a purchased part. The assembly file is available from the CD in the book.

AIR RESERVOIR SUPPORT Assembly
Courtesy of Gears Educational Systems & SMC
Corporation of America

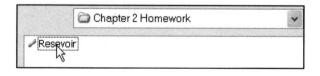

- Create a new assembly named AIR RESERVOIR SUPPORT AND PLATE.

- Two M15-MOUNT parts and two ANGLE-BRACKET parts hold the SMC AIR RESERVOIR.

- The ANGLE-BRACKET parts are fastened to the FLAT-PLATE.

Exercise 2.7a: **FLAT-PLATE Part**.

- Create the FLAT-PLATE Part on the Top Plane. The FLAT-PLATE is machined from .090, [2.3] 6061 Alloy flat stock. The default units are inches.

- Utilize the Top Plane for the Sketch plane.

- Locate the Origin at the Midpoint of the left vertical line.

- The 8.688, [220.68mm] x 5.688, [144.48mm] FLAT PLATE contains a Linear Pattern of ∅.190, [4.83mm] Thru holes.

- The Holes are equally spaced, .500, [12.70mm] apart.

- Determine the maximum number of holes contained in the FLAT-PLATE.

  Maximum # of holes_____.

- Utilize a Linear Pattern in two Directions to create the holes.

- Utilize the Geometric Pattern Option.

Direction 2

Direction 1

Exercise 2.7b: IM15-MOUNT Part.

- Create the IM15-MOUNT part on the Right plane.

- Center the part on the Origin. Utilize the features in the FeatureManager.

The IM15-MOUNT Part is machined from 0.060, [1.5mm] 6061 Alloy flat stock. The default units are inches.

Exercise 2.7c: **ANGLE BRACKET Part**.

- Create the ANGLE BRACKET part.

- The Extruded Base feature is sketched with an L-Shaped
  profile on the Right Plane. The ANGLE BRACKET Part is
  machined from 0.060, [1.5mm] 6061 Alloy flat stock. The
  default units are inches.

Exercise 2.7d: Reservoir Assembly.

The Reservoir stores compressed air. Air is pumped through a Schrader Valve into the Reservoir.

A Quick Connect Straight Fitting is utilized to supply air to the Pneumatic Test Module Assembly. Quick Connect Fittings allow air tubing to be assembled and disassembled without removing the fitting.

Copy the Pneumatic Components folder from the CD in the book to the SW-TUTORIAL folder.

Open the part, Reservoir from the Pneumatics Components folder or from the Chapter 2 Homework folder. The Reservoir default units are in millimeters.

Schrader Valve

Quick Connect
Straight Fitting

Reservoir and Fittings
Courtesy of SMC Corporation of America and
Gears Educational Systems

Engineers and designers work in metric and english units. Always verify your units for parts and other engineering data. In pneumatic systems, common units for volume, pressure and temperature are defined in the below table.

Magnitude	Metric Unit (m)	English (e)
Mass	kg	pound
	g	ounce
Length	m	foot
	m	yard
	mm	inch
Temperature	°C	°F
Area, Section	m ^{2}	sq.ft
	cm ^{2}	sq.inch
Volume	m ^{3}	cu.yard
	cm ^{3}	cu.inch
	dm ^{3}	cu.ft.
Volume Flow	m ^{3}n / min	scfm
	dm ^{3}n /min (ℓ/min)	scfm
Force	N	pound force (ℓbf.)
Pressure	bar	ℓbf./sq.inch (psi)

Common Metric and English Units

The ISO unit of pressure is the Pa (Pascal). $1 Pa = 1 N/m$.

Exercise 2.4e: AIR RESERVOIR SUPPORT AND PLATE Assembly.

Create the AIR RESERVOIR SUPPORT AND PLATE assembly. Note: There is more than one solution for the mate types illustrated below.

The FLAT-PLATE is the first component in the AIR RESERVOIR SUPPORT AND PLATE assembly. Insert the FLAT-PLATE. The FLAT-PLATE is fixed to the Origin.

AIR RESERVOIR SUPPORT AND PLATE Assembly
Courtesy of SMC Corporation of America

- Insert the ANGLE BRACKET.

- Mate the ANGLE BRACKET to the FLAT-PLATE. The bottom flat face of the ANGLE BRACKET is coincident to the top face of the FLAT-PLATE.

- The center hole of the ANGLE BRACKET is concentric to the upper left hole of the FLAT-PLATE.

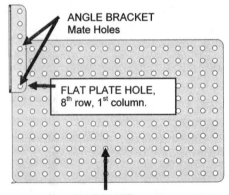

- The first hole of the ANGLE bracket is concentric with the hole in the 8th row, 1st column of the FLAT-PLATE.

- Insert the IM15-MOUNT.

- Mate the IM15-MOUNT. The IM15-MOUNT flat back face is coincident to the flat inside front face of the ANGLE BRACKET.

- The bottom right hole of the IM15-MOUNT is concentric with the right hole of the ANGLE BRACKET.

- The bottom edge of the IM15-MOUNT is parallel to bottom edge of the ANGLE BRACKET.

- Insert the Reservoir Assembly.

- Mate the Reservoir Assembly. The conical face of the Reservoir is concentric to the IM15-MOUNT center hole.

- The left end cap of the Reservoir Assembly is coincident to the front face of the IM15-MOUNT.

- The Hex Nut flat face is parallel to the top face of the FLAT-PLATE.

- Insert the second ANGLE BRACKET.

- Mate the ANGLE BRACKET to the FLAT-PLATE. The bottom flat face of the ANGLE BRACKET is coincident to the top face of the FLAT-PLATE.

- The center hole of the ANGLE BRACKET is concentric with the hole in the 11th row, 13th column of the FLAT-PLATE.

- The first hole of the ANGLE bracket is concentric with the hole in the 8th row, 13th column of the FLAT-PLATE.

- Insert the second IM15-MOUNT.

- Mate the IM15-MOUNT to the outside face of the ANGLE BRACKET. The bottom right hole of the IM15-MOUNT is concentric with the right hole of the ANGLE BRACKET.

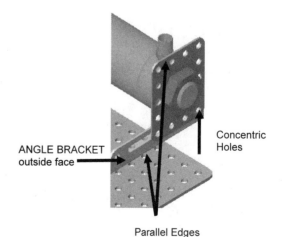

- The top edge of the IM15-MOUNT is parallel to the top edge of the ANGLE BRACKET.

- Save the assembly. Insert the required SCREWS. The AIR RESERVOIR SUPPORT AND PLATE assembly is complete.

Notes:

Project 3

Fundamentals of Drawing

Below are the desired outcomes and usage competencies based on the completion of Project 3.

Desired Outcomes:	Usage Competencies:
• CUSTOM-A Sheet Format. • A-ANSI-MM Drawing Template. • FLATBAR configurations. • FLATBAR part drawing. • LINKAGE assembly drawing. • FLATBAR-SHAFTCOLLAR assembly.	• Ability to create a Custom Sheet Format, Drawing Template, Company logo, and Title block.
	• Understand Standard, Isometric, Detail, Section, and Exploded views. • Knowledge of the View Palette. • Ability to incorporate a Bill of Materials with Custom Properties
	• Proficiency to create and edit drawing dimensions and annotations. • Aptitude to create a Design Table.

Notes:

Project 3 – Fundamentals of Drawing

Project Objective

Create a FLATBAR drawing with a customized Sheet Format and a Drawing Template containing a Company logo and Title block.

Obtain an understanding to display the following views with the ability to insert, add, and edit dimensions and annotations:

- Standard: Top, Front, and Right

- Isometric, Detail, and Section

- Exploded

Create a LINKAGE assembly drawing with a Bill of Materials. Obtain knowledge to develop and incorporate a Bill of Materials with Custom Properties. Create a FLATBAR-SHAFTCOLLAR assembly.

On the completion of this project, you will be able to:

- Create a customized Sheet Format.

- Generate a custom Drawing Template.

- Produce a Bill of Materials with Custom Properties.

- Develop various drawing views.

- Reposition views on a drawing.

- Move dimensions in the same view.

- Apply Edit Sheet Format mode and Edit Sheet mode.

- Modify the dimension scheme.

- Create a Parametric drawing note.

- Link notes in the Title block to SolidWorks properties.

- Generate an Exploded view.

- Create and edit a Design Table.

Project Overview

Generate two drawings in this project:

- FLATBAR part drawing and a LINKAGE assembly drawing.

The FLATBAR drawing utilizes a custom
Drawing Template and a custom Sheet Format. The FLATBAR drawing contains two
sheets:

- Sheet1 contains a Front, Top, and Isometric view with dimensions and a linked
  Parametric note.

- Sheet2 contains the 3HOLE configuration of the FLATBAR. Configurations are
  created with a Design Table.

The LINKAGE assembly drawing contains two sheets:

- Sheet1 contains the LINKAGE assembly in an Exploded view with a Bill of
  Materials.

- Sheet2 contains the AirCylinder assembly with a Section view, Detail view, and a
  Scale view.

Create the FLATBAR-SHAFTCOLLAR assembly. Utilize a Design Table to create four new configurations of the assembly.

There are two major design modes used to develop a drawing:

- *Edit Sheet Format*

- *Edit Sheet*

The *Edit Sheet Format* mode provides the ability to:

- Change the Title block size and text headings.

- Incorporate a Company logo.

- Add Custom Properties and text.

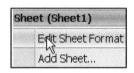

The *Edit Sheet* mode provides the ability to:

- Add or modify views.

- Add or modify dimensions.

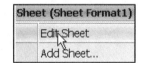

- Add or modify notes.

Drawing Template and Sheet Format

The foundation of a SolidWorks drawing is the Drawing Template. Drawing size, drawing standards, company information, manufacturing and or assembly requirements, units and other properties are defined in the Drawing Template.

The Sheet Format is incorporated into the Drawing Template. The Sheet Format contains the border, Title block information, Revision block information, Company name and or Logo information, Custom Properties, and SolidWorks Properties.

Custom Properties and SolidWorks Properties are shared values between documents. Utilize an A-size Drawing Template with Sheet format for the FLATBAR drawing and LINKAGE assembly drawing.

Views from the part or assembly are inserted into the SolidWorks drawing.

Create Sheet Formats for different parts types. Example: sheet metal parts, plastic parts, and high precision machined parts.

Create Sheet Formats for each category of parts that are manufactured with unique sets of title block notes.

Note: A Third Angle Projection scheme is illustrated in this project.

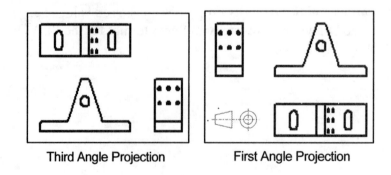

Third Angle Projection   First Angle Projection

For non-ANSI dimension standards, the dimensioning techniques are the same, even if the displayed arrows and text size are different. For printers supporting millimeter paper sizes, select A4-Landscape (297mm × 210mm).

The default Drawing Templates contain predefined Title block Notes linked to Custom Properties and SolidWorks Properties.

Activity: New Drawing

Create a new drawing. Close all parts and drawings.

1)   Click **Windows**, **Close All** from the Menu bar.

2)   Click **New** ⬜ from the Menu bar.

3)   Double-click **Drawing** from the Templates tab.

4)   Select **A-Landscape**.

5)   Click **OK** from the Sheet Format/Size box.

6)   If required, click **Cancel** ✖ from the Model View PropertyManager. The Draw FeatureManager is displayed.

☼ A new drawing invokes the Model View PropertyManager if the Start Command When Creating New Drawing option is checked.

The A-Landscape paper is displayed in a new Graphics window. The sheet border defines the drawing size, 11″ × 8.5″ or (279.4mm × 215.9mm).

☼ To view the sheet properties, right-click Properties in the drawing sheet. View the Sheet Properties dialog box. Click OK to return to the drawing sheet.

💡 Draw1 is the default drawing name. Sheet1 is the default first Sheet name. For an active drawing document, the View Layout and Annotation tabs are displayed in the CommandManager.

💡 Utilize the CommandManager tabs or individual toolbars to access the needed features in this Project.

Set the Sheet Properties.

7)   Right-click in the **Graphics window**.

8)   Click **Properties**. The Sheet Properties are
          displayed.

9)   Enter Sheet Scale **1:1**.

10)   Click **Third Angle** for Type of projection.

11)   Click **OK** from the Sheet Properties dialog box.

Activity: Drawing-Document Properties

Set the drawing document properties.

12)   Click **Options** , **Document Properties** tab from
          the Menu bar.

13)   Select **ANSI** for Overall drafting standard from the
          drop-down menu.

14)   Click **Units**.

15)   Click **MMGS** (millimeter, gram, second) for Unit
          system.

16)   Select **.12** for Length units Decimal places.

17)   Select **None** for Angular units Decimal places.

View the available Document Properties options.
Click each folder under the Document Properties
tab.

Available Document Properties are document
dependent.

Companies develop drawing format standards and
use specific text height for Metric and English
drawings. Numerous engineering drawings use the
following format:

- Font: Century Gothic – All capitals.

- Text height: 3mm for drawings up to B Size, 17in. × 22in.

- Text height: 5mm for drawings larger than B Size, 17in × 22in.

- Arrow heads: Solid filled with a 1:3 ratio of arrow width to arrow height.

Set the dimension font.
18) Click **Annotations** folder as illustrated.

19) Click the **Font** button. The Choose Font dialog box is displayed.

Set the dimension text height.
20) Click the **Units** box from the Choose Font dialog box.

21) Enter **3.0**mm for Height.

22) Click **OK** from the Choose Font dialog box.

Set the arrow size.
23) Click the **Dimensions** folder as illustrated.

24) Enter **1**mm for arrow Height.

25) Enter **3**mm for arrow Width.

26) Enter **6**mm for arrow Length.

27) Click **OK** from the Document Properties dialog box.

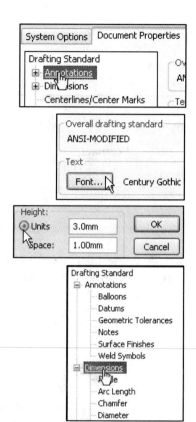

There are three dimension style type buttons: Outside, Inside, and Smart. Smart is the default option.

Check the Dual dimensions display box to display dual dimensions for your model or drawing.

Title Block

The Title block contains text fields linked to System Properties and Custom Properties. System Properties are determined from the SolidWorks documents. Custom Property values are assigned to named variables.

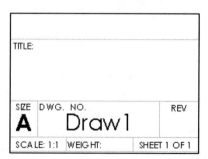

Save time. Utilize System Properties and define Custom Properties in your Sheet Formats.

System Properties Linked to fields in default Sheet Formats:	Custom Properties of drawings linked to fields in default Sheet Formats:		Custom Properties of parts and assemblies linked to fields in default Sheet Formats:
SW-File Name (in DWG. NO. field):	CompanyName:	EngineeringApproval:	Description (in TITLE field):
SW-Sheet Scale:	CheckedBy:	EngAppDate:	Weight:
SW-Current Sheet:	CheckedDate:	ManufacturingApproval:	Material:
SW-Total Sheets:	DrawnBy:	MfgAppDate:	Finish:
	DrawnDate:	QAApproval:	Revision:
	EngineeringApproval:	QAAppDate:	

The Title block is located in the lower right hand corner of Sheet1.

The Drawing contains two modes:

1. *Edit Sheet Format*

2. *Edit Sheet*

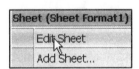

Insert views and dimensions in the Edit Sheet mode. Modify the Sheet Format text, lines or title block information in the Edit Sheet Format mode.

The CompanyName Custom Property is located in the title block above the TITLE box. There is no value defined for CompanyName. A small text box indicates an empty field.

Define a value for the Custom Property CompanyName. Example: D&M ENGINEERING.

Activity: Title Box

Activate the Edit Sheet Format Mode.
28)   Right-click in **Sheet1**.

29)   Click **Edit Sheet Format**. The Title block lines turn blue.

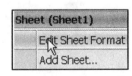

View the right side of the Title block.

30)   Click the **Zoom to Area** tool from the Heads-up View toolbar.

31)   **Zoom in** on the Title block.

32) Click the **Zoom to Area** tool to deactivate.

Define CompanyName Custom Property.

33) Position the **mouse pointer** in the middle of the box above the TITLE box as illustrated.

34) Click **File**, **Properties** from the Menu bar. The Summary Information dialog box is displayed.

35) Click the **Custom** tab.

36) Click inside the **Property Name box**.

37) Click the **drop down arrow** in the Property Name box.

38) Select **CompanyName** from the Property menu.

39) Enter **D&M ENGINEERING** (or your company name) in the Value/Text Expression box.

40) Click inside the **Evaluated Value** box. The CompanyName is displayed in the Evaluated Value box.

41) Click **OK** from the dialog box.

42) Move your **mouse pointer** in the center of the block as illustrated. The Custom Property, $PRP: "COMPANYNAME", is displayed in the Title block.

Modify the font size.

43) Double-click the **D&M ENGINEERING** text. The Formatting dialog box is displayed.

44) Click the **drop down arrows** to set the Text Font and Height from the Formatting toolbar.

45) Click the **Style buttons** and **Justification buttons** to modify the selected text.

46) Close the Formatting dialog box.

47) Click **OK** from the Note PropertyManager.

Click a position outside the selected text box to save and exit the text.

The Tolerance block is located in the Title block. The Tolerance block provides information to the manufacturer on the minimum and maximum variation for each dimension on the drawing. If a specific tolerance or note is provided on the drawing, the specific tolerance or note will override the information in the Tolerance block.

General tolerance values are based on the design requirements and the manufacturing process.

Create Sheet Formats for different part types; examples: sheet metal parts, plastic parts, and high precision machined parts. Create Sheet Formats for each category of parts that are manufactured with unique sets of Title block notes.

Modify the Tolerance block in the Sheet Format for ASME Y14.5 machined, millimeter parts. Delete unnecessary text. The FRACTIONAL text refers to inches. The BEND text refers to sheet metal parts. The Three Decimal Place text is not required for this millimeter part in the Project.

Modify the Tolerance Note.
48) Double-click the text **INTERPRET GEOMETRIC TOLERANCING PER:**

49) Enter **ASME Y14.5**.

50) Click **OK** from the Note PropertyManager.

51) Double-click inside the **Tolerance block** text. The Formatting dialog box and the Note PropertyManager is displayed.

52) Delete the text **INCHES**.

53) Enter **MILLIMETERS**.

54) Delete the line **FRACTIONAL ±**.

55) Delete the text **BEND ±**.

56)   Click a **position** at the end of the ᴬᴺᴳᵁᴸᴬᴿ: ᴹᴬᶜᴴ ± line.

57)   Enter **0**. Click the **Add Symbol** button from the Text Format box. The Symbols dialog box is displayed.

58)   Select **Degree** from the Symbols dialog box. Click **OK** from the Symbols dialog box.

59)   Enter **30'** for minutes of a degree.

Modify the TWO and THREE PLACE DECIMAL LINES.
60)   Delete the **TWO** and **THREE PLACE DECIMAL lines**.

61)   Enter **ONE PLACE DECIMAL ± 0.5**.

62)   Enter **TWO PLACE DECIMAL ± 0.15**.

63)   Click **OK** ✔ from the Note PropertyManager.

Fit the drawing to the Graphics window.
64)   Press the **f** key.

Save Draw1.
65)   Click **Save** 🖫. Accept the default name.

66)   Click **Save** from the Save As box.

💡 Draw1 is the default drawing file name. This name is temporary. In the next activity, invoke Microsoft Word. Always save before selecting another software application.

Various symbols are available through the Symbol dialog box. The ± symbol is located in the Modify Symbols list. The ± symbol is sometimes displayed as <MOD-PM>. The degree symbol ° is sometimes displayed as <MOD-DEG>.

Interpretation of tolerances is as follows:

* The angular dimension 110° is machined between 109.5° and 110.5°.

* The dimension 2.5 is machined between 2.0 and 3.0.

* The dimension 2.05 is machined between 1.90 and 2.20.

Company Logo

A Company logo is normally located in the Title block. Create a Company logo. Copy a picture file from Microsoft ClipArt using Microsoft Word. Paste the logo into the SolidWorks drawing. Note: The following logo example was created in Microsoft Word 2003 using the COMPASS.wmf file. You can utilize any ClipArt picture, scanned image, or bitmap for a logo in this activity.

The Compass logo clipart and finished Compass logo for the drawing is located on the CD enclosed in the book. Click **Insert**, **Picture**, and **browse** to the Logo folder. Click the **Logo** Logo file. **Move** and **re-size** the finished logo in the drawing.

Activity: Drawing Logo

Create a New Microsoft Word Document. In the next step, MS Office Word 2003 is used.

67) Click **Start** from the Microsoft desktop.

68) Click **All Programs**. Click **Microsoft Office Word 2003**.

69) Click **File**, **New** from the Standard toolbar in MS Word.

70) Click **Insert, Picture, ClipArt** from the Main menu. The Insert Clip Art menu is displayed.

71) In the Search text enter **compass**. Note: Enter any name for Clip Art to Search For. If you do not have the Clip Art loaded on your system, click **Clips Online** to obtain additional Clip Art. Follow the provided directions to select and download.

The Compass logo clipart is located in the Logo folder provided on the CD enclosed in the book.

Rectangle   Insert WordArt   Insert ClipArt

Locate the picture file.

72) Click **Go**. Locate the **Compass.wmf** file. **Double-click** the file. The picture is displayed in the Word document. Note: You can use any picture file. The Compass Logo file is also located on the CD enclosed in the book.

Redefine the picture layout.

73) Click the **picture**. Right-click **Format Picture**. The Format Picture dialog box is displayed.

Display the drag handles.

74) Click the **Layout** tab. Click **Square**.

75) Click **OK** from the Format Picture dialog box.

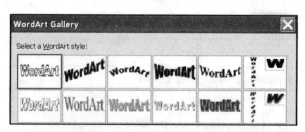

Add text to the logo picture.

76) Click the **picture**. Click **Insert WordArt** 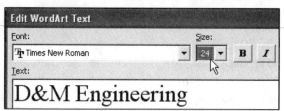 from the Draw toolbar. The WordArt Gallery dialog box is displayed.

77) Click a **WordArt** style. Click **OK**.

78) Enter **D&M Engineering** in the text box.

79) Click **24** from the Size drop down list.

80) Click **OK** from the Edit WordArt Text dialog box.

81) Click the **Word Art text**. A WordArt toolbar is displayed.

82) Click **Text Wrapping** . Click **Square**.

83) Click and drag the **Word Art text** under the Compass picture.

84) Size the **Word Art text** by dragging the picture handles.

Group the Word Art text and the picture to create the logo.

85) Click on the **Word Art text**.

86) Hold the **Ctrl** key down.

87) Click the **compass** picture. Release the **Ctrl** key. Right-click and select **Grouping**.

88) Click **Group**. The Word Art text and the picture are grouped. The logo is created.

Copy the new logo.
89)   Click the **logo**.

90)   Click **Edit**, **Copy** from the Main menu.

91)   The logo is placed into the Clipboard. **Minimize** the
            Microsoft Word Graphics window.

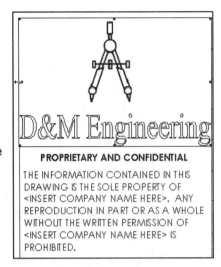

Return to the SolidWorks Title block.
92)   Click a **position** on the left side of the Title block in the
            SolidWorks Graphics window. **Zoom out** if required.

Paste the logo.
93)   Click **Edit**, **Paste** from the Menu bar.

94)   **Move** and **Size** the logo to the SolidWorks Title block
            by dragging the picture handles.

Return to the Edit Sheet mode.
95)   Right-click in the **Graphics window**.

96)   Click **Edit Sheet**. The Title block is displayed in black/gray.

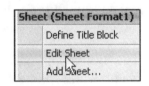

Fit the Sheet Format to the Graphics window.
97)   Press the **f** key.

Draw1 displays Editing Sheet1 in the Status bar. The Title
block is displayed in black when in Edit Sheet mode.

Save Sheet Format and Save As Drawing Template

Save the drawing document in the Graphics window in two forms: Sheet Format and Drawing Template. Save the Sheet Format as a custom Sheet Format named CUSTOM-A. Use the CUSTOM-A Sheet Format for the drawings in this project. The Sheet Format file extension is .slddrt.

The Drawing Template can be displayed with or without the Sheet Format. Combine the Sheet Format with the Drawing Template to create a custom Drawing Template named A-ANSI-MM. Utilize the Save As option to save a Drawing Template. The Drawing Template file extension is .drwdot.

💡 Always select the Save as type option first, then select the Save in folder to avoid saving in default SolidWorks installation directories.

The System Options, File Locations, Document Templates option is only valid for the current session of SolidWorks in some network locations. Set the File Locations option in order to view the SW-TUTORIAL-2009 tab in the New Document dialog box.

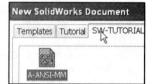

Activity: Save Sheet Format and Save As Drawing Template

Save the Sheet Format.
98) Click **File, Save Sheet Format** from the Menu bar. The Save Sheet Format dialog box appears.

99) Click **drop down arrow** from the Save Sheet Format dialog box.

The default Sheet Format folder is called SolidWorks 2009 on a new installation. Do not select this folder. The file extension for Sheet Format is .slddrt.

100) Select **SW-TUTORIAL-2009** for the Save in folder.

101) Enter **CUSTOM-A** for File name.

102) Click **Save** from the Save Sheet Format dialog box.

Save the Drawing Template.
103) Click **Save As** from the Menu bar.

104) Click **Drawing Templates (*.drwdot)** from the Save as type box.

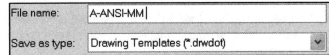

105) Select **SW-TUTORIAL-2009** for the Save in folder.

106) Enter **A-ANSI-MM** for File name.

107) Click **Save**.

The A-ANSI-MM.drwdot drawing template is displayed in the Graphics window. Add the SW-TUTORIAL-2009 folder to the File Locations Document Template System Option.

Set System Options - File Locations.
108) Click **Options** 📇 , **File Locations** from the Menu bar.

109) Click **Add**.

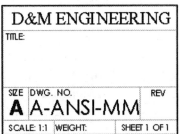

110) Select the **SW-TUTORIAL-2009** folder.

111) Click **OK** from the Browse for Folder menu.

112) Click **OK** to exit System Options.

113) Click **Yes**.

Close all files.
114) Click **Windows**, **Close All** from the Menu bar.

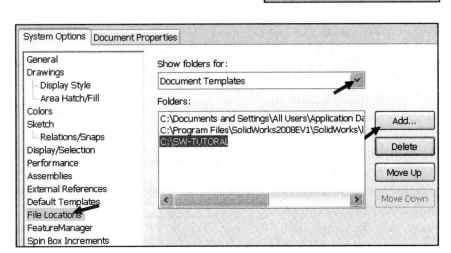

Open a new drawing.

115) Click **New** ☐ from the Menu bar.

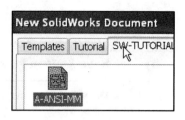

116) Select the **SW-TUTORIAL-2009** tab.

117) Double-click the **A-ANSI-MM** Drawing Template.

118) If required, click **Cancel** ✖ from the Model View
PropertyManager. Draw2 is displayed in the Graphics
window.

🔅 The Draw2-Sheet1 drawing is displayed in the Graphics
window. You have successfully created a new drawing
Template with a Custom sheet format.

Close all files.
119) Click **Windows**, **Close All** from the Menu bar.

🔅 Combine customize
Drawing Templates and Sheet
Formats to match your
company's drawing standards.
Save the empty Drawing
Template and Sheet Format
separately to reuse
information.

🔍 Additional details on
Drawing Templates, Sheet
Format and Custom Properties
are available in SolidWorks
Help Topics. Keywords:
Documents (templates,
properties) Sheet Formats
(new, new drawings, note
text), Properties (drawing
sheets), Customize Drawing
Sheet Formats.

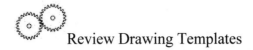 Review Drawing Templates

The Custom Drawing Template was created from the default Drawing Template. You modified Sheet Properties and Document Properties to control the Sheet size, Scale, Annotations, and Dimensions.

The Sheet Format contained a Title block and Custom Property information. You inserted a Company Logo and modified the Title block.

The Save Sheet Format option was utilized to save the CUSTOM-A.slddrt Sheet Format. The Save As option was utilized to save the A-ANSI-MM.drwdot template.

The Sheet Format and Drawing Template were saved in the SW-TUTORIAL-2009 folder.

FLATBAR Drawing

A drawing contains part views, geometric dimensioning and tolerances, notes and other related design information. When a part is modified, the drawing automatically updates. When a dimension in the drawing is modified, the part is automatically updated.

Create the FLATBAR drawing from the FLATBAR part. Display the Front, Top, Right, and Isometric views. Utilize the Model View tool from the View Layout toolbar.

Insert dimensions from the part. Utilize the Insert Model Items tool from the Annotation toolbar. Insert and modify dimensions and notes.

Insert a Parametric note that links the dimension text to the part depth. Utilize a user defined Part Number. Define the part material with the Material Editor. Add Custom Properties for Material and Number.

Activity: FLATBAR Drawing-Open the FLATBAR Part

Open the FLATBAR part.

120) Click **Open** from the Menu bar.

121) Select the **SW-TUTORIAL-2009** folder.

122) Select **Part** for Files of type.

123) Double-click **FLATBAR**. The FLATBAR FeatureManager is displayed.

Create a new drawing.

124) Click **New** ⬜ from the Menu bar.

125) Select the **SW-TUTORIAL-2009** tab.

126) Double-click **A-ANSI-MM**.

The Model View PropertyManager is displayed if the Start
command when creating new drawing box is checked. If the Model
View PropertyManager is not displayed, click the Model View tool
from the View Layout toolbar.

The FLATBAR **FLATBAR** part icon is displayed in the Open
documents box. Drawing view names are based on the part view
orientation. The Front view is the first view inserted into the
drawing. The Top view and Right view are projected from the
Front view.

Insert the Front, Top, and Right view.

127) Click **Next** ⊕ from the Model View PropertyManager.

128) Click **Multiple views**.

129) Deactivate the Isometric view. Click the ***Isometric** icon from the
Standard views box.

130) Click ***Front**, ***Top** and ***Right** view from the Standard views box.

131) Click **OK** ✅ from the Model View PropertyManager. Click **Yes**.
The three views are displayed on Sheet1.

A part cannot be inserted into a drawing when the Edit Sheet Format is selected. You are required to be in the Edit Sheet mode.

Insert an Isometric view using the View Palette.
132) Click the **View Palette** tab on the right side of the Graphics window.

133) Select **FLATBAR** from the View Palette drop-down menu as illustrated. View the available views.

134) Click and drag the **Isometric view** in the top right corner as illustrated.

135) Click **OK** ✔ from the Drawing View PropertyManager.

Click the View Palette tab in the Task Pane. Click the drop-down arrow to view any active documents or click the Browse button to locate a document. Click and drag the desired view/views into the active drawing sheet.

Modify the Sheet Scale.
136) Right-click a **position** inside the Sheet1 boundary.

137) Click **Properties**. The Sheet Properties dialog box is displayed.

138) Enter **1:1** for Sheet Scale.

139) Click **OK** from the Sheet Properties dialog box.

If needed, hide the Origins.
140) Click **View**, uncheck **Origins** from the Menu bar.

Save the drawing.
141) Click **Save As** from the Menu bar.

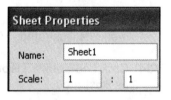

142) Enter **FLATBAR** in the SW-TUTORIAL-2009 folder.

143) Click **Save**.

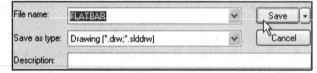

144) Click **Save** 💾.

Text in the Title block is linked to the Filename and Description created in the part. The DWG. NO. text box utilizes the Property, $PRP:"SW-File Name" passed from the FLATBAR part to the FLATBAR drawing.

The Title text box utilizes the Property, $PRPSHEET: "Description".

The filename FLATBAR is displayed in the DWG. NO. box. The Description FLATBAR 9 HOLE is displayed in the Title box. The FLATBAR drawing contains three Principle views (Standard views): Front, Top, Right, and an Isometric view.

Insert drawing views as follows:

- Utilize the Model View tool.

  o Drag a part into the drawing to create three Standard views.

  o Predefine views in a custom Drawing Template.

  o Drag a hyperlink through Internet Explorer.

- Drag an active part view from the View Palette. The View Palette is located in the Task Pane. With an open part, drag the selected view into the active drawing sheet.

The View Palette populates when you:

- Click Make Drawing from Part/Assembly.

- Browse to a document from the View Palette.

- Select from a list of open documents in the View Palette.

Move Views and Properties of the Sheet

Move Views on Sheet1 to create space for additional Drawing View placement.

The mouse pointer provides feedback in both the Drawing Sheet

<img> and Drawing View <img> modes.

The mouse pointer displays the Drawing Sheet <img> icon when the Sheet properties and commands are executed.

The mouse pointer displays the Drawing View <img> icon when the View properties and commands are executed.

View the mouse pointer icon for feedback to select Sheet, View, and Component and Edge properties in the Drawing.

Sheet Properties

- Sheet Properties display properties of the selected sheet.

  Right-click in the sheet boundary to view the available commands.

View Properties

- View Properties display properties of the selected view.

  Right-click inside the view boundary. Modify the View Properties in the Display Style box or the View Toolbar.

Component Properties

- Component Properties display properties of the selected component. Right-click to on the face of the component . View the available options.

Edge Properties

- Edge Properties display properties of the selected geometry.

  Right-click on an edge inside the view boundary. View the available options.

Reposition the views on the drawing. Provide approximately 25mm - 50mm between each view for dimension placement.

Activity: FLATBAR Drawing-Position Views

Position the views.
145) Click inside the view boundary of **Drawing View1** (Front). The mouse pointer displays the Drawing View icon.

146) Position the **mouse pointer** on the edge of the view boundary until the Drawing View icon is displayed.

147) Drag **Drawing View1** in an upward vertical direction. The Top and Right views move aligned to Drawing View1 (Front).

148) Press **Shift + Z** key to Zoom in on Sheet1.

149) Click the **Right view** boundary.

150) Position the **mouse pointer** on the edge of the view until the Drawing Move View icon is displayed.

151) Drag the **Right view** in a right to left direction towards the Front view.

Move the Top view in a downward vertical direction.
152) Click the **Top view**, "Drawing View3" boundary.

153) Drag the **Top view** in a downward direction towards Drawing View1.

Fit Sheet1 to the Graphics window.
154) Press the **f** key.

Detail Drawing

The design intent of this project is to work with dimensions inserted from parts and to incorporate them into the drawings. Explore methods to move, hide and recreate dimensions to adhere to a drawing standard.

There are other solutions to the dimensioning schemes illustrated in this project. Detail drawings require dimensions, annotations, tolerance, materials, Engineering Change Orders, authorization, etc. to release the part to manufacturing and other notes prior to production.

Review a hypothetical "worse case" drawing situation. You just inserted dimensions from a part into a drawing. The dimensions, extensions lines and arrows are not in the correct locations. How can you address the position of these details? Answer: Dimension to an ASME Y14.5M standard.

No.	Situation:
1	Extension line crosses dimension line. Dimensions not evenly spaced.
2	Largest dimension placed closest to profile.
3	Leader lines overlapping.
4	Extension line crossing arrowhead.
5	Arrow gap too large.
6	Dimension pointing to feature in another view. Missing dimension – inserted into Detail view (not shown).
7	Dimension text over centerline, too close to profile.
8	Dimension from other view – leader line too long.
9	Dimension inside section lines.
10	No visible gap.
11	Arrows overlapping text.
12	Incorrect decimal display with whole number (millimeter), no specified tolerance.

Worse Case Drawing Situation

The ASME Y14.5M standard defines an engineering drawing standard.

Review the twelve changes made to the drawing to meet the standard.

Dimensions are displayed in MILLIMETERS.

No.	Preferred Application of the Dimensions:
1	Extension lines do not cross unless situation is unavoidable. Stagger dimension text.
2	Largest dimension placed farthest from profile. Dimensions are evenly spaced and grouped.
3	Arrow heads do not overlap.
4	Break extension lines that cross close to arrowhead.
5	Flip arrows to the inside.
6	Move dimensions to the view that displays the outline of the feature. Insure that all dimensions are accounted for.
7	Move text off of reference geometry (centerline).
8	Drag dimensions into their correct view boundary. Create reference dimensions if required. Slant extension lines to clearly illustrate feature.
9	Locate dimensions outside off section lines.
10	Create a visible gap between extension lines and profile lines.
11	Arrows do not overlap the text.
12	Whole numbers displayed with no zero and no decimal point (millimeter).

Apply these dimension practices to the FLATBAR and other drawings in this project.

A Detailed drawing is used to manufacture a part. A mistake on a drawing can cost your company substantial loss in revenue. The mistake could result in a customer liability lawsuit.

Dimension and annotate your parts clearly to avoid common problems and mistakes.

Dimensions and Annotations

Dimensions and annotations are inserted from the part. The annotations are not in the correct location. Additional dimensions and annotations are required.

Dimensions and annotations are inserted by selecting individual features, views or the entire sheet. Select the entire sheet. Insert Model Items command from the Annotations toolbar.

Activity: FLATBAR Drawing-Dimensions and Annotations

Insert dimensions.

155) Click **Sheet1** in the center of the drawing. The mouse pointer

displays the Sheet ⬚ icon.

156) Click the **Annotation** tab from the CommandManager.

157) Click the **Model Items** ✏ tool from the Annotation toolbar. The Model Items PropertyManager is displayed. The Import items into all views option is checked.

158) Select **Entire model** from the Source box.

159) Click **OK** ✔ from the Model Items PropertyManager. Dimensions are inserted into the drawing.

Remove Trailing zeroes.

160) Click **Options** ▤ , **Document Properties** tab from the Menu bar.

161) Click the **Dimensions** folder.

162) Select **Remove** for the Trailing zeroes drop-down menu.

163) Click **OK** from the Document Properties – Dimensions dialog box.

🔅 Dimensions are inserted into the drawing. The dimensions are not in the correct location with respect to the profile lines. Move them later in the project.

The dimensions and text in the next section have been enlarged for visibility. Drawing dimension location is dependent on: *Feature dimension creation* and *Selected drawing views*.

Move dimensions within the same view. Use the mouse pointer to drag dimensions and leader lines to a new location. Leader lines reference the size of the profile. A gap must exist between the profile lines and the leader lines. Shorten the leader lines to maintain a drawing standard. Use the blue Arrow buttons to flip the dimension arrows.

Plan ahead for general drawing notes. Notes provide relative part or assembly information. Example: Material type, material finish, special manufacturing procedure or considerations, preferred supplier, etc.

Below are a few helpful guidelines to create general drawing notes:

- Use capitol letters.

- Use left text justification.

- Font size should be the same as the dimension text.

Create Parametric notes by selecting dimensions in the drawing. Example: Specify the material thickness of the FLATBAR as a note in the drawing. If the thickness is modified, the corresponding note is also modified.

Hide superfluous feature dimensions. Do not delete feature dimensions. Recall hidden dimension with the View, Show Annotations command. Move redundant, dependent views outside the sheet boundary.

Move the linear dimensions in Drawing View1, (Front).
164) Click the vertical dimension text **101.6**. The dimension text turns blue.

165) Drag the **dimension text** downward.

166) Click the horizontal dimension **12.7**.

167) Drag the **text** approximately 10mm's from the profile. The smallest linear dimensions are closest to the profile.

168) Click the radial dimension **R6.35**.

169) Drag the **text** diagonally off the profile if required.

Modify dimension text.
170) Click the diameter dimension **4.83**. It turns blue. The Dimension PropertyManager is displayed.

171) Click inside the **Dimension Text** box.

172) Enter **9X** before <MOD-DIAM>. Enter **EQ SP** after <DIM>.

173) Click **OK** ✔ from the Dimension PropertyManager.

Inserted dimensions can be moved from one drawing view to another. Hold the Shift key down. Click and drag the dimension text from one view into the other view boundary. Release the Shift key.

Modify the precision of the material thickness.
174) Click the depth dimension text **1.52** in the Top view.

175) Select **.1** from the Tolerance/Precision box.

176) Click **OK** ✔ from the Dimension PropertyManager. The text displays 1.5.

Insert a Parametric note.
177) Click the **Annotation** tab from the CommandManager.

178) Click the **Note** **A** tool from the Annotation toolbar. The Note icon is displayed.

179) Click a **position** above Front view. Enter **MATERIAL THICKNESS**.

180) Click the depth dimension text **1.5** in the Top view. The variable name for the dimension is displayed in the text box.

181) Enter **MM**.

182) Click **OK** ✔ from the Note PropertyManager.

Hide superfluous dimensions.
183) Right-click the **1.5** dimension text in the Top view.

184) Click **Hide**.

Hide the Right view.
185) Right-click the **Right view** boundary.

186) Click **Hide**. Note: If required, expand the drop-down menu. The
Right view is not displayed in the Graphics window.

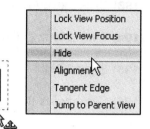

187) Click **OK** ✔ from the Drawing View PropertyManager.

Fit the model to the drawing.
188) Press the **f** key.

Save the drawing.
189) Click **Save** 💾.

Locate the Top view off of Sheet1.
190) Click and drag the **Top view boundary** off of the Sheet1 boundary as
illustrated.

Views and notes outside the sheet boundary do not print. The
Parametric note is controlled through the FLATBAR part Extrude1
depth. Modify the depth to update the note.

Open the FLATBAR part.
191) Right-click inside the **Front view** boundary.

192) Click **Open flatbar.sldprt**. The FLATBAR part is displayed.

Modify the Extrude1 depth dimension.
193) Click **Extrude1** from the FeatureManager.

194) Click **.060**in, [1.52].

195) Enter **2.3MM** as illustrated. Note: You need to enter MM.

196) Click **inside** the Graphics window.

197) Click **Save** .

Return to the drawing.
198) Click **Window**, **FLATBAR –Sheet1** from the Menu bar. The
Parametric note is updated to reflect the dimension change in
the part.

The FLATBAR drawing references the FLATBAR part. Do
not delete the part or move the part location. Work between
multiple documents:

- Press Ctrl-Tab to toggle between open SolidWorks
documents.

- Right-click inside the Drawing view boundary. Select
Open Part. Example: Open flatbar.sldprt.

- Right-click the part icon in the FeatureManager. Select
Open Drawing.

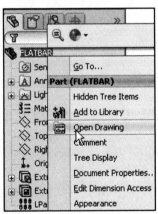

Commands are accessed through the toolbars and drop-
down menus. Commands are also accessed with a Right-click
in the Graphics window and FeatureManager.

A majority of FLATBAR drawing dimensions are inserted from the FLATBAR part. An overall dimension is required to dimension the slot shape profile. Add a dimension in the drawing.

Add a dimension to Drawing View1.

199) Click the **Smart Dimension** ⬨ tool from the Annotation toolbar. The Autodimension tab is selected by default.

200) Click the **Smart dimensioning** box.

201) Click the **top horizontal line** of the FLATBAR.

202) Click the **bottom horizontal line** of the FLATBAR.

203) Click a **position** to the right of the Front view as illustrated.

Modify the Radius text.
204) Click the **R6.36** dimension text.

205) Delete **R<DIM>** in the Dimension Text box.

206) Click **Yes** to confirm dimension override.

207) Enter **2X R** for Dimension text. Do not enter the radius value.

208) Click **OK** ✔ from the Dimension PropertyManager.

Save the FLATBAR drawing.

209) Click **Save** 🖫. Note: Click Options, Document Properties, Dimensions from the Menu bar. Uncheck the Add parentheses by default box.

Part Number and Document Properties

Engineers manage the parts they create and modify. Each part requires a Part Number and Part Name. A part number is a numeric representation of the part. Each part has a unique number. Each drawing has a unique number. Drawings incorporate numerous part numbers or assembly numbers.

There are software applications that incorporate unique part numbers to create and perform:

- Bill of Materials

- Manufacturing procedures

- Cost analysis

- Inventory control / Just in Time, JIT

You are required to procure the part and drawing numbers from the documentation control manager. Utilize the following prefix codes to categorize created parts and drawings. The part name, part number and drawing numbers are as follows:

Category:	Prefix:	Part Name:	Part Number:	Drawing Number:
Machined Parts	56-	FLATEPLATE	GIDS-SC-10001-9	56-10222
		AXLE	GIDS-SC-10017	56-10223
		SHAFT-COLLAR	GIDS-SC-10012-3-16	56-10224
Purchased Parts	99-	AIRCYLINDER	99-FBM8x1.25	999-101-8
Assemblies	10-	LINKAGE ASM	GIDS-SC-1000	10-10123

Link notes in the Title block to SolidWorks Properties. Properties are variables shared between documents and applications.

The machined parts are manufactured from Aluminum. Specify the Material Property in the part. Link the Material Property to the drawing title block. Create a part number that is utilized in the Bill of Materials. Create additional notes in the title block to complete the drawing.

Activity: FLATBAR Drawing-Part Number and Document Properties

Return to the FLATEBAR part.
210) Right-click in the **Front view** boundary.

211) Click **Open flabar.sldprt**.

212) Right-click **Material** in the FLATBAR FeatureManager.

213) Click **Edit Material**. The Material dialog box is displayed.

214) Expand the Aluminum Alloys folder.

215) Select **2014 Alloy**. View the material properties.

216) Click the **Apply** button.

217) Click **Close**. The 2014 Alloy is displayed in the FeatureManager.

Save the FLATBAR.

218) Click **Save** 🖫.

Define the part number property for the BOM.

219) Click the FLATBAR **ConfigurationManager** 🖿 tab.

220) Right-click **Default**.

221) Click **Properties**. The Configuration Properties PropertyManager is displayed.

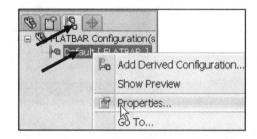

222) Click **User Specified Name** from the drop-down box under Document Name.

223) Enter **GIDS-SC-10001-9** in the Part number text box.

Define a material property.
224) Click the **Custom Properties** button.

225) Click inside the **Property Name** box.

226) Click the **down arrow**.

227) Select **Material** from the Property Name list.

228) Click inside the **Value / Text Expression** box.

229) Click the **down arrow**.

230) Select **Material**.

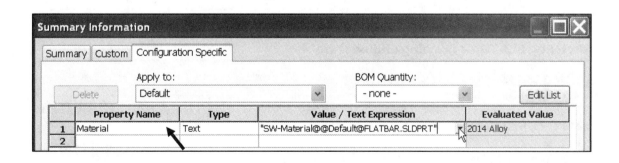

Define the Number Property.
231) Click inside the **second Property Name** box.

232) Click the **down arrow**.

233) Select **Number** from the Name list.

234) Click inside the **Value / Text Expression** box.

235) Enter **56-10222** for Drawing Number.

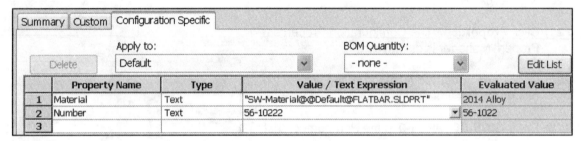

	Property Name	Type	Value / Text Expression	Evaluated Value
1	Material	Text	"SW-Material@@Default@FLATBAR.SLDPRT"	2014 Alloy
2	Number	Text	56-10222	56-1022
3				

236) Click **OK** from the Summary Information dialog box.

237) Click **OK** ✔ from the Configuration Properties PropertyManager.

Return to the FeatureManager.
238) Click the FLATBAR **FeatureManager** tab.

Save the FLATBAR part.
239) Click **Save** 💾.

Return to the drawing.
240) Click **Windows**, **FLATBAR - Sheet1** from the Main menu.

The Material Property is inserted into the Title block.

INTERPRET GEOMETRIC
TOLERANCING PER: ASME Y14.5

MATERIAL
2014 Alloy

Activity: FLATBAR Drawing-Linked Note

Create a Linked Note.
241) Right-click in **Sheet1**.

242) Click **Edit Sheet Format**.

243) **Zoom in** on the lower right corner of the drawing.

244) Double-click on the DWG. NO. text **FLATBAR**. The Note PropertyManager is displayed.

D&M ENGINEERING
TITLE
FLAT BAR 9 HOLES
SIZE DWG. NO.   REV
A   FLATBAR
SCALE: 1:1 WEIGHT: SHEET 1 OF 1

245) Click **Link to Property** from the Text Format box.

246) Select **Model in view specified in sheet properties**.

247) Select **Number** from the Link to Property drop-down menu.

248) Click **OK** from the Link to Property box.

249) Click **OK** ✔ from the Note PropertyManager.

Return to the drawing sheet.
250) Right-click a **position** in the Graphics window.

251) Click **Edit Sheet**.

Save the FLATBAR drawing.
252) Click **Save** 🖫 .

Custom Properties such as Revision and Drawn By are created in the project exercises.

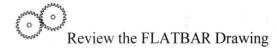 Additional details on Drawing Views, New Drawing, Details, Dimensions, Dimensions and Annotations are available in SolidWorks Help.

Keywords: Drawing Views (overview), Drawing Views (model), Move (drawing views), Dimensions (circles, extension lines, inserting into drawings, move, parenthesis), Annotations (Note, Hole Callout, Centerline, Centermark), Notes (linked to properties, in sheet formats, parametric).

 Review the FLATBAR Drawing

You created the FLATBAR drawing with the A-ANSI-MM Drawing Template. The FLATBAR drawing utilized the FLATBAR part with the Model View tool and the View Palette tool.

The Model View PropertyManager provided the ability to insert new views of a document. You selected the Front, Top, and Right, views. You applied the View Palette to insert an Isometric view.

You moved the views by dragging the blue view boundary. You inserted part dimensions and annotations into the drawing with the Insert Model Items tool. Dimensions were moved to new positions. Leader lines and dimension text were repositioned. Annotations were edited to reflect the dimension standard.

You created a Parametric note that referenced part dimensions in the drawing text. Aluminum 2014 was assigned in the FLATBAR part. The Material Custom Property and Number Custom Property were assigned in the FLATBAR part and referenced in the drawing Title block.

Know inch/mm decimal display. The ASME Y14.5 standard states:

- For millimeter dimensions < 1, display the leading zero. Remove trailing zeros.

- For inch dimensions < 1, delete the leading zero. The dimension is displayed with the same number of decimal places as its tolerance.

Note: The FLATBAR drawing linked Title block notes to Custom Properties in the drawing and in the part. The additional drawings in this project utilize drawing numbers linked to the model file name. The Title of the drawing utilizes a Note.

LINKAGE Assembly Drawing – Sheet1

The LINKAGE assembly drawing Sheet 1 utilizes the LINKAGE assembly. Add an Exploded view and a Bill of Materials to the drawing.

Create an Exploded view in the LINKAGE assembly. The Bill of Materials reflects the components of the LINKAGE assembly. Create a drawing with a Bill of Materials. Perform the following steps:

- Create a new drawing with the custom A-ANSI-MM size Drawing Template with the CUSTOM-A sheet format.

- Create and display the Exploded view of the LINKAGE assembly.

- Insert the Exploded view of the assembly into the drawing.

- Insert a Bill of Materials.

- Label each component with Balloon text.

Activity: LINKAGE Assembly Drawing-Sheet1

Close all parts and drawings.
253) Click **Windows, Close All** from the Menu bar.

Create a new drawing.
254) Click **New** ⬚ from the Menu bar.

255) Double-click **A-ANSI-MM** from the SW-TUTORIAL-2009 folder. The Model View PropertyManager is displayed.

Open the LINKAGE assembly.
256) Click the **Browse** button.

257) Select **Assembly** for Files of type in the SW-TUTORIAL-2009 folder.

258) Double-click **LINKAGE**. Note: Single view is selected by default.

259) Click **Isometric view** from the Standard views box.

260) Select **Shaded With Edges** from the Display Style box.

261) Check the **Use custom scale** box.

262) Select **User Defined** from the drop down menu.

263) Enter **2:3** for Scale.

264) Click a **position** on the right side of Sheet1 as illustrated.

265) Click **OK** from the Drawing View1 PropertyManager.

Deactivate the Origins if needed.
266) Click **View**, uncheck **Origin** from the Menu bar.

Save the LINKAGE assembly drawing.

267) Click **Save**. Accept the default file name.

268) Click **Save**.

Display modes for a Drawing view are similar to a part document. The 3D Drawing View 🖱 tool provides the ability to manipulate the model view in 3D, to select a difficult face, edge, or point.

Wireframe and Shaded Display modes provide the best graphic performance. Mechanical details require Hidden Lines Visible display and Hidden Lines Removed display. Select Shaded/Hidden Lines Removed to display Auxiliary Views to avoid confusion.

Tangent Edges Visible provides clarity for the start of a Fillet edge. Tangent Edges Removed provides the best graphic performance.

Right-click in the view boundary to access the Tangent Edge options.

💡 Utilize the Lightweight Drawing option to improve performance for large assemblies.

Wireframe   Hidden Lines Visible   Hidden Lines Removed   Shaded

Tangent Edges Visible   Tangent Edges With Font   Tangent Edges Removed

To address Tangent lines views:

- Right-click in a Drawing view.

- Click Tangent Edge.

- Click a Tangent Edge view option.

Return to the LINKAGE assembly.

269) Right-click inside the **Isometric view** boundary.

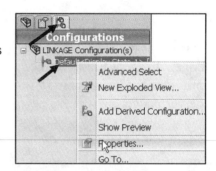

270) Click **Open linkage.sldasm**. The LINKAGE assembly is displayed. Click the **ConfigurationManager** tab.

271) Right-click **Default [LINKAGE]**.

272) Click **Properties**. The Configuration Properties PropertyManager is displayed.

273) Select **User Specified Name** from the Part number displayed when used in Bill of Materials.

274) Enter **GIDS-SC-1000** in the Part number text box.

275) Click **OK** ✔ from the Configuration Properties PropertyManager.

276) Click the LINKAGE **FeatureManager** tab.

277) Click **Save** .

Exploded View

The Exploded View illustrates how to assemble the components in an assembly. Create an Exploded View with four steps. Click and drag components in the Graphics window.

The Manipulator icon indicates the direction to explode. Select an alternate component edge for the Explode direction. Drag the component in the Graphics window or enter an exact value in the Explode distance box.

Manipulate the top-level components in the assembly. Access the Explode view option as follows:

- Right-click the configuration name in the ConfigurationManager.

- Select the Exploded View tool in the Assemble toolbar.

- Select Insert, Exploded View from the Menu bar.

Activity: LINKAGE Assembly Drawing-Exploded View

Insert an Exploded view.

278) Click the **ConfigurationManager** ⊞ tab.

279) Right-click **Default [GIDS-SC-1000]**.

280) Click **New Exploded view** 🗗 New Exploded View... The Explode PropertyManager is displayed.

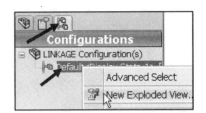

Create Explode Step 1. Use the distance box option.
281) Click the back **SHAFT-COLLAR** as illustrated.

282) Enter **50**mm in the Explode distance box.

283) Click **Apply**. The SHAFT-COLLAR moves 50mms to the back of the model. If required, click the **Reverse direction** button.

284) Click **Done**. Explode Step1 is created.

Create Explode Step 2. Use the Manipulator icon.
285) Click the front **SHAFT-COLLAR** in the Graphics window as illustrated.

286) Drag the blue **Manipulator icon** ⊥ to the front of the assembly approximately 50mms.

287) Click **inside** the Graphics window. Explode Step2 is created.

Create Explode Step 3.
288) Click the **back FLATBAR** in the Graphics window as illustrated.

289) Drag the blue **Manipulator icon** ⊥ to the back of the assembly. Explode Step3 is created.

Create Explode Step 4.
290) Click the front **FLATBAR** in the Graphics window.

291) Drag the blue **Manipulator icon** ⊥ to the front of the assembly. Explode Step4 is created.

292) Click **inside** the Graphics window.

293) **Expand** each Explode Step to review.

294) Click **OK** ✔ from the Explode PropertyManager.

Save the LINKAGE part in the Exploded State.
295) Click **Save** 💾 .

Activity: LINKAGE Assembly Drawing-Animation

Animate the Exploded view.
296) Expand Default [GIDS-SC-1000].

297) Right-click **ExplView1** in the ConfigurationManager.

298) Click **Animate collapse** to play the animation. View the Animation.

Return the Exploded view in its collapsed state.

299) Close ☒ the Animation Controller dialog box.

Return to the Assembly FeatureManager
300) Click the LINKAGE **FeatureManager** tab.

301) Click **Save** .

Open the LINKAGE drawing.
302) Click **Window, LINKAGE – SHEET1** from the Menu bar.

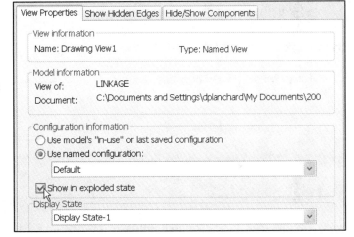

Display the Exploded view in the drawing.
303) Right-click inside the **Isometric view**.

304) Click **Properties**.

305) Check the **Show in exploded state** box.

306) Click **OK** from the Drawing Views Properties box.

307) Click **OK** ✔ from the Drawing View1 PropertyManager. View the exploded state in the drawing on Sheet1.

308) Rebuild the model.

Bill of Materials

A Bill of Materials (BOM) is a table inserted into a drawing to keep a record of the parts used in an assembly. The default BOM template contains the Item Number, Quantity, Part No. and Description. The default Item number is determined by the order in which the component is inserted into the assembly. Quantity is the number of instances of a part or assembly.

Part No. is determined by the following: file name, default and the User Defined option, Part number used by the Bill of Materials. Description is determined by the description entered when the document is saved.

Activity: LINKAGE Assembly Drawing-Bill of Materials

Create a Bill of Materials.

309) Click inside the **Isometric view** boundary.

310) Click the **Annotation** tab from the CommandManager.

311) Click the **Bill of Materials** tool from the Consolidated Tables toolbar. The Bill of Materials PropertyManager is displayed.

312) Select **bom-material** for Table Template.

313) Select **Top Level only** for BOM Type.

314) Click **OK** from the Bill of Materials PropertyManager.

315) Double-click a position in the **upper left corner** of the Sheet1.

316) Click a **position** in Sheet1.

ITEM NO.	PART NUMBER	DESCRIPTION	MATERIAL	QTY.
1	GIDS-PC-10001	LINEAR ACTUATOR		1
2	AXLE	AXLE ROD		1
3	GIDS-SC-10001-9	FLAT BAR 9 HOLES	2014 Alloy	2
4	SHAFT-COLLAR	SHAFT-COLLAR		2

The Bill of Materials requires some editing. The AXLE and SHAFT-COLLAR PART NUMBER values are not defined. The current part file name determines the PART NUMBER value.

The current part description determines the DESCRIPTION values. Redefine the PART NUMBER for the Bill of Materials. Note: You will also scale the LINKAGE assembly.

Modify the AXLE Part number.
317) Right-click the **AXLE** part in the LINKAGE drawing. Click **Open Part**. The AXLE FeatureManager is displayed.

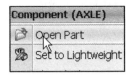

318) Click the AXLE **ConfigurationManager** tab.

319) Right-click **Default [AXLE]** in the ConfigurationManager.

320) Click **Properties**.

321) Select **User Specified Name** from the Configuration Properties dialog box.

322) Enter **GIDS-SC-10017** for the Part Number to be utilized in the Bill of Materials.

323) Click **OK** from the Configuration Properties PropertyManager. **Return** to the FeatureManager.

324) Click **Save**.

Return to the LINKAGE drawing.
325) Click **Window**, **LINKAGE - Sheet1** from the Menu bar.

Modify the SHAFT-COLLAR PART NUMBER.
326) Right-click the left **SHAFT-COLLAR** part in the LINKAGE drawing.

327) Click **Open Part**. The SHAFT-COLLAR FeatureManager is displayed.

328) Click the SHAFT-COLLAR **ConfigurationManager** tab.

329) Right-click **Default [SHAFT-COLLAR]** from the ConfigurationManager.

330) Click **Properties**. Select the **User Specified Name** from the Configuration Properties box.

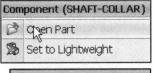

331) Enter **GIDS-SC-10012-3-16** for the Part Number in the Bill of Materials.

332) Click **OK** from the Configuration Properties PropertyManager.

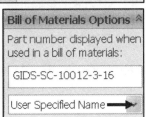

333) **Return** to the FeatureManager.

334) Click **Save**.

Return to the LINKAGE assembly drawing.
335) Click **Window, LINKAGE - Sheet1** from the Menu bar.

336) Rebuild the drawing and update the BOM.

Modify the LINKAGE assembly scale.
337) Click inside the **Isometric view** boundary.

338) Enter **1:2** for Scale.

339) Click **OK** ✅ from the Drawing View1 PropertyManager.

340) Click **Save** 💾.

ITEM NO.	PART NUMBER	DESCRIPTION	MATERIAL	QTY.
1	GIDS-PC-10001	LINEAR ACTUATOR		1
2	GIDS-SC-10017	AXLE ROD		1
3	GIDS-SC-10001-9	FLAT BAR 9 HOLES	2014 Alloy	2
4	GIDS-SC-10012-3-16	SHAFT-COLLAR		2

Note: As an exercise, complete the Bill of Materials. Label each component with a unique item number. The item number is placed inside a circle. The circle is called Balloon text. List each item in a Bill of Materials table. Utilize Auto Balloon to apply Balloon text to all BOM components.

The Circle Split Line option contains the Item Number and Quantity. Item number is determined by the order listed in the assembly FeatureManager. Quantity lists the number of instances in the assembly.

Activity: LINKAGE Assembly Drawing-Automatic Balloons

Insert the Automatic Balloons.
341) Click inside the **Isometric view** boundary of the LINKAGE.

342) Click the **Auto Balloons** 🎈 tool from the Annotation toolbar. The Auto Balloon PropertyManager is displayed. Accept the Square default Balloon Layout.

343) Click **OK** ✅ from the Auto Balloon PropertyManager.

Reposition the Balloon text.
344) Click and drag each **Balloon** to the desired position.

345) Click and drag the **Balloon arrowhead** to reposition the arrow on a component edge.

346) Click **OK** ✔ from the Balloon PropertyManager.

Display Item Number/Quantity.
347) Ctrl-Select the **four Balloon text** in the Graphics window. The Balloon PropertyManager is displayed.

348) Select **Circular Split Line** for Style.

349) Click **OK** ✔ from the Balloon PropertyManager.

Save the LINKAGE assembly drawing.
350) Click **Save** 🖫 .

☀ Select the BOM table in the drawing and Right-click Properties to modify entries and display table parameters.

LINKAGE Assembly Drawing – Sheet2

A drawing consists of one or more sheets. Utilize the Model View tool in the View Layout toolbar to insert the AirCylinder assembly. The LINKAGE drawing Sheet2 displays the Front view and Top view of the AirCylinder assembly.

Insert a Section View to display the internal features of the AirCylinder. Insert a Detail View to display an enlarged area of the AirCylinder.

Activity: LINKAGE Assembly Drawing-Sheet2

Add Sheet2.
351) Right-click in the Graphics window.

352) Click **Add Sheet**. Sheet2 is displayed. **Right-click** in Sheet2.

☀ You can also add a sheet by clicking the Add Sheet icon in the lower left corner of the Graphics window.

353) Click **Properties**.

354) Enter **1:2** for Scale.

Select the CUSTOM-A Sheet Format.
355) Click **Browse** from the Sheet Properties box.

356) Select **SW-TUTORIAL-2009** for Look in folder.

357) Double-click **CUSTOM-A**.

358) Click **OK** from the Sheet Properties box. Sheet 2 of 2 is displayed in the Graphics window.

Insert the AirCylinder assembly.
359) Click the **View Layout** tab from the CommandManager.

360) Click the **Model View** tool from the View Layout toolbar. The Model View PropertyManager is displayed.

361) Click the **Browse** button.

362) Double-click the **AirCylinder** assembly from the SW-TUTORIAL-2009 folder.

363) Click the **Multiple views** box.

364) Click **Top view** as illustrated in the Standard views box. Note: Front view is selected by default. Both views should be active.

365) Click **OK** from the Model View PropertyManager.

Save Sheet2.
366) Click **Save** .

Modify the Title Name font size.
367) **Right-click** in the Graphics window.

368) Click **Edit Sheet Format**.

369) Double-click on the Title: **LINEAR ACTUATOR**.

370) Resize the text to the Title block. Enter **5**mm for text height.

371) Click inside the **Graphics window**.

372) **Right-click** in the Graphics window.

373) Click **Edit Sheet**.

Section views display the interior features. Define a cutting plane with a sketched line in a view perpendicular to the Section view. Create a full Section view by sketching a section line in the Top view. Detailed views enlarge an area of an existing view. Specify location, shape and scale. Create a Detail view from a Section view at a 2:1 scale.

Activity: LINKAGE Assembly Drawing-Sheet2 Section view

Add a Section View to the drawing.
374) Click the **Drawing View3** boundary.

375) Click the **Section View** tool from the View Layout toolbar. The Section View PropertyManager is displayed. The Sketch line icon is displayed.

376) Sketch a section line through the **midpoints** of the view boundary.

377) Click the **end point**. The Section line extends beyond the left and right profile lines. The Section View dialog box is displayed.

Position Section View A-A.
378) Click **OK** from the Section View dialog box.

379) Click a **location** above the Top view. The section arrows points downward.

380) Check the **Flip direction** box.

381) Click **OK** from the Section View PropertyManager.

SECTION A-A

Fit the views to the drawing.
382) Press the **f** key.

Activity: LINKAGE Assembly Drawing-Sheet2 Detail view

Add a Detail view to the drawing.
383) Click inside the **Section View** boundary. The Section View A-A PropertyManager is displayed.

384) **Zoom in** to enlarge the view.

SECTION A-A

385) Click the **Detail View** tool from the View Layout toolbar. The Circle Sketch tool is selected.

386) Click the **center** of the air fitting on the left side in the Section View as illustrated.

387) Sketch a **Circle** to encompass the air fitting.

388) If required, enter **B** for Detail View Name in the Label text box.

Position Detail View B.
389) Press the **f** key.

390) Click a **location** on Sheet2 to the right of the SECTION View.

391) Enter **2:1** for Scale.

392) Click **OK** from the Detail View B PropertyManager.

SECTION A-A

DETAIL B
SCALE 2 : 1

Select a view boundary before creating Projected Views, Section Views or Detail Views.

Move views if required.
393) Click and drag the **view boundary** to allow for approximately 1 inch, [25mm] spacing between views.

Save the LINKAGE assembly drawing.
394) Click **Save** .

Close all parts and assemblies.
395) Click **Window, Close All** from the Menu bar.

Additional details on Exploded View, Notes, Properties, Bill of Materials, Balloons, Section View and Detail View are available in SolidWorks Help. Keywords: Exploded, Notes, Properties (configurations), Bill of Materials, Balloons, Auto Balloon, Section, and Detail.

Review the LINKAGE Assembly Drawing

The LINKAGE Assembly drawing consisted of two sheets. Sheet1 contained an Exploded view. The Exploded view was created in the LINKAGE assembly.

The Bill of Materials listed the Item Number, Part Number, Description, Material and Quantity of components in the assembly. Balloons were inserted to label top level components in the LINKAGE assembly. You developed Custom Properties in the part and utilized the Properties in the drawing and Bill of Materials.

Sheet2 contained the Front view, Top view, Section view, and Detail view of the AirCylinder assembly.

Design Tables

A Design Table is a spreadsheet used to create multiple configurations in a part or assembly. The Design Table controls the dimensions and parameters in the part. Utilize the Design Table to modify the overall length and number of holes in each FLATBAR.

Create three configurations of the FLATBAR:

- 3HOLE

- 5HOLE

- 7HOLE

Utilize the Design Table to control the Part Number and Description in the Bill of Materials. Insert the custom parameter $PRP@DESCRIPTION into the Design Table. Insert the system parameter $PARTNUMBER into the Design Table.

Activity: FLATBAR Part-Design Table

Open the FLATBAR part.
396) Click **Open** from the Menu bar.

397) Double-click the **FLATBAR** part from the SW-TUTORIAL-2009 folder. The FLATBAR FeatureManager is displayed.

Insert a Design Table.
398) Click **Insert**, **Tables**, **Design Table** from the Menu bar. The Auto-create option is selected. Accept the default settings.

399) Click **OK** from the Design Table PropertyManager.

Select the input dimension.
400) Hold the **Ctrl key** down.

401) Click the **D1@Sketch1**, **D2@Sketch1**, **D1@Extude1**, **D1@Sketch2**, **D3@LPattern1** and **D1@LPattern1** from the Dimensions box.

402) Release the **Ctrl key**.

403) Click **OK** from the Dimensions dialog box.

The illustrated dimension variable names in the Dimensions dialog box will be different if sketches or features were deleted when creating the FLATBAR part.

The input dimension names and default values are automatically entered into the Design Table. The Design Table displays the Primary Units of the Part. Example: Inches. The value Default is entered in Cell A3.

The values for the FLATBAR are entered in Cells B3 through G9. The FLATBAR length is controlled in Column B. The Number of Holes is controlled in Column G.

Enter the three configuration names.
404) Click **Cell A4**.

405) Enter **3HOLE**.

406) Click **Cell A5**.

407) Enter **5HOLE**.

408) Click **Cell A6**.

409) Enter **7HOLE**.

410) Click Cell **D3**.

411) Enter **0.09** to round off the Thickness value.

Enter the dimension values for the 3HOLE configuration.
412) Click **Cell B4**. Enter **1**.

413) Click **Cell G4**. Enter **3**.

Enter the dimension values for the 5HOLE configuration.
414) Click **Cell B5**.

415) Enter **2**.

416) Click **Cell G5**.

417) Enter **5**.

Enter the dimension values for the 7HOLE
configuration.
418) Click **Cell B6**.

419) Enter **3**.

420) Click **Cell G6**.

421) Enter **7**.

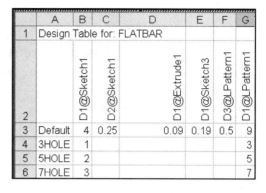

	A	B	C	D	E	F	G
1	Design Table for: FLATBAR						
2		D1@Sketch1	D2@Sketch1		D1@Extrude1	D1@Sketch3	D3@LPattern1	D1@LPattern1
3	Default	4	0.25		0.09	0.19	0.5	9
4	3HOLE	1						3
5	5HOLE	2						5
6	7HOLE	3						7

Build the three configurations.
422) Click a **position** outside the EXCEL Design Table in
the Graphics window.

423) Click **OK** to generate the configurations. The
Design Table icon is displayed in the FLATBAR
FeatureManager.

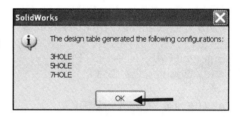

Display the configurations.
424) Double-click **3HOLE**.

425) Double-click **5HOLE**.

426) Double-click **7HOLE**.

427) Double-click **Default**.

428) Click **Save** 💾.

Edit the Design Table.
429) Right-click **Design Table** in the
ConfigurationManager.

430) Click **Edit Table**. The Add Rows and Columns dialog
box is displayed.

431) Click **Cancel** from the Add Rows and Columns dialog
box.

Columns C through F are filled with the default FLATBAR values.

Enter parameters for DESCRIPTION and PARTNUMBER. Custom Properties begin with the prefix, "$PRP@". SolidWorks Properties begin with the prefix, "$".

Enter DESCRIPTION custom Property.
432) Double-click **Cell H2**.

433) Enter **$PRP@DESCRIPTION**.

434) Click **Cell H3**. Enter **9HOLES**.

435) Click **Cell H4**. Enter **3HOLES**.

436) Click **Cell H5**. Enter **5HOLES**.

437) Click **Cell H6**. Enter **7HOLES**.

Enter the PARTNUMBER Property.
438) Double-click **Cell I2**.

439) Enter **$PARTNUMBER**.

440) Click **Cell I3**.

441) Enter **GIDS-SC-10009-9**.

442) Click **Cell I4**.

443) Enter **GIDS-SC-10009-3**.

444) Click **Cell I5**.

445) Enter **GIDS-SC-10009-5**.

446) Click **Cell I6**.

447) Enter **GIDS-SC-10009-7**.

448) Click a **position** in the Graphics window to update the Design Table.

	D3@LPattern1	D1@LPattern1	$PRP@DESCRIPTION
	0.5	9	9HOLES
	0.5	3	3HOLES
	0.5	5	5HOLES
	0.5	7	7HOLES

D1@Sketch3	D3@LPattern1	D1@LPattern1	$PRP@DESCRIPTION	$PARTNUMBER	
0.19	0.5	9	9HOLES	GIDS-SC-10009-9	
0.19	0.5	3	3HOLES	GIDS-SC-10009-3	
0.19	0.5	5	5HOLES	GIDS-SC-10009-5	
0.19	0.5	7	7HOLES	GIDS-SC-10009-7	

Activity: FLATBAR Drawing-Sheet2

Select configurations in the drawing. The Properties option in the Drawing view displays a list of configuration names.

Open the FLATBAR drawing.
449) Click **Open** 📂 from the Menu bar.

450) Select Files of type: **Drawing (*drw,*slddrw)**.

451) Double-click **FLATBAR** from the SW-TUTORIAL-2009 folder. The FLATBAR drawing is displayed. The dimensions tied to the Design table are displayed in a different color. The dimension color is controlled from the System Options, Colors section.

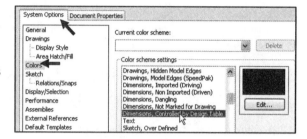

Copy the Front view.
452) Click inside the FLATBAR **Front view** boundary.

453) Press **Ctrl C**.

454) **Right-click** in the Graphics window.

455) Click **Add Sheet**. Sheet2 is displayed.

456) Right-click **Properties**.

457) Click **Browse** from the Sheet Properties dialog box.

458) Double-click **CUSTOM-A** Sheet Format from the SW-TUTORIAL-2009 folder.

459) Click **OK** from the Sheet Properties box.

Paste the Front view from Sheet1.
460) Click a **position** inside the Sheet2 boundary.

461) Press **Ctrl V**. The Front view is displayed.

Display the 3HOLE FLATBAR configuration on Sheet2.
462) Right-click inside the **Front view** boundary.

463) Click **Properties**.

464) Select **3HOLE** from the Use named configuration list.

465) Click **OK** from the Drawing View Properties dialog box. The 3HOLE FLATBAR configuration is displayed.

466) Right-click inside the **Drawing View** boundary.

467) Click **Open flatbar.sldprt**.

468) Double-click the **3HOLE** configuration from the ConfigurationManager tab.

Return to the FLATBAR Drawing Sheet2.

469) Click **Window**, **FLATBAR – Sheet2** from the Menu bar.

470) Click on the **9X** dimension text in the Graphics window. The Dimension PropertyManager is displayed.

471) Replace the 9X dimension text with **3X** in the Dimension Text box as illustrated.

472) Click **OK** ✔ from the Dimension PropertyManager.

Save the FLATBAR Sheet2 drawing.

473) Click **Save** 💾.

The 5HOLE and 7HOLE configurations are explored as an exercise. Combine the FLATBAR configurations with the SHAFT-COLLAR part to create three different assemblies. Select configuration in the assembly. The Properties in the FeatureManager option displays a list of configuration names.

The FLATBAR-SHAFTCOLLAR assembly contains a FLATBAR fixed to the assembly Origin and a SHAFTCOLLAR mated to the FLATBAR left hole. The default configuration utilizes the FLATBAR-9HOLE part.

Design Tables exist in the assembly. Utilize a Design Table to control part configurations, 3HOLE, 5HOLE, and 7HOLE. Utilize the Design Table to Control Suppress/Resolve state of a component in an assembly. Insert the parameter $STATE into the Design Table.

Activity: FLATBAR-SHAFTCOLLAR Assembly

Return to the Default FLATBAR configuration.
474) Right-click in the **3HOLE FLATBAR** view boundary.

475) Click **Open flatbar**.

476) Click the **ConfigurationManager** tab.

477) Double-click the **Default** configuration.

478) Click the **FeatureManager** tab. The FLATBAR (Default) FeatureManager is displayed.

479) Click **Save**.

Create the FLATBAR-SHAFTCOLLAR assembly.
480) Click **New** from the Menu bar.

481) Double-click **Assembly** from the Templates tab. The Begin Assembly PropertyManager is displayed. FLATBAR is an active document. FLATBAR is displayed in the Open documents box.

482) Click **FLATBAR** from the Open documents box.

483) Click **OK** from the Begin Assembly PropertyManager. The FLATBAR is fixed to the Origin.

Save the FLATBAR-SHAFTCOLLAR assembly.
484) Click **Save**.

485) Enter **FLATBAR-SHAFTCOLLAR** for
Assembly name.

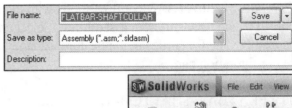

486) Click **Save**.

Insert the SHAFTCOLLAR part.

487) Click the **Insert Components** tool
from the Assembly toolbar. The Insert
Component PropertyManager is displayed.

488) Click **BROWSE**.

489) Double-click the **SHAFT-COLLAR** part.

490) Click a **position** to the front left of the FLATBAR as
illustrated in the Graphics window.

Fit the model to the Graphics window.
491) Press the **f** key.

492) Click **Save** .

Mate the SHAFTCOLLAR.

493) Click the **Mate** tool from the Assembly toolbar.
The Mate PropertyManager is displayed.

Insert a Concentric mate.
494) Click the **left hole face** of the FLATBAR.

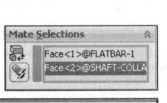

495) Click the outside **cylindrical face** of
the SHAFT-COLLAR. The selected
faces are displayed in the Mate
Selections box. Concentric is selected
by default.

496) Click the **Green Check mark** .

Insert a Coincident mate.
497) Click the **back flat face** of the SHAFT-COLLAR.

498) Click the **front face** of the FLATBAR as illustrated.
Coincident is selected by default.

499) Click the **Green Check mark** .

500) Click **OK** from the Mate PropertyManager.

Insert and mate the second SHAFT-COLLAR to the right hole.

501) Click the **Insert Components** tool from the Assembly toolbar. The Insert Component PropertyManager is displayed.

502) Click the **Browse** button.

503) Double-click the **SHAFT-COLLAR** part.

504) Click a **position** to the front right of the FLATBAR as illustrated.

Mate the second SHAFTCOLLAR.

505) Click the **Mate** tool from the Assembly toolbar. The Mate PropertyManager is displayed.

Insert a Concentric mate.
506) Click the **right hole face** of the FLATBAR.

507) Click the outside **cylindrical face** of the SHAFT-COLLAR. Concentric is selected by default.

508) Click the **Green Check mark** .

Insert a Coincident mate.
509) Click the **back flat face** of the SHAFT-COLLAR.

510) Click the **front face** of the FLATBAR. Coincident is selected by default.

511) Click the **Green Check mark** .

512) Click **OK** from the Mate PropertyManager.

Save the FLATBAR-SHAFTCOLLAR assembly.

513) Click **Save** .

The FLATBAR-SHAFTCOLLAR FeatureManager displays the Default configuration of the FLATBAR in parenthesis, FLATBAR<1> (Default).

The instance number, <1> indicates the first instance of the FLATBAR. Note: Your instance number will be different, if you delete the FLATBAR and then reinsert into the assembly. The exact instance number is required for the Design Table.

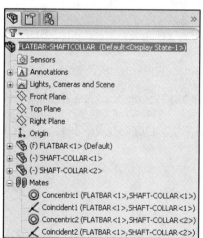

Create a Design Table that contains three new configurations. Each configuration utilizes a different FLATBAR configuration. Control the Suppress/Resolve State of the second SHAFT-COLLAR.

Insert a Design Table.

514) Click **Insert**, **Tables**, **Design Table** from the Menu bar. The Auto-create option is selected by default.

515) Click **OK** ✔ from the Design Table PropertyManager.

Enter the Design Table values.

516) Default is displayed in Cell A3. Click **Cell A4**.

517) Enter **NO SHAFT-COLLAR**.

518) Double-click **CELL B2**.

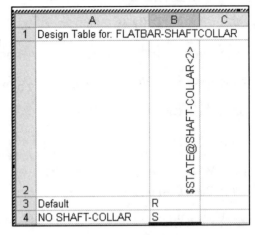

519) Enter **$STATE@SHAFT-COLLAR<2>**.

520) Click **Cell B3**.

521) Enter **R** for Resolved.

522) Click **Cell B4**.

523) Enter **S** for Suppressed.

524) Click a **position** outside the Design Table in the Graphics window.

525) Click **OK** to display the NO SHAFT-COLLAR configuration.

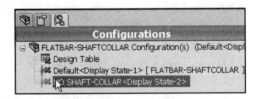

Display the configurations.

526) Click the **ConfigurationManager** tab.

527) Double-click the **NO SHAFT-COLLAR** configuration. The second SHAFT-COLLAR is suppressed in the Graphics window.

528) Double-click the **Default** configuration. The second SHAFT-COLLAR is resolved. Both SHAFT-COLLARs are displayed in the Graphics window.

Insert FLATBAR configurations.
529) Right-click **Design Table**.

530) Click **Edit Table**.

531) Click **Cancel** from the Add Rows and Columns dialog box.

Enter Configuration names.
532) Click **Cell A5**. Enter **3HOLE FLATBAR**.

533) Click **Cell A6**. Enter **5HOLE FLATBAR**.

534) Click **Cell A7**. Enter **7HOLE FLATBAR**.

Enter STATE values.
535) Click **Cell B5**. Enter **S** for Suppress.

536) Click Cell **B6**. Enter **S**.

537) Click Cell **B7**. Enter **S**.

Enter Design Table values.
538) Double-click **Cell C2**.

539) Enter **$CONFIGURATION@FLATBAR<1>**.

540) Click **Cell C5**.

541) Enter **3HOLE**.

542) Click **Cell C6**.

543) Enter **5HOLE**.

544) Click **Cell C7**.

545) Enter **7HOLE**.

546) Click a **position** in the Graphics window to exit.

547) Click **OK** to create the three configurations.

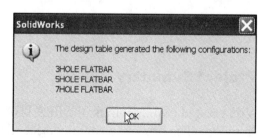

Display the configurations.
548) Double-click the **3HOLE FLATBAR** configuration.

549) Double-click the **5HOLE FLATBAR** configuration.

550) Double-click the **7HOLE FLATBAR** configuration.

551) Double-click the **Default** configuration.

552) Click the **Assembly FeatureManager** 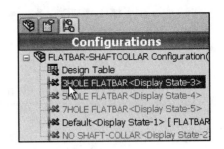 tab.

Save the FLATBAR-SHAFTCOLLAR assembly.
553) Click **Isometric view** from the Heads-up View toolbar.

554) Click **Save** .

Close all documents.
555) Click **Windows**, **Close All** from the Menu bar.

Always return to the Default configuration in the assembly. Control the individual configuration through properties of a view in a drawing and properties of a component in the assembly.

To modify configuration specific notes or dimensions in an assembly drawing, the configuration in the assembly must be the active configuration.

If an assembly or component is loaded in a Lightweight state, right-click the **assembly name** or **component name** from the FeatureManager. Click **Set Lightweight to Resolved**.

Additional details on Design Tables and Configurations are available in SolidWorks Help.

Project Summary

You created two drawings: the FLATBAR drawing and the LINKAGE assembly drawing. The drawings contained Standard views, a Detail view, a Section view, and an Isometric view.

The drawings utilized a Custom Sheet Format and a Custom Drawing Template. The Sheet Format contained the Company logo and Title block information.

The FLATBAR drawing consisted of two Sheets: Sheet1 and Sheet2. You obtained an understanding of displaying views with the ability to insert, add, and modify dimensions. You used two major design modes in the drawings: Edit Sheet Format and Edit Sheet.

The LINKAGE assembly drawing contained two sheets. Sheet1 contained an Exploded view and a Bill of Materials. The Properties for the Bill of Materials were developed in each part and assembly. Sheet2 utilized a Detail view and a Section view of the AirCylinder assembly.

You created three configurations of the FLATBAR part with a Design Table. The Design Table controlled parameters and dimensions of the FLATBAR part. You utilized these three configurations in the FLATBAR-SHAFTCOLLAR assembly.

Drawings are an integral part of the design process. Part, assemblies, and drawings all work together. From your initial design concepts, you created parts and drawings that fulfilled the design requirements of your customer.

Additional SolidWorks examples are provided in the text **Drawing and Detailing with SolidWorks**, Planchard & Planchard, SDC Publications.

Project Terminology

Bill of Materials (BOM): A BOM is a EXCEL table in a drawing that lists the item, quantity, part number and description of the components in an assembly. Balloon labels are placed on items in the drawing that correspond to the number in the table. A BOM template controls additional information such as Material or Cost.

Center marks: Represents two perpendicular intersecting centerlines.

Design Table: A Design Table is a spreadsheet used to create multiple configurations in a part or assembly. The Design Table controls the dimensions and parameters in the part.

Detailed view: Detailed views enlarge an area of an existing view. Specify location, shape, and scale.

Drawing file name: Drawing file names end with a .slddrw suffix.

Drawing Layers: Contain dimensions, annotations, and geometry.

Drawing Template: The foundation of a SolidWorks drawing is the Drawing Template. Drawing size, drawing standards, company information, manufacturing and or assembly requirements, units and other properties are defined in the Drawing Template. In this project, the Drawing Template contained the drawing Size and Document Properties.

Edit Sheet Format Mode: Provides the ability to:

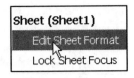

- Change the Title block size and text headings.

- Incorporate a Company logo.

- Add a drawing, design or company text.

Remember: A part cannot be inserted into a drawing when the Edit Sheet Format mode is selected.

Edit Sheet Mode: Provides the ability to:

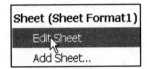

- Add or modify views.

- Add or modify dimensions.

- Add or modify text.

General Notes: Below are a few helpful guidelines to create general drawing notes:

- Use capitol letters.

- Use left text justification.

- Font size should be the same as the dimension text.

Hole Callout: The Hole Callout function creates additional notes required to dimension the holes.

Hole centerlines: Are composed of alternating long and short dash lines. The lines identify the center of a circle, axes or other cylindrical geometry.

Insert Model Items: The tool utilized to insert part dimensions and annotations into drawing views. The Insert Model Items tool is located in the Annotate toolbar.

Leader lines: Reference the size of the profile. A gap must exist between the profile lines and the leader lines.

Model View: The tool utilized to insert named views into a drawing. The Model View tool is located in the Layout View toolbar.

Notes: Notes can be used to add text with leaders or as a stand-alone text string. If an edge, face or vertex is selected prior to adding the note, a leader is created to that location.

Part file name: Part file names end with a .sldprt suffix. Note: A drawing or part file can have the same prefix. A drawing or part file cannot have the same suffix. Example: Drawing file name: FLATBAR.slddrw. Part file name: FLATBAR.sldprt

Section view: Section views display the interior features. Define a cutting plane with a sketched line in a view perpendicular to the Section view.

Sheet Format: The Sheet Format is incorporated into the Drawing Template. The Sheet Format contains the border, title block information, revision block information, company name and or logo information, Custom Properties and SolidWorks Properties. In this project the Sheet Format contained the title block information.

Title block: Contains vital part or assembly information. Each company can have a unique version of a title block.

View Appearance: There are two important factors that affect the appearance of views:

1. Whether the view is shown wireframe, hidden lines removed, or hidden lines visible.

2. How tangent edges on entities such as fillets are displayed.

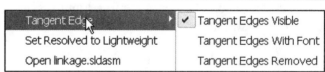

Questions

1. Describe a Bill of Materials and its contents.

2. Name the two major design modes used to develop a drawing in SolidWorks.

3. True or False. Units, Dimensioning Standards, Arrow size, Font size are modified in the Options, Document Properties section.

4. How do you save a Sheet Format?

5. Identify seven components that are commonly found in a title block.

6. Describe the procedure to insert an Isometric view to the drawing?

7. In SolidWorks, drawing file names end with a _____ suffix. Part file names end with a _____ suffix.

8. True or False. In SolidWorks, if a part is modified, the drawing is updated with a Rebuild command.

9. True or False. In SolidWorks, when a dimension in the drawing is modified, the part is updated with a Rebuild command.

10. Name three guidelines to create General Notes on a drawing.

11. True or False. Most engineering drawings use the following font: Times New Roman – All small letters.

12. What are Leader lines? Provide an example.

13. Describe the key differences between a Detail view and a Section view on a drawing.

14. Identify the procedure to create an Exploded view.

15. Describe the purpose of a Design Table in a part and in an assembly.

16. Review the Design Intent section in the Introduction. Identify how you incorporated design intent into the drawing.

17. Identify how you incorporate design intent into configurations with a Design Table.

18. Review the Keyboard Short Cut keys in the Appendix. Identify the Short Cut keys you incorporated into this project.

19. Discuss why a part designed in inch units would utilize a drawing detailed in millimeter units.

Exercises

Exercise 3.1: FLATBAR – 3 HOLE Drawing.

Note: Dimensions are enlarged for clarity. Utilize inch, millimeter, or dual dimensioning.

- Create the FLATBAR – 3HOLE drawing.

- Insert a Shaded Isometric view.

- Insert a Front and Top view.

- Insert dimensions. Insert 3X – EQ. SP.

- Add a Parametric Note for MATERIAL THICKNESS.

- Click the Thickness dimension is the Top view.

- Hide the Thickness dimension in the Top view.

- Enter 2014 Alloy material to the part.

Exercise 3.2: AXLE Drawing.

Create the AXLE drawing.

- Insert a Front, Top, and Shaded Isometric view. Fit the part to the drawing.

- Insert dual dimensions from the part. Add a centerline in the Top view. Add a Sheet.

- Modify the Dimension Font to 18 points.

- Utilize the Material Editor. The Material is 2014 Alloy.

- Set Decimal places to 4.

- Utilize the Mass Properties tool from the Evaluate toolbar to calculate the volume and mass of the AXLE part.

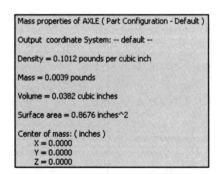

Mass properties of AXLE (Part Configuration - Default)

Output coordinate System: -- default --

Density = 0.1012 pounds per cubic inch

Mass = 0.0039 pounds

Volume = 0.0382 cubic inches

Surface area = 0.8676 inches^2

Center of mass: (inches)
    X = 0.0000
    Y = 0.0000
    Z = 0.0000

Exercise 3.3: SHAFT COLLAR Drawing.

Create the SHAFT COLLAR Drawing. Insert a Front, Top, and Shaded Isometric view. Add a 4:1 scale to the Isometric view.

- Insert and add dimensions as illustrated. Add a centerline to the Isometric and Top views. Add a Sheet.

- Add a Revision table. Add a Row. Input the fields for the first row of the revision table.

Exercise 3.4: 3LINKS Assembly drawing.

- Utilize three different FLATBAR configurations and a SHAFT-COLLAR.

- Create a 3LINKS assembly.

- Create a 3LINKS assembly drawing.

- Insert a Bill of Materials as illustrated.

- Add balloons.

ITEM NO.	PART NUMBER	DESCRIPTION	QTY.
1	GIDS-SC-10009-7	7HOLES	1
2	GIDS-SC-10012-3-16	SHAFT-COLLAR	1
3	GIDS-SC-10009-5	5HOLES	1
4	GIDS-SC-10009-3	3HOLES	1

Exercise 3.5: SHAFT-COLLAR1 Drawing: Design Tables.

Utilize a Design Table to create three configurations of the SHAFT-COLLAR1:

- Small

- Medium

- Large

Note: The dimension variable name will be different if sketches or features were deleted.

- Add a Sheet to the SHAFT-COLLAR1 drawing.

- Insert three different configurations: Small, Medium, and Large as illustrated.

Exercise 3.6: Create a FLATBAR-5HOLE Drawing.

- Create the drawing as illustrated.

- Insert a Shaded Isometric view.

- Insert a Front and Top view.

- Insert dimensions from the part.

- Modify the hole dimension to include 5X # EQ. SP.

- Add a Parametric Note for MATERIAL THICKNESS.

- Add a reference dimension.

Exercise 3.7: LINKAGE-2 Drawing.

- Create a new drawing named, LINKAGE-2.

- Insert an Isometric view, shaded view of the LINKAGE-2 Assembly created in the Project 1 exercises.

- Define the PART NO. Property and the DESCRIPTION Property for the AXLE, FLATBAR- 9HOLE, FLATBAR – 3HOLE and SHAFT COLLAR.

- Save the LINKAGE-2 assembly to update the properties. Return to the LINKAGE-2 Drawing. Insert a Bill of Materials with Auto Balloons.

ITEM NO.	PART NUMBER	DESCRIPTION	MATERIAL	QTY.
1	GIDS-PC-10001	LINEAR ACTUATOR		1
2	GIDS-SC-10017	AXLE ROD	2014 Alloy	3
3	GIDS-SC-10009-9	9HOLES	2014 Alloy	2
4	GIDS-SC-10012-3-16	SHAFT-COLLAR	2014 Alloy	6
5	GIDS-SC-10009-3	FLAT BAR 3 HOLES	6061 Alloy	2

Exercise 3.8: eDrawing Exercise.

Create an eDrawing of the LINKAGE-2 drawing. A SolidWorks eDrawing is a compressed document that does not require the corresponding part or assembly. SolidWorks eDrawing is animated to display multiple views and dimensions. Review the eDrawing On-line Help for additional functionality.

- Active eDrawings.

- Click Publish eDrawing 2009 File from the Menu bar menu.

- Click the Play button.

- Click the Stop button.

- Save the LINKAGE-2 eDrawing.

- Return to the LINKAGE2 drawing.

Project 4

Advanced Features

Below are the desired outcomes and usage competencies based on the completion of Project 4.

Desired Outcomes:	Usage Competencies:

• Six parts for the PNEUMATIC-TEST-MODULE assembly:
   o WEIGHT
   o HOOK
   o WHEEL
   o HEX-ADAPTER
   o AXLE-3000
   o SHAFTCOLLAR-500
	• Apply the following Advanced modeling features: Plane, Lofted Base, Extruded Cut, Swept Base, Dome, Helix and Spiral, Swept Cut, Extruded Base, Revolved Cut, Extruded Cut, Circular Pattern, Axis, and Hole Wizard.
	
	• Reuse geometry.
	
	• Modify existing parts to create new parts with the Save as copy command.

Notes:

Project 4 – Advanced Features

Project Objective

Obtain an understanding to create parts for the configuration of the PNEUMATIC-TEST-MODULE assembly. Attain the ability to reuse geometry by modifying existing parts and to create new parts. Knowledge of the following SolidWorks features: *Extruded Boss/Base, Extruded Cut, Dome, Plane, Axis, Lofted Boss/Base, Swept Boss/Base, Helix and Spiral Swept Cut, Revolved Cut, Hole Wizard, and Circular Pattern.*

Create six individual parts:

- WEIGHT

- HOOK

- WHEEL

- HEX-ADAPTER

- AXLE-3000

- SHAFTCOLLAR-500

In Project 5, develop a working understanding with multiple documents in an assembly. Build on sound assembly modeling techniques that utilize symmetry, component patterns, and mirrored components.

Create five assemblies:

- 3HOLE-SHAFTCOLLAR assembly

- 5HOLE-SHAFTCOLLAR assembly

- WHEEL-FLATBAR assembly

- WHEEL-AND-AXLE assembly

- PNEUMATIC-TEST-MODULE assembly

On the completion of this project, you will be able to:

- Create new parts and copy parts with the Save As command to reuse similar geometry.

- Utilize Construction geometry in a sketch.

- Apply the following SolidWorks features:

  o Extruded Boss/Base

  o Extruded Cut

  o Dome

  o Plane

  o Lofted Boss/Base

  o Swept Boss/Base

  o Swept Cut

  o Revolved Cut

  o Hole Wizard

  o Helix and Spiral

  o Axis

  o Circular Pattern

Project Overview

Six additional parts are required for the final
PNEUMATIC-TEST-MODULE assembly. Each
part explores various modeling techniques.

Create three new parts in this project:

- WEIGHT

- HOOK

- WHEEL

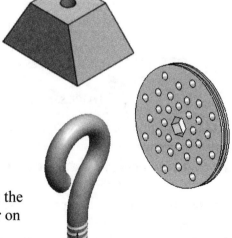

The WEIGHT and HOOK parts were applied in the
Project 2 exercises. See Chapter 2 Homework folder on
the CD in the book.

Utilize the Save As command and modify existing parts that
were created in the previous Projects to create three additional
parts for the PNEUMATIC-TEST-MODULE assembly.

- HEX-ADAPTER

- AXLE-3000

- SHAFTCOLLAR-500

The HEX-ADAPTER part utilizes modified
geometry from the HEX-STANDOFF part.

The AXLE-3000 part utilizes modified geometry from the
AXLE part.

The SHAFTCOLLAR-500 part utilizes modified geometry
from the SHAFT-COLLAR part.

HEX-STANDOFF

HEX-ADAPTER

Press the **g** key to activate the Magnifying glass tool.
Use the Magnifying glass tool to inspect a model
and make selections without changing the overall
view of your model in the Graphics window.

WEIGHT Part

The WEIGHT part is a machined part. Utilize the Loft feature tool. Create a Loft by blending two or more profiles. Each profile is sketched on a separate plane.

Create Plane1. Offset Plane1 from the Top Plane.

Sketch a rectangle for the first profile on the Top Plane.

Sketch a square for the second profile on Plane1.

Select the corner of each profile to create the Loft feature.

Utilize the Extruded Cut feature 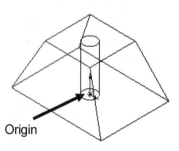 tool with a Through All End Condition to create a hole centered on the top face of the Loft feature.

All parts in this project utilize a custom part template. Create the custom part template from the default part template. Save the Custom Part template in the SW-TUTORIAL-2009 folder.

Activity: Create the WEIGHT Part

Create a new part template.

1)   Click **New** ⬜ from the Menu bar.

2)   Double-click **Part** from the Templates tab. The Part FeatureManager is displayed.

Set the Dimensioning standard.

3)   Click **Options** 🔲, **Document Properties** tab from the Menu bar.

4)   Select **ANSI** from the Overall drafting standard drop-down menu.

Set units.

5)   Click **Units**.

6)   Select **IPS**, **[MMGS]** for Unit system.

7)   Select **.123**, **[.12]** for Linear units Decimal places.

8)   Select **None** for Angular units Decimal places.

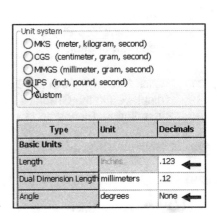

Set Leader arrow direction.

9)   Click **Dimensions**.

10)   Check the **Smart** box as illustrated.

11)   Click **OK** from the Document Properties - Detailing - Dimensions dialog box.

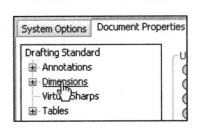

Save the part template.

12)   Click **Save As** from the Menu bar.

13)   Select **Part Templates (*.prtdot)** for Save as type.

14)   Select **SW-TUTORIAL-2009** for Save in folder.

15)   Enter **PART-ANSI-IN**, **[PART-ANSI-MM]** for File name.

16)   Click **Save**.

17)   Click **File**, **Close** from the Menu bar.

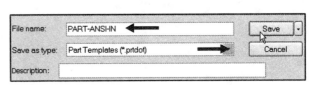

Create a new part.

18) Click **New** 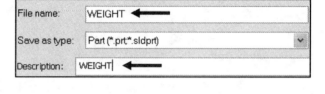 from the Menu bar.

19) Click the **SW-TUTORIAL-2009** tab.

20) Double-click **PART-ANSI-IN**, [PART-ANSI-MM]. The Part FeatureManager is displayed.

Save the part.
21) Click **Save As** from the Menu bar.

22) Select the **SW-TUTORIAL-2009** folder.

23) Enter **WEIGHT** for File name.

24) Enter **WEIGHT** for Description.

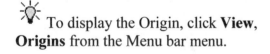

25) Click **Save**.

Insert Plane1.
26) Right-click **Top Plane** from the FeatureManager.

27) Click **Show** from the Context toolbar. The Front Plane is displayed in the Graphics window. Note: In a new installation, Planes and Origins may be displayed by default.

28) Hold the **Ctrl** key down.

29) Click the **boundary** of the Top Plane as illustrated.

30) Drag the **mouse pointer** upward.

31) Release the **mouse pointer**.

32) Release the **Ctrl** key. The Plane PropertyManager is displayed. Top Plane is displayed in the Selections box.

💡 To display the Origin, click **View**, **Origins** from the Menu bar menu.

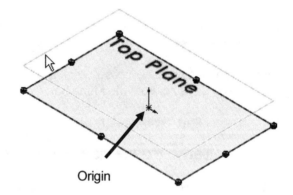

Origin

33)   Enter **.500**in, **[12.70]** for Distance.

34)   Click **OK** ✅ from the Plane PropertyManager.

Plane1 is displayed in the Graphics window and is listed in the FeatureManager. Plane1 is offset from the Top Plane.

A Loft feature requires two sketches. The first sketch, Sketch1 is a rectangle sketched on the Top Plane centered about the Origin ⌐. The second sketch, Sketch2 is a square sketched on Plane1 centered about the Origin.

Create Sketch1.
35)   Right-click **Top Plane** from the FeatureManager.

36)   Click **Sketch** ⌐ from the Context toolbar. The Sketch toolbar is displayed.

37)   Click **Center Rectangle** ▣ from the Consolidated Sketch

tool. The Center Rectangle ▣ icon is displayed.

38)   Click the **Origin** ⌐.

39)   Click a **position** to the top right as illustrated.

💡 The Center Rectangle tool provides the ability to sketch a rectangle located at a center point, in this case the Origin. This eliminates the need for centerlines to the Origin with a Midpoint geometric relation.

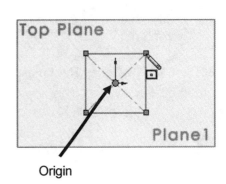

Origin

Add dimensions.

40)   Click the **Smart Dimension** ✎ Sketch tool.

41)   Click the **top horizontal** line.

42)   Click a **position** above the line.

43)   Enter **1.000**in, [25.40].

44)   Click the **Green Check mark** ✔ .

45)   Click the **right vertical** line.

46)   Click a **position** to the right.

47)   Enter **.750**in, [19.05].

48)   Click the **Green Check mark** ✔ .

Close Sketch1.

49)   Click **Exit Sketch** ⌐ from the Sketch toolbar. The sketch
           is fully defined and is displayed in black.

Rename Sketch1.

50)   Click **Sketch1** from the FeatureManager.

51)   Enter **Sketch-Rectangle** for name.

Save the part

52)   Click **Save** 🖫.

Display an Isometric view.

53)   Click **Isometric view** ⬡ from the Heads-
           up View toolbar.

Create Sketch2.

54)   Right-click **Plane1** from the
           FeatureManager. Plane1 is your Sketch
           plane.

55)   Click **Sketch** ⌐ from the Context toolbar. The Sketch toolbar is
           displayed.

56)   Click the **Center Rectangle** ▢ Consolidated Sketch tool. The

           Center Rectangle ▢ icon is displayed.

57)   Click the **Origin** ⌐. Note: If needed, zoom in to select the Origin.

58)   Click a **position** as illustrated.

59)   Right-click **Select** to deselect the
          Center Rectangle tool.

Add an Equal relation between the left vertical
line and the top horizontal line.

60)   Click the **left vertical line** of the
          rectangle.

61)   Hold the **Ctrl** key down.

62)   Click the **top horizontal line** of the rectangle.

63)   Release the **Ctrl** key.

64)   Right-click **Make Equal** = from the Context toolbar.

65)   Click **OK** ✅ from the Properties PropertyManager.

Add a dimension.

66)   Click the **Smart Dimension** ◇ Sketch tool.

67)   Click the **top horizontal** line.

68)   Click a **position** above the line.

69)   Enter .**500**in, [**12.70**].

70)   Click the **Green Check mark** ✅ .

Close Sketch2.

71)   Click **Exit Sketch** ⤴ from the
          Sketch toolbar. Sketch2 is fully
          defined and is displayed in black.

🔆 If you did not select the Origin,
insert a Coincident relation between
the rectangle and the Origin to fully
define Sketch2.

Rename Sketch2.

72)   Click **Sketch2** from the FeatureManager.

73)   Enter **Sketch-Square** for name.

Save the WEIGHT part.

74)   Click **Save** 🖫.

🔅 Loft features are comprised of multiple sketches. Name
sketches for clarity.

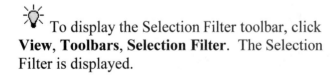

Insert a Loft feature.

75)   Click the **Features** tab from the
CommandManager.

76)   Click the **Lofted Boss/Base** 🛆 Feature tool. The
Loft PropertyManager is displayed.

77)   Clear the **Profiles** box.

78)   Click the **back right corner** of Sketch-Rectangle
as illustrated.

79)   Click the **back right corner** of Sketch-
Square. Sketch-Rectangle and
Sketch-Square are displayed in the
Profiles box.

80)   Click **OK** ✅ from the Loft
PropertyManager. Loft1 is displayed
in the FeatureManager.

🔅 A Loft feature creates transitions
between profiles. A Loft feature can be a
Base, Boss, Cut, or Surface. Create a
Loft feature by using two or more profiles. Only the
first and last profiles can be points.

🔅 To display the Selection Filter toolbar, click
View, **Toolbars**, **Selection Filter**. The Selection
Filter is displayed.

🔅 To clear a Filter icon ⬚🝆, click **Clear All Filters** from the
Selection Filter toolbar.

81)   **Expand** Loft1 in the FeatureManager. Sketch-Rectangle and Sketch-Square are the two sketches that contain the Loft feature.

82)   **Zoom in** on the Loft1 feature.

Activity: WEIGHT Part-Extruded Cut Feature

Insert a new sketch for the Extruded Cut feature.

83)   Right-click the **top square face** of the Loft1 feature for the Sketch plane.

84)   Click **Sketch** E from the Context toolbar. The Sketch toolbar is displayed.

85)   Click the **Circle** ⊘ Sketch tool. The circle ⊘ icon is displayed.

86)   Click the **Origin** ↳ as illustrated.

Origin

87)   Click a **position** to the right of the Origin as illustrated.

Add a dimension.

88)   Click the **Smart Dimension** ✧ Sketch tool.

89)   Click the **circumference** of the circle.

[3.81]
Ø.150

90)   Click a **position** in the Graphics window above the circle to locate the dimension.

91)   Enter **.150**in, **[3.81]** in the Modify box.

Insert an Extruded Cut feature.

92)   Click the **Features** tab from the CommandManager.

93)   Click **Extruded Cut** 🔲 from the Features toolbar. The Extrude PropertyManager is displayed.

94)   Select **Through All** for End Condition in Direction 1. The direction arrow points downward.

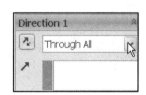

Direction 1
Through All

95)   Click **OK** ✔ from the Extrude PropertyManager. Extrude1 is displayed in the FeatureManager.

96)   Click **Wireframe** ⬚ from the Heads-up View toolbar. View the Extrude1 feature.

Rename the Extrude1 feature.
97) Click **Extrude1** from the FeatureManager.

98) Enter **Hole-for-Hook** for name.

Save the WEIGHT part.
99) Click **Isometric view** from the Heads-up View toolbar.

100) Click **Shaded With Edges** from the Heads-up View toolbar.

101) Right-click **Top Plane** from the FeatureManager.

102) Click **Hide** from the Context toolbar.

103) Right-click **Plane1** from the FeatureManager.

104) Click **Hide** from the Context toolbar.

105) Click **Save**. The WEIGHT part is complete.

 Review the WEIGHT Part

The WEIGHT part was created with the Loft feature. The Loft feature required two planes: Top Plane and Plane1. Profiles were sketched on each plane. Profiles were selected to create the Loft feature.

An Extruded Cut feature with the Through All option was utilized to create a center hole in the WEIGHT.

HOOK Part

The HOOK part fastens to the WEIGHT part. The HOOK is created with a Swept Boss/Base feature.

The Swept Boss/Base feature adds material by moving a profile along a path. A simple Swept feature requires two sketches. The first sketch is called the path. The second sketch is called the profile.

The profile and path are sketched on perpendicular planes.

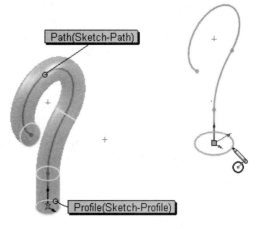

Create the HOOK part with a Swept Base feature.

The Swept Base feature uses:

- A path sketched on the Right Plane

- A profile sketched on the Top Plane

Utilize the Dome feature tool to create a spherical feature on a circular face.

Utilize the Swept Cut feature tool to create the thread for the HOOK part as illustrated. The Swept Cut feature removes material.

Activity: Create the HOOK Part

Create the new part.

106) Click **New** from the Menu bar.

107) Select the **SW-TUTORIAL-2009** tab.

108) Double-click **PART-ANSI-IN**, [PART-ANSI-MM].

Save the part.

109) Click **Save**.

110) Select the **SW-TUTORIAL-2009** folder.

111) Enter **HOOK** for File name.

112) Enter **HOOK** for Description.

113) Click **Save**. The HOOK FeatureManager is displayed.

The Swept feature requires two sketches.
Sketch1 is the Sweep Path sketched on the Right Plane.
Sketch2 is the Sweep Profile sketched on the Top Plane.

Sketch the Sweep Path.
114)   Right-click **Right Plane** from the FeatureManager.

115)   Click **Sketch** ⌐ from the Context toolbar.

116)   Click the **Line** ＼ Sketch tool. The Insert Line
PropertyManager is displayed.

117)   Sketch a **vertical line** from the Origin ⌐ as illustrated.

Add a dimension.
118)   Click the **Smart Dimension** ⬦ Sketch tool.

119)   Click the **vertical line**.

120)   Click a **position** to the right.

121)   Enter .250in, [**6.35**].

122)   Click the **Green Check mark** ✅ .

Fit the model to the Graphics window.
123)   Press the **f** key. Size the model to the Graphics window.

Create the Centerpoint arc.
124)   Click the **Centerpoint Arc** Sketch
tool from the Consolidated Sketch

toolbar. The Centerpoint Arc icon
is displayed.

125)   Click the **arc centerpoint**
vertically aligned to the Origin.

126)   Click the **arc start point** as
illustrated.

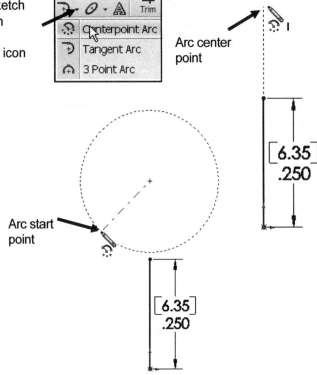

127) Drag the **mouse pointer** clockwise approximately 260°.

128) Release the mouse pointer **horizontally aligned** to the arc start point.

129) Click the **3 Point Arc** ⌒ Sketch tool from the Consolidated Sketch toolbar. The Arc PropertyManager is displayed.

130) Click the **vertical line endpoint**.

131) Click the **Centerpoint arc endpoint**.

132) Drag and pull the center of the **3 Point Arc downwards**.

133) Click the center of the **Centerpoint arc line** as illustrated.

134) Click **OK** ✔ from the Arc PropertyManager.

🔆 It is important to draw the correct shape with the 3 Point Arc tool as illustrated.

Add a Vertical relation between the Origin and the center point of the arc.

135) Click the **Origin** ⌐.

136) Hold the **Ctrl** key down.

Correct shape   **Incorrect shape**

137) Click the **centerpoint** of the Centerpoint arc.

138) Release the **Ctrl** key.

139) Click **Vertical** ∣ from the Add Relations box.

Add a Horizontal relation.

140)   Click the **start point** of the Center point arc.

141)   Hold the **Ctrl** key down.

142)   Click the **end point** of the Center point arc.

143)   Release the **Ctrl** key.

144)   Click **Horizontal** ▬ from the Add Relations box.

Add a Tangent relation.

145)   Click the **vertical line**.

146)   Hold the **Ctrl** key down.

147)   Click the **3 Point Arc**.

148)   Release the **Ctrl** key.

149)   Click **Tangent** ⌒ from the Add Relations box.

Add a second Tangent relation.

150)   Click the **3 Point Arc**.

151)   Hold the **Ctrl** key down.

152)   Click the **Center point arc**.

153)   Release the **Ctrl** key.

154)   Click **Tangent** ⌒ from the Add Relations box.

Add dimensions.

155)   Click the **Smart Dimension** ✎ Sketch tool.

156)   Click the **3 Point Arc**.

157)   Click a **position** to the left.

158)   Enter **.500**in, [**12.70**].

159)   Click the **Green Check mark** ✔ .

Dimension the overall length of the sketch.
160) Click the **top of the arc**.

161) Click the **Origin** 〰.

162) Click a **position** to the right of the profile. Accept the default dimension.

163) Click the **Green Check mark** ✓.

164) Click the **Leaders** tab in the Dimension PropertyManager.

Modify the Arc condition.
165) Click the First arc condition: **Max**.

166) Click **OK** ✓ from the Dimension PropertyManager.

Modify the overall length.
167) Double-click the default **dimension**.

168) Enter **1.000**in, **[25.40]**.

169) Click the **Green Check mark** ✓.

Fit the model to the Graphics window.
170) Press the **f** key.

171) Move the **dimensions** to the correct location.

By default, the Dimension tool utilizes the center point of an arc or circle. Select the circle profile during dimensioning. Utilize the Leaders tab in the Dimension PropertyManager to modify the arc condition to Minimum or Maximum.

Close the sketch.

172) Click **Exit Sketch** from the Sketch toolbar.

173) Rename **Sketch1** to **Sketch-Path**.

Save the HOOK.
174) Click **Save** 💾.

Center point

Minimum
Arc Conditions

Maximum

Activity: HOOK Part-Sweep Profile

Create the Sweep profile (cross section).

175) Click **Isometric view**. Right-click **Top Plane** from the FeatureManager.

176) Click **Sketch** from the Context toolbar.

177) Click the **Circle** Sketch tool. The Circle PropertyManager is displayed.

178) Click the **Origin**. Click a **position** to the right of the Origin.

Add a dimension.

179) Click the **Smart Dimension** Sketch tool.

180) Click the **circumference** of the small circle.

181) Click a **position** diagonally to the right.

182) Enter **.150**in, [**3.81**].

183) Click the **Green Check mark**.

184) Click **OK** from the Dimension PropertyManager.

Vertical line of Sketch-Path

$[3.81]$
$\varnothing.150$

A Pierce Geometric relation positions the center of the cross section on the sketched path. The center point of the small circle pierces the sketch-path, (vertical line).

Add a Pierce relation.

185) Click the **Origin**.

186) Hold the **Ctrl** key down.

187) Click the **vertical line** of the Sketch-Path.

188) Release the **Ctrl** key.

189) Click **Pierce** from the Add Relations box.

190) Click **OK** from the Properties PropertyManager

Close the sketch.

191) Click **Exit Sketch** from the Sketch toolbar.

192) Rename **Sketch2** to **Sketch-Profile**.

Save the part.

193) Click **Save** 🖫.

Activity: HOOK Part-Swept Base Feature

Insert a Swept feature.

194) Click **Sketch-Profile** in the FeatureManager.

195) Click the **Swept Boss/Base** ⟲ Features tool. The Sweep PropertyManager is displayed. Sketch-Profile is displayed in the Profile box.

196) **Expand** HOOK from the fly-out FeatureManager.

197) Click inside the **Path** box.

198) Click **Sketch-Path** from the fly-out FeatureManager. Sketch-Path is displayed in the Path box.

199) Click **OK** ✔ from the Sweep PropertyManager. Sweep1 is displayed in the FeatureManager.

Save the HOOK part.

200) Click **Save** 🖫.

🔅 Sketch the path, then sketch the profile or cross section for the Swept Base feature. Pierce the profile at the start of the path trajectory.

Activity: HOOK Part-Dome Feature

Insert a Dome feature.

201) **Rotate** the model with the middle mouse button and click the **flat face** of the Sweep1 feature in the Graphics window as illustrated.

202) Click the **Dome** ⬭ Features tool. The Dome PropertyManager is displayed. Face<1> is displayed in the Parameters box.

203) Enter **.050**in, **[1.27]** for Distance.

204) Click **OK** ✔ from the Dome PropertyManager. Dome1 is displayed in the FeatureManager.

The HOOK requires threads. Use the Swept Cut feature to create the required threads. The thread requires a spiral path. The path is called the Threadpath. The thread requires a sketched profile. The circular cross section is called the Threadprofile.

There are numerous steps required to create a thread. The thread is not flush with the bottom face. Use an offset plane to start the thread. Create a new offset Sketch plane, ThreadPlane.

Use the below steps to create the thread: Note: Steps on threads for plastic parts, springs, and coils. **1.)** *Create a new plane for the thread.* **2.)** *Create the spiral path.* **3.)** *Create a large cross section circular profile to improve visibility.* **4.)** *Pierce the cross section circular profile to the spiral path.* **5.)** *Dimension the circular profile.* **6.)** *Create the Swept feature.*

Activity: HOOK Part-Threads with Swept Cut Feature

Create the Offset Reference Plane.
205) **Rotate** the model with the middle mouse button.

206) Click the **bottom circular** face of Sweep1. Do not click the Origin.

207) Click **Insert**, **Reference Geometry**, **Plane** from the Menu bar. The Plane PropertyManager is displayed. Face<1> is displayed in the Selections box.

208) Enter **.020**in, [**0.51**] for Distance.

209) Check the **Reverse direction** box. Plane1 is located above the Top Plane.

210) Click **OK** from the Plane PropertyManager. Plane1 is displayed in the FeatureManager.

211) Rename **Plane1** to **Threadplane**.

212) **Rebuild** the model.

You can also access the Plane PropertyManager by using the Consolidated Reference Geometry drop-down menu from the Features toolbar.

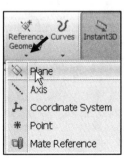

Display the Isometric view.

213) Click **Isometric view** 🔷 from the Heads-up View toolbar.

214) Click **Hidden Lines Removed** ⬚ from the Heads-up View toolbar.

Create the Thread path.

215) **Rotate** and **Zoom in** on the bottom of Sweep1.

216) Right-click **Threadplane** from the FeatureManager.

217) Click **Sketch** ✎ from the Context toolbar.

218) Click the **bottom** of Sweep1 as illustrated.

219) Click the **Convert Entities** ⬚ Sketch tool.

Create the Thread Path.

220) Click **Insert**, **Curve**, **Helix/Spiral** from the Menu bar. The Helix/Spiral PropertyManager is displayed.

221) Enter .050in, [1.27] for Pitch.

222) Check the **Reverse direction** box.

223) Enter 4 for Revolutions.

224) Enter 0deg for the Start angle.

225) Click the **Clockwise** box.

226) Click **OK** ✓ from the Helix/Spiral PropertyManager. Helix/Spiral1 is displayed in the FeatureManager.

227) Rename **Helix/Spiral1** to **Threadpath**.

228) Click **Isometric view** 🔷 from the Heads-up View toolbar.

229) Click **Save** 💾.

💡 You can also access the Helix/Spiral PropertyManager through the Consolidated Curves drop-down menu from the Features toolbar.

Create the Thread Profile, (cross section).

230) Right-click **Right Plane** from the FeatureManager.

231) Click **Sketch** 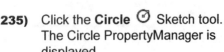 from the Context toolbar. The Sketch toolbar is displayed.

232) Click **Right view** 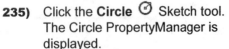 from the Heads-up View toolbar.

233) Right-click **Threadplane** from the FeatureManager.

234) Click **Hide** from the Context toolbar.

235) Click the **Circle** ⊘ Sketch tool. The Circle PropertyManager is displayed.

236) Sketch a **circle** to the right of the profile as illustrated.

Deselect the Circle Sketch tool.

237) Right-click **Select**.

Add a Pierce relation.

238) Click the **Threadpath** at the start of the helical curve as illustrated.

239) Hold the **Ctrl** key down.

240) Click the **center point** of the circle.

241) Release the **Ctrl** key. The Properties PropertyManager is displayed. The selected sketch entities are displayed in the Properties box.

242) Click **Pierce** from the Add Relations box.

243) Click **OK** ✔ from the Properties PropertyManager. View the results.

Add a dimension.

244)   Click the **Smart Dimension** Sketch tool.

245)   Click the **circumference**.

246)   Click a **position** off the profile.

247)   Enter .030in, [0.76].

248)   Click the **Green Check mark** .

Close the sketch.

249)   Click **Exit Sketch** from the Sketch toolbar.

250)   Click **Isometric view** from the Heads-up View toolbar.

251)   Rename **Sketch3** to **Threadprofile**.

252)   Click **Threadprofile** in the FeatureManager.

Insert the Swept Cut feature.

253)   Click **Swept Cut** from the Features toolbar. The Cut-Sweep PropertyManager is displayed. Threadprofile is displayed in the Profile box.

254)   Click inside the **Path** box.

255)   Click **Threadpath** from the fly-out FeatureManager. Threadpath is displayed in the Path box.

256)   Click **OK** from the Cut-Sweep PropertyManager. Cut-Sweep1 is displayed in the FeatureManager.

257)   Rename **Cut-Sweep1** to **Thread**.

Save the HOOK part.

258)   Click **Shaded** from the Heads-up View toolbar.

259)   Click **Save** 🖫. The HOOK part is complete.

💡 Utilize Insert, Feature from the Menu bar to select other Feature tools which are not located on the Features tab in the CommandManager.

💡 Utilize Tools, Customize, Command, Features to modify the Features toolbar.

 Review the HOOK Part

The HOOK part was created with two Swept features. A Swept Base feature added material by moving a profile along a path. The Swept feature required two sketches. The first sketch was called the path. The path was sketched on the Right Plane. The second sketch was called profile. The profile was sketched on the Top Plane. The path and profile were sketched on perpendicular planes. The path was sweep along the profile to create the Swept Base feature.

The Dome feature created a spherical face on the end of the Swept Base feature.

A Swept Cut feature removed material to create the thread. The thread required a spiral path and a circular profile. The path was created on a reference plane, parallel to the Top Plane. The path utilized a Helical Curve. The thread required a sketched profile. This circular cross section was sketched perpendicular to the Front Plane. The thread profile was pierced to the thread path.

🔍 Additional details on Loft, Swept, Swept Cut, Helix and Spiral, Relations, Pierce and Reference planes are available in SolidWorks Help.

WHEEL Part

The WHEEL part is a machined part.

Create the WHEEL part with the Extruded Base feature tool. Utilize the Mid Plane option to center the WHEEL on the Front Plane.

Utilize the Revolved Cut feature tool to remove material from the WHEEL and to create a groove for a belt.

The WHEEL contains a complex pattern of holes. Apply the Extruded Cut feature tool.

Simplify the geometry by dividing the four holes into two Extruded Cut features.

The first Extruded Cut feature contains two small circles sketched on two bolt circles. The bolt circles utilize Construction geometry.

The second Extruded Cut feature utilizes two small circles sketched on two bolt circles. The bolt circles utilize Construction geometry.

Utilize the Circular Pattern Feature 🔁 tool. The two Extruded Cut features are contained in the Circular Pattern. Revolve the Extruded Cut features about the Temporary Axis located at the center of the Hexagon.

Create a Reference Axis. The Reference Axis is utilized in the WHEEL-AXLE assembly.

💡 Construction geometry is used only to assist in creating the sketch entities and geometry that are ultimately incorporated into the part. Construction geometry is ignored when the sketch is used to create a feature. Construction geometry uses the same line style as centerlines.

Activity: WHEEL Part

Create the new part.

260)   Click **New** ⬚ from the Menu bar.

261)   Click the **SW-TUTORIAL-2009** tab.

262)   Double-click **PART-ANSI-IN**, [PART-ANSI-MM].

Save the part.

263)   Click **Save** 📷.

264)   Select the **SW-TUTORIAL-2009** folder.

265)   Enter **WHEEL** for File name.

266)   Enter **WHEEL** for Description.

267)   Click **Save**. The WHEEL FeatureManager is displayed.

Insert the sketch for the Extruded Base feature.

268)   Right-click **Front Plane** from the FeatureManager.

269)   Click **Sketch** ✐ from the Context toolbar. The Sketch toolbar is displayed.

270)   Click the **Circle** ⊘ Sketch tool. The Circle PropertyManager is displayed.

271)   Click the **Origin** ↳ as illustrated.

272)   Click a **position** to the right of the Origin.

Insert a polygon.

273)   Click the **Polygon** ⊕ Sketch tool. The Polygon PropertyManager is displayed.

Origin

274)   Click the **Origin** ↳.

275)   Drag and click the **mouse pointer** horizontally to the right of the Origin to create the hexagon as illustrated.

276)   Click **OK** ✅ from the Polygon PropertyManager.

Deselect the Polygon Sketch tool.

277)   Right-click **Select**.

Add a Horizontal relation.

278) Click the **Origin** └.

279) Hold the **Ctrl** key down.

280) Click the **right point** of the hexagon.

281) Release the **Ctrl** key.

282) Right-click **Make Horizontal** ━ from the Context toolbar.

283) Click **OK** ✔ from the Properties PropertyManager.

Add dimensions.

284) Click the **Smart Dimension** ✏ Sketch tool.

285) Click the **circumference** of the large circle.

286) Click a **position** above the circle.

287) Enter **3.000**in, [**76.20**].

288) Click the **Green Check mark** ✔ .

289) Click the **circumference** of the inscribed circle for the Hexagon.

290) Click a **position** above the Hexagon.

291) Enter **.438**in, [**11.13**].

292) Click the **Green Check mark** ✔ .

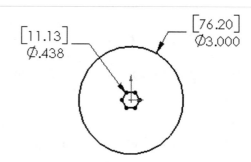

Activity: WHEEL Part-Extruded Base Feature

Insert an Extruded Base feature.

293) Click **Extruded Boss/Base** 🗔 from the Features toolbar. The Extrude PropertyManager is displayed.

294) Select **Mid Plane** for End Condition in Direction 1.

295) Enter **.250**in, [**6.35**] for Depth.

296) Click **OK** ✔ from the Extrude PropertyManager. Extrude1 is displayed in the FeatureManager.

Fit the model to the Graphics window.

297) Press the **f** key.

Save the WHEEL part.

298) Click **Save** 🖫.

Activity: WHEEL Part-Revolved Cut Feature

Insert a new sketch for the Revolved Cut feature.

299) Right-click **Right Plane** from the FeatureManager.

300) Click **Sketch** ✏ from the Context toolbar. The Sketch toolbar is displayed.

301) Click **Right view** 🗇 from the Heads-up View toolbar.

Sketch the axis of revolution.

302) Click the **Centerline** ┊ Sketch tool from the Consolidated Sketch toolbar. The Insert Line PropertyManager is displayed.

303) Click the **Origin** ⌊.

304) Click a **position** horizontally to the right of the Origin.

Deselect the sketch tool.

305) Right-click **Select**.

306) **Zoom in** on the top edge.

Sketch the profile.

307) Click the **Line** ╲ Sketch tool.

308) Sketch the **first vertical line** as illustrated.

309) Click the **Tangent Arc** ⊃ Sketch tool. The Arc PropertyManager is displayed.

310) Click the **end point** of the vertical line.

311) Sketch a **180° arc** as illustrated.

Deselect the sketch tool.

312) Right-click **Select**.

313)   Click the **Line** ╲ Sketch tool.

314)   Sketch the **second vertical line** as illustrated. The end point of the line is Coincident with the top horizontal edge of Extrude1.

315)   Sketch a **horizontal line** collinear with the top edge to close the profile.

Add a Vertical relation.
316)   Right-click **Select**.

317)   Click the **Origin** ↳ from the FeatureManager.

318)   Hold the **Ctrl** key down.

319)   Click the **center point** of the arc.

Center point
of the arc

320)   Release the **Ctrl** key. Click **Vertical** ❙ from the Add Relations box.

If needed, add a Collinear relation.
321)   Click the **horizontal line**. Hold the **Ctrl** key down.

322)   Click the **horizontal silhouette edge** as illustrated.

323)   Release the **Ctrl** key.

324)   Click **Collinear** ✐ from the Add Relations box.

Add an Equal relation.
325)   Click the **left vertical** line. Hold the **Ctrl** key down.

326)   Click the **right vertical** line.

327)   Release the **Ctrl** key.

328)   Click **Equal** from the Add Relations box.

Add dimensions.
329)   Click the **Smart Dimension** ✧ Sketch tool.

330)   Click the **arc**.

331)   Click a position to the **left** of the profile.

332)   Enter .063in, [**1.60**].

333)   Click the **Green Check mark** ✔ .

[1.60]
R.063

334) Click the **right vertical line**.

335) Click a position to the **right** of the profile.

336) Enter .078in, [**1.98**].

337) Click the **Green Check mark** ✓.

Fit the model to the Graphics window.
338) Press the **f** key.

Deselect the sketch tool.
339) Right-click **Select**.

Activity: WHEEL Part-Revolved Cut Feature

Insert a Revolved Cut feature.
340) Select the axis of revolution. Click the **centerline** in the Graphics window as illustrated.

341) Click **Revolved Cut** 🔧 from the Features toolbar. The Cut-Revolve PropertyManager is displayed. The Cut-Revolve PropertyManager displays 360 degrees for the Angle of Revolution.

342) Click **OK** ✓ from the Cut-Revolve PropertyManager. Cut-Revolve1 is displayed in the FeatureManager.

Save the WHEEL part.
343) Click **Save** 💾.

Four bolt circles, spaced 0.5in, [12.7] apart locate the 8 - Ø.190, [4.83] holes. Simplify the situation. Utilize two Extruded Cut features on each bolt circle.

Position the first Extruded Cut feature hole on the first bolt circle and third bolt circle.

Position the second Extruded Cut feature hole on the second bolt circle and forth bolt circle.

| **Activity: WHEEL Part- First Extruded Cut Feature** |

Display the Top Plane.
344) Right-click **Top Plane** from the FeatureManager.

345) Click **Show** 👓 from the Context toolbar.

346) Click **Front view** 📦 from the Heads-up View toolbar.

347) Click **Hidden Lines Visible** 📦 from the Heads-up View toolbar.

Insert a new sketch for the first Extruded Cut feature.
348) Right-click the Extrude1 **front face** as illustrated.

349) Click **Sketch** 📝 from the Context toolbar. The Sketch toolbar is displayed.

Create the first construction bolt circle.
350) Click the **Circle** ⊘ Sketch tool. The Circle PropertyManager is displayed.

351) Click the **Origin** ↳.

352) Click a **position** to the right of the hexagon as illustrated.

353) Check the **For construction** box.

Create the second construction bolt circle.
354) Click the **Origin** ↳.

355) Click a **position** to the right of the first construction bolt circle as illustrated.

356) Check the **For construction** box. The two bolt circles are displayed with Construction style lines.

💡 Construction geometry is used only to assist in creating the sketch entities and geometry that are ultimately incorporated into the part. Construction geometry is ignored when the sketch is used to create a feature. Construction geometry uses the same line style as centerlines.

Deselect the circle Sketch tool.
357) Right-click **Select**.

Insert a centerline.

358) Click the **Centerline** ⋮ Sketch tool. The Insert Line PropertyManager is displayed.

359) Sketch a **45° centerline** (approximately) from the Origin to the second bolt circle as illustrated.

Sketch the two circle profiles.

360) Click the **Circle** ⊘ Sketch tool. The Circle PropertyManager is displayed.

361) Sketch a **circle** at the intersection of the centerline and the first bolt circle.

362) Sketch a **circle** at the intersection of the centerline and the second bolt circle.

Deselect the Circle Sketch tool.
363) Right-click **Select**.

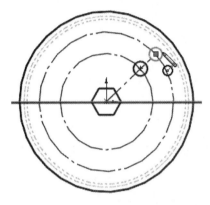

Note: An Intersection relation is created between three entities: the center point of the small circle, the centerline, and the bolt circle.

Add an Equal relation.
364) Click the **first circle**.

365) Hold the **Ctrl** key down.

366) Click the **second circle**.

367) Release the **Ctrl** key.

368) Right-click **Make Equal** = from the Context toolbar.

Add dimensions.
369) Click the **Smart Dimension** ⬦ Sketch tool.

370) Click the **first construction circle**.

371) Click a **position** above the profile.

372) Enter **1.000**in, [**25.4**].

373) Click the **Green Check mark** ✔ .

374) Click the **second construction circle**.

375) Click a **position** above the profile.

376) Enter **2.000**in, [**50.80**].

377) Click the **Green Check mark** ✔.

378) Click the **second small circle**.

379) Click a **position** above the profile.

380) Enter **.190**in, [**4.83**].

381) Click the **Green Check mark** ✔.

382) Click **Top Plane** from the fly-out FeatureManager.

383) Click the **45° centerline**.

384) Click a **position** between the two lines.

385) Enter **45**deg for angle.

386) Click the **Green Check mark** ✔.

Note: If the sketch is not fully defined, you may need to add an Intersection relation between the center point of the small circle, the centerline, and the bolt circle.

Insert an Extruded Cut feature.

387) Click **Extruded Cut** from the Features toolbar. The Extrude PropertyManager is displayed.

388) Select **Through All** for the End Condition in Direction 1.

389) Click **OK** ✔ from the Extrude PropertyManager. Extrude2 is displayed in the FeatureManager.

Activity: WHEEL Part- Second Extruded Cut Feature

Insert a new sketch for the second Extruded Cut feature.
390) Right-click the **Extrude1** front face.

391) Click **Sketch** ⌐ from the Context toolbar.

Sketch two additional Construction line bolt circles, 1.500in, [38.10] and 2.500in, [63.50]. Create the first Construction bolt circle.

392) Click the **Circle** ⊘ Sketch tool. The Circle PropertyManager is displayed.

393) Click the **Origin** ⌐.

394) Click a **position** between the two small circles.

395) Check the **For construction** box.

Create the second additional construction bolt circle.

396) Click the **Origin** ⌐.

397) Click a **position** to the right of the large construction bolt circle as illustrated.

398) Check the **For construction** box from the Circle PropertyManager. The two bolt circles are displayed with the two construction lines.

Insert a centerline.

399) Click the **Centerline** ⁝ Sketch tool. The Insert Line PropertyManager is displayed.

400) Sketch a **22.5° centerline** to the right from the Origin to the second bolt circle as illustrated.

401) Select **.1** from the Primary Unit Precision box.

402) Click **Hidden Lines Removed** ⬜ from the Heads-up View toolbar.

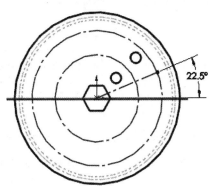

Sketch the two circle profiles.

403) Click the **Circle** ⊘ Sketch tool. The Circle
PropertyManager is displayed

404) Sketch a **circle** at the intersection of the
centerline and the first bolt circle.

405) Sketch a **circle** at the intersection of the
centerline and the second bolt circle.

Deselect the Circle Sketch tool.
406) Right-click **Select**.

Add an Equal relation.
407) Click the **first circle**.

408) Hold the **Ctrl** key down.

409) Click the **second circle**. Release the **Ctrl** key.

410) Right-click **Make Equal** = from the shortcut
toolbar.

Add dimensions.
411) Click the **Smart Dimension** ✧ Sketch tool. The

Smart Dimension ↖ icon is displayed.

412) Click the **first construction circle**.

413) Click a **position** above the profile.

414) Enter **1.500**in, **[38.10]**.

415) Click the **second construction circle**.

416) Click a **position** above the profile.

417) Enter **2.500**in, **[63.50]**.

418) Click the **small circle** as illustrated.

419) Click a **position** above the profile.

420) Enter **.190**in, **[4.83]**.

🔅 If the sketch is not fully defined, you may
need to add an Intersection relation between the
center point of the small circle, the centerline, and
the bolt circle.

Insert an Extruded Cut feature.

421)   Click **Extruded Cut** from the Features toolbar. The Extrude PropertyManager is displayed.

422)   Select **Through All** for End Condition in Direction 1.

423)   Click **OK** ✔ from the Extrude PropertyManager. Exturde3 is displayed in the FeatureManager.

424)   Click **Save** 🖫.

View the Temporary Axes.
425)   Click **View**, check **Temporary Axes** from the Menu bar.

Activity: WHEEL Part-Circular Pattern Feature

Insert a Circular Pattern.

426)   Click **Isometric view** 🟦 from the Heads-up View toolbar.

427)   Click **Circular Pattern** ⊕ from the Consolidated Features toolbar. The Circular Pattern PropertyManager is displayed.

428)   Click **inside** the Pattern Axis box.

429)   Click the **Temporary Axis** in the Graphics window at the center of the Hexagon. Axis<1> is displayed in the Pattern Axis box.

430)   Enter **360**deg for Angle.

431)   Enter **8** for Number of Instances.

432)   Click inside the **Features to Pattern** box.

433)   Click **Extrude2** and **Extrude3** from the fly-out FeatureManager. Extrude2 and Extrude3 are displayed in the Features to Pattern box.

434) Check the **Geometry pattern** box.

435) Click **OK** ✔ from the Circular Pattern PropertyManager. CirPattern1 is displayed in the FeatureManager.

Save the WHEEL part.

436) Click **Save** 💾.

Utilize a Reference Axis to locate the WHEEL in the PNEUMATIC-TEST-MODULE assembly. The Reference Axis is located in the FeatureManager and Graphics window. The Reference Axis is a construction axis defined between two planes.

Insert a Reference axis.

437) Click the **Axis** tool from the Reference Geometry Consolidated Features toolbar. The Axis PropertyManager is displayed.

438) Click **Top Plane** from the fly-out FeatureManager.

439) Click **Right Plane** from the fly-out FeatureManager. The selected planes are displayed in the Selections box.

440) Click **OK** ✔ from the Axis PropertyManager. Axis1 is displayed in the FeatureManager.

Axis1 is positioned through the Hex

Cut centered at the Origin ⌐.

441) Click and drag the **Axis1 handles** outward to extend the length on both sides as illustrated.

Save the WHEEL part.

442) Click **Isometric view** .

443) Click **View**, uncheck **Temporary Axes** from the Menu bar.

444) **Hide** all Planes.

445) Click **Shaded With Edges** from the Heads-up View toolbar.

446) Click **Save** .

The Geometry pattern option in the Circular Pattern PropertyManager and the Linear Pattern PropertyManager saves rebuild time. The End Conditions are not recalculated. For extruded parts, utilize the Geometry pattern option.

Sketched lines, arcs or circles are modified from profile geometry to construction geometry. Select the geometry in the sketch. Check the For construction box option.

 Review the WHEEL Part

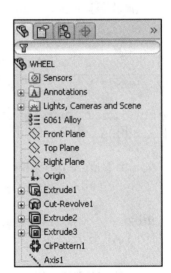

The WHEEL part was created with the Extruded Base feature. You sketched a circular sketch on the Front Plane and extruded the sketch with the Mid Plane option.

A Revolved Cut feature removed material from the WHEEL and created the groove. The Revolved Cut feature utilized an arc sketched on the Right Plane. A sketched centerline was required to create the Revolved Cut feature.

The WHEEL contained a complex pattern of holes. The first Extruded Cut feature contained two small circles sketched on two bolt circles. The bolt circles utilized construction geometry. Geometric relationships and dimensions were used in the sketch. The second Extruded Cut feature utilized two small circles sketched on two bolt circles.

The two Extruded Cut features were contained in one Circular Pattern and revolved about the Temporary Axis. The Reference Axis was created with two perpendicular planes. Utilize the Reference Axis, Axis1 in the WHEEL-AXLE assembly.

Modify a Part

Conserve design time and cost. Modify existing parts and assemblies to create new parts and assemblies. Utilize the Save as copy tool to avoid updating the existing assemblies with new file names.

The HEX-STANDOFF part was created in Project 2. The HEX-ADAPTER is required to fasten the WHEEL to the AXLE. Start with the HEX-STANDOFF part.

Utilize the Save As command and enter the HEX-ADAPTER for the new file name. Important: Check the Save as copy check box. The HEX-ADAPTER is the new part name. Open the HEX-ADAPTER. Modify the dimensions of the Extruded Base feature.

Utilize Edit Definition to modify the Hole Wizard Tap Hole to a Standard Hole. Insert an Extruded Boss feature to create the head of the HEX-ADAPTER.

Insert an Extruded Cut feature. Sketch a circle on the Right Plane. Extrude the circle in Direction1 and Direction2 with the Through All End Condition option.

Feature order determines the internal geometry of the Hole. If the Hole feature is created before the Extrude2-Head feature, the Through All End Condition will extend through the Extrude1 feature.

If the Hole feature is created after the Extrude2-Head feature, the Through All End Condition will extend through the Extrude1 feature and the Extrude2-Head feature.

Modify feature order by dragging feature names in the FeatureManager. Utilize the Save As command to create the AXLE3000 part from the AXLE part.

Utilize the Save As command to create the SHAFTCOLLAR-500 part from the SHAFT-COLLAR part. Save the HEX-STANDOFF as the HEX-ADAPTER part.

Activity: HEX-ADAPTER Part

Create the HEX-ADAPTER.

447) Click **Open** 📂 from the Menu bar.

448) Select **Part** for Files of type from the SW-TUTORIAL-2009 folder.

449) Double-click **HEX-STANDOFF**. The HEX-STANDOFF FeatureManager is displayed.

450) Click **Save As** from the Menu bar.

451) Select the **SW-TUTORIAL-2009** folder.

452) Enter **HEX-ADAPTER** for File name.

453) Enter **HEX-ADAPTER** for Description.

454) Check the **Save as copy** box.

455) Click **Save**.

456) Click **File**, **Close** from the Menu bar.

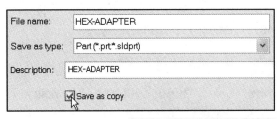

Open the HEX-ADAPTER.

457) Click **Open** 🖰 from the Menu bar.

458) Double-click **HEX-ADAPTER** from the SW-TUTORIAL-2009 folder. The HEX-ADAPTER FeatureManager is displayed.

Modify the Extrude1 dimensions.

459) Double-click **Extrude1** from the FeatureManager.

460) Click **.735**in, [**18.67**].

461) Enter **.700**in, [**17.78**] for depth.

462) Click **.313**in, [**7.95**].

463) Enter **.438**in, [**11.13**] for diameter.

Modify the #10-24 Tapped Hole1 feature.

464) Right-click **#10-24 Tapped Hole1** from the FeatureManager.

465) Click **Edit Feature** 🖰 from the Context toolbar. The Hole Specification PropertyManager is displayed.

💡 The Hole Specification PropertyManager is part of the Hole Wizard tool located in the Features toolbar.

The Type tab is selected by default. Select the **Hole** tab from the Hole Specification box.

466) Select **Ansi Inch** for Standard.

467) Select **Tap Drills** for Type.

468) Select **#10-24** for Size.

469) Select **Through All** for End Condition.

470) Click **OK** ✔ from the Hole Specification PropertyManager. The Tap Hole is modified.

Insert a sketch for the Extruded Boss feature.
471) Press the **Up Arrow key** approximately four times.

472) Right-click the **bottom hexagonal face** of the Extrude1 feature as illustrated. Note: The face icon feedback symbol.

473) Click **Sketch** from the Context toolbar.

474) Click **Bottom view** from the Heads-up View toolbar.

475) Click the **Circle** ⊘ Sketch tool. The Circle PropertyManager is displayed.

476) Click the **Origin** ↳ as illustrated.

477) Click a **position** in the Graphics window to the right of the Origin.

Add a dimension.
478) Click the **Smart Dimension** ⬦ Sketch tool.

479) Click the circumference of the **circle**.

480) Click a **position** above the circle to locate the dimension.

481) Enter **.625**in, [**15.88**] in the Modify dialog box.

[15.88]
⌀.625

Fit the model to the Graphics window.
482) Press the **f** key.

Activity: HEX-ADAPTER Part-Extruded Boss Feature

Extrude the sketch to create the Extruded Boss feature.

483) Click **Isometric view** 🧊 from the Heads-up View toolbar.

484) Click **Extruded Boss/Base** 🗔 from the Features toolbar. The Extrude PropertyManager is displayed.

485) Enter **.200**in, **[6.35]** for Depth. The Direction arrow points downward. Flip the **Direction arrow** if required.

486) Click **OK** ✔ from the Extrude PropertyManager. Extrude2 is displayed in the FeatureManager.

487) Rename **Extrude2** to **Extrude2-Head**.

488) Click **Save** 💾.

Direction 1	
🡕	Blind ∨
🡕	
⬇D1	0.200in ⬅

Activity: HEX-ADAPTER Part-Extruded Cut Feature

Insert a new sketch for the Extruded Cut on the Right Plane.

489) Right-click **Right Plane** from the FeatureManager.

490) Click **Sketch** ✎ from the Context toolbar.

491) Click **Right view** 📐 from the Heads-up View toolbar. Note the location of the Origin.

492) Click the **Circle** ⊙ Sketch tool. The Circle PropertyManager is displayed.

493) Sketch a **circle** below the Origin ↳. The centerpoint is vertically aligned to the Origin as illustrated. If required, add a Vertical relation between the centerpoint of the circle and the Origin.

Origin

Add dimensions.

494) Click the **Smart Dimension** ◇ Sketch tool.

495) Click the **middle horizontal edge**.

496) Click the **centerpoint** of the circle.

497) Click a **position** to the right of the profile.

498) Enter **.100**in, [**2.54**].

499) Click the **Green Check mark** ✔ .

500) Click the circumference of the **circle**.

501) Click a **position** below the profile.

502) Enter **.120**in, [**3.95**].

503) Click the **Green Check mark** ✔ .

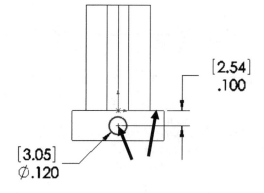

Insert an Extruded Cut feature.

504) Click **Extruded Cut** 📄 from the Features toolbar. The Extrude PropertyManager is displayed.

505) Select **Through All** for End Condition in Direction 1.

506) Check the **Direction 2** box.

507) Select **Through All** for End Condition in Direction 2.

508) Click **OK** ✔ from the Extrude PropertyManager. Extrude3 is displayed in the FeatureManager.

509) Click **Isometric view** 🔲 from the Heads-up View toolbar.

510) Rename **Extrude3** to **Extrude3-SetScrew**.

Save the HEX-ADAPTER part.

511) Click **Save** 💾 .

The Through All End Condition is required to penetrate both the
Extrude1 and Extrude2 features. Reorder features in the
FeatureManager. Position the Extrude2 feature before the Tap
Drill for # 10 Tap 1 feature in the FeatureManager.

Reorder Extrude2.
512) Click and drag **Extrude2-Head** from the
FeatureManager upward as illustrated.

513) Click a **position** below Extrude1. The
Through All End Condition option for the
Tap Drill for # 10 Tap 1 feature creates a
hole through both Extrude1 and
Extrude2.

Display a Section view.
514) Click **Front Plane** from the
FeatureManager.

515) Click **Section view** from the Heads-up View toolbar in
the Graphics window. The Section View
PropertyManager is displayed. View the results.

516) Click **OK** from the Section View PropertyManager.

Display the full view.
517) Click **Section view** from the Heads-up View toolbar in
the Graphics window.

518) Click **Shaded With Edges** from the Heads-up View
toolbar.

Save the HEX-ADAPTER.
519) Click **Save**. Note the location of the Origin in the
model.

Close all documents.
520) Click **Windows**, **Close All** from the Menu bar.

Origin

Utilize the Save As command and work on the copied
version of the document before making any changes to the
original. Keep the original document in tact.

Review the HEX-ADAPTER Part

The HEX-ADAPTER part was created by utilizing the Save As, and the Save as copy command with the HEX-STANDOFF part. The Extruded Base feature dimensions were modified. Edit Definition was utilized to modify the Hole type from the Hole Wizard feature.

An Extruded Boss feature added material. An Extruded Cut feature, sketched on the Right Plane with the Through All End Condition for both Direction1 and Direction2, created a hole through the Extruded Boss feature. Reordering features in the FeatureManager modified the Hole. Utilizing existing geometry saved time with the Save as copy command. The original part and its references to other assemblies are not affected with the Save as copy command.

You require additional work before completing the PNEUMATIC-TEST-MODULE assembly. The AXLE and SHAFT-COLLAR were created in Project 1. Utilize the Save as copy command to save the parts.

Additional details on Save (Save as copy), Reorder (features), Section View PropertyManager are available in SolidWorks Help.

Utilize Design Table configurations for the AXLE part and SHAFT-COLLAR part developed in the previous Project.

Note: The AXLE-3000 part and SHAFT-COLLAR-500 part utilize the Save as copy option in the next section. Utilize the Save as copy components or the configurations developed with Design Tables in Project 3 for the WHEEL-AXLE assembly.

Activity: AXLE-3000 Part

Create the AXLE-3000 part from the AXLE part.

521) Click **Open** from the Menu bar.

522) Double-click **AXLE** from the SW-TUTORIAL-2009 folder. The AXLE FeatureManager is displayed.

523) Click **Save As** from the Menu bar.

524) Select the **SW-TUTORIAL-2009** folder.

525) Enter **AXLE-3000** for File name.

526) Enter **AXLE-3000** for Description.

527) Click **Save as copy** check box.

528) Click **Save**.

Close the AXLE part
529) Click **File, Close** from the Menu bar.

Open AXLE-3000 part.
530) Click **Open** 🖻 from the Menu bar.

531) Double-click **AXLE-3000** from the SW-TUTORIAL-2009 folder. The AXLE-3000 FeatureManager is displayed.

Modify the depth dimension.
532) Double-click the **cylindrical face** in the Graphics window. Dimensions are displayed.

533) Click **1.375**in, [**34.93**].

534) Enter **3.000**in, [**76.20**].

Fit the model to the Graphics window.
535) Press the **f** key.

Save the AXLE-3000 part.
536) Click **Save** 🖫.

537) Click **inside** the Graphics window.

Activity: SHAFTCOLLAR-500 Part

Create the SHAFTCOLLAR-500 part.
538) Click **Open** 🖻 from the Menu bar.

539) Double-click **SHAFT-COLLAR** from the SW-TUTORIAL-2009 folder.

540) Click **Save As** from the Menu bar.

541) Enter **SHAFT-COLLAR-500** for File name.

542) Enter **SHAFT-COLLAR-500** for Description.

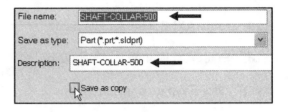

543) Click **Save as copy** check box.

544) Click **Save**.

Close the SHAFT-COLLAR part.
545) Click **File**, **Close** from the Menu bar.

Open the SHAFT-COLLAR-500 part.

546) Click **Open** 📂 from the Menu bar.

547) Double-click **SHAFT-COLLAR-500** from the SW-TUTORIAL-2009 folder. SHAFT-COLLAR-500 is displayed in the Graphics window.

Modify the diameter dimensions.
548) Right-click **Annotations** in the FeatureManager.

549) Check the **Show Feature Dimensions** box.

550) Press the **f** key to fit the model to the graphics area.

551) Click **.438**in, [**11.11**].

552) Enter **.750**in, [**19.05**] for outside diameter.

553) Click **.190**in, [**4.83**].

554) Enter **.500**in, [**12.70**] for inside diameter. View the results.

555) Right-click **Annotations** in the FeatureManager.

556) Uncheck the **Show Feature Dimensions** box.

557) **Rebuild** the model.

Fit the model to the Graphics window.
558) Press the **f** key.

Save the SHAFT-COLLAR-500 part.
559) Click **Save** .

Close all documents.
560) Click **Windows, Close All** from the Menu bar.

Press the **s** key in the Graphics window. A Context Pop-up features toolbar is displayed. The features toolbar displays the last few feature tools applied.

You can select the types of Annotations that you want to display and set text scale and other Annotations options. In the FeatureManager design tree, right-click the **Annotations** folder, and click **details**. View the options from the Annotation Properties dialog box.

Project Summary

In this Project you created six parts. The WEIGHT part utilized the Plane feature, Lofted Base feature and the Extruded Cut feature. The HOOK part utilized the Swept Base feature, Dome feature, Plane feature, Helix and Spiral feature, and Swept Cut feature. The WHEEL part utilized the Extruded Base feature, Revolved Cut feature, Extruded Cut feature, Circular Pattern feature and Axis feature.

The second three parts utilized existing parts created in early projects. The HEX-ADAPTER part, AXLE-3000 part and the SHAFTCOLLAR-500 part utilized existing part geometry along with the Hole Wizard feature.

You applied the following Sketch tools in this Project: Circle, Line, Centerline, Tangent Arc, Polygon, Smart Dimension, Center Rectangle, Centerpoint Arc, 3 Point Arc and Convert Entities.

Project Terminology

Circular Pattern: A Circular Pattern repeats features or geometry in a polar array. A Circular Patten requires an axis of revolution, the number of instances and an angle.

ConfigurationManager: The ConfigurationManager on the left side of the Graphics window is utilized to create, select, and view the configurations of parts and assemblies.

Dome: A Dome feature creates a spherical or elliptical feature from a selected face.

Loft: A Loft feature blends two or more profiles. Each profile is sketched on a separate plane.

Mirror Component: A mirror component creates a mirrored or copied part or assembly. A mirrored component is sometimes called a "right-hand" version of the original "left hand" version.

Replace: The Replace command substitutes one or more open instances of a component in an assembly with a different component.

Revolved Cut: A Revolved Cut removes material. A sketched profile is revolved around a centerline. The Revolved Cut requires a direction and an angle of revolution.

Swept Boss/Base: A Swept Boss/Base feature adds material by moving a profile along a path. A basic Swept feature requires two sketches. The first sketch is called the path. The second sketch is called profile. The profile and path are sketched on perpendicular planes.

Swept Cut: A Swept Cut feature removes material by moving a profile along a path. A basic Swept feature requires two sketches. The first sketch is called the path. The second sketch is called profile. The profile and path are sketched on perpendicular planes.

1. Sketch various **FLATBAR Parts**.

Sketch the front view of the FLATBAR
configurations that contain 11, 13, 15,
and 17 holes. Determine the center-to-
center distance between the first hole and
the last hole for each FLATBAR
configuration.

Center-to-Center Distance

FLATBAR-11HOLE.

FLATBAR-13HOLE.

FLATBAR-15HOLE.

FLATBAR-17HOLE.

Questions

1. What is the minimum number of profiles and planes required for a Loft feature?

2. A Swept Boss/Base feature requires a _____ and a _____.

3. Describe the differences between a Loft feature and a Swept feature.

4. Identify the three default reference planes in an assembly.

5. True of False. A Revolved-Cut feature (Cut-Revolve1) requires an axis of revolution.

6. True or False. A Circular Pattern contains only one feature to pattern.

7. Describe the difference between a Swept Boss/Base feature and a Swept Cut feature.

8. Identify the type of Geometric relations that can be added to a sketch.

9. What function does the Save as copy check box perform when saving a part under a new name?

10. True or False. Never reuse geometry from one part to create another part.

Exercises

Exercise 4.1:

Build the illustrated model. Calculate the volume of the part and locate the Center of mass with the provided information. Insert three features: Extruded Base, Extruded Boss, and Mirror. Three holes are displayed with an Ø1.00in. Set the document properties for the model.

Given:
A = Ø1.00
All Thru Holes
Material: Brass
Density = .307 lb/in^3
Units: IPS
Decimal places = 2

Exercise 4.2:

Build the illustrated model. Calculate the overall mass of the part and locate the Center of mass with the provided information. Insert a Revolved Base feature and Extruded Cut feature to build this part.

Note: Select the Front Plane as the Sketch plane. Apply the Centerline Sketch tool for the Revolve1 feature. Insert the required geometric relations and dimensions. Sketch1 is the profile for the Revolve1 feature.

Given:
A = Ø12
Material: Cast Alloy Steel
Density = .0073 g/mm^3
Units: MMGS

Exercise 4.3:

Build the illustrated model. Calculate the overall mass of the part and locate the Center of mass with the provided information.

Note: Insert two features: Extruded Base and Revolved Boss.

Given:
A = 60, B = 40, C = 8
Material: Cast Alloy
Steel
Density = .0073
g/mm^3
Units: MMGS

Exercise 4.4:

Build the illustrated model. Calculate the overall mass of the part and locate the Center of mass with the provided information.

Think about the various features that create the model. Insert seven features to build this model: Extruded Base, Extruded Cut, Extruded Boss, Fillet, second Extruded Cut, Mirror, and a second Fillet. Apply symmetry. Create the left half of the model first, and then apply the Mirror feature.

38 DIA
57 DIA SF
1 DEEP
2 HOLES

Given:
A = 76, B = 127
Material: 2014 Alloy
Density: .0028
g/mm^3
Units: MMGS
ALL ROUNDS
EQUAL 6MM

Exercise 4.5:

Build the illustrated model. Calculate the overall mass of the part and locate the Center of mass with the provided information.

Think about the various features that create the part. Insert seven features to build this part: Extruded-Thin, Extruded Boss, two Extruded Cuts, and three Fillets. Apply reference construction planes to build the circular features.

Given:
A = 52, B = 58
ALL-ROUNDS R 4MM
Material: 6061 Alloy
Density: .0027 g/mm^3
Units: MMGS

Origin

Exercise 4.6:

Build the illustrated model.
Build this model. Calculate the volume of the part and locate the Center of mass with the provided information.

Think about the various features that create this model. Insert five features to build this part: Extruded Base, two Extruded Bosses, Extruded Cut, and a Rib. Insert a reference plane to create the Extrude2 feature.

Given:
A = Ø3.00, B = 1.00
Material: 6061 Alloy
Density: .097 lb/in^3
Units: IPS
Decimal places = 2

Origin

Exercise 4.7: Build the illustrated model.

Calculate the overall mass and locate the Center of mass of the illustrated model.

Insert seven features: Extruded Base, two Extruded Bosses, two Extruded Cuts, Chamfer and a Fillet.

Think about the steps that you would take to build the illustrated part.

Identify the location of the part Origin. Start with the back base flange. Review the provided dimensions and annotations in the part illustration.

Given:
A = 2.00, B = Ø.35
Material: 1060 Alloy
Density: 0.097 lb/in^3
Units: IPS
Decimal places = 2

Project 5

PNEUMATIC-TEST-MODULE and Final ROBOT Assembly

Below are the desired outcomes and usage competencies based on the completion of Project 5.

Desired Outcomes:	Usage Competencies:

• Create five sub-assemblies:
   ○ WHEEL-AND-AXLE
   ○ WHEEL-FLATBAR
   ○ 3HOLE-SHAFTCOLLAR
   ○ 5HOLE-SHAFTCOLLAR
   ○ PNEUMATIC-TEST-MODULE
• Create the final ROBOT assembly
	• Reuse geometry.
	
	• Apply Standard Mate types.
	
	• Modify existing assemblies to create new assemblies.
	
	• Utilize the following Assembly tools: Mate, Linear Component Pattern, Feature Driven Component Pattern, Mirror Components, Replace Components, and AssemblyXpert.
	
	• Work with multiple documents in an assembly.

Notes:

Project 5 – PNEUMATIC-TEST-MODULE and ROBOT Assembly

Project Objective

Develop a working understanding with multiple documents in an assembly. Build on sound assembly modeling techniques that utilize symmetry, component patterns, and mirrored components.

Create five sub-assemblies and the final ROBOT assembly:

* 3HOLE-SHAFTCOLLAR sub-assembly

* 5HOLE-SHAFTCOLLAR sub-assembly

* WHEEL-FLATBAR sub-assembly

* WHEEL-AND-AXLE sub-assembly

* PNEUMATIC-TEST-MODULE sub-assembly

* ROBOT final assembly

On the completion of this project, you will be able to:

* Utilize various Assembly techniques

* Suppress and hide components

* Create new assemblies and copy assemblies to reuse similar parts

* Use the following Assembly tools:

  o Insert Component

  o Standard Mates: Concentric, Coincident, and Parallel

  o Linear Component Pattern

  o Feature Driven Component Pattern

  o Circular Component Pattern

  o Mirror Components

  o Replace Components

  o AssemblyXpert

Project Overview

Create the 3HOLE-SHAFTCOLLAR sub-assembly.

Utilize the 3HOLE-SHAFTCOLLAR sub-assembly to create the 5HOLE-SHAFTCOLLAR sub-assembly.

The WHEEL-FLATBAR sub-assembly contains the following items:

- 3HOLE-SHAFTCOLLAR assembly

- 5HOLE-SHAFTCOLLAR assembly

- WHEEL part

☼ If an assembly or component is loaded in a Lightweight 🔲 state, right-click the **assembly name** or **component name** from the FeatureManager. Click **Set Lightweight to Resolved**.

The WHEEL-AND-AXLE assembly contains the following items:

- WHEEL-FLATBAR assembly

- AXLE-3000 part

- SHAFTCOLLAR-500 part

- HEX-ADAPTER part

Combine the created new assemblies and parts to develop the PNEUMATIC-TEST-MODULE assembly.

Create the final ROBOT assembly. Insert the Robot-platform assembly, PNEUMATIC-TEST-MODULE assembly, basic_integration assembly and the HEX-STANDOFF components. All assemblies and components for the final ROBOT assembly are located on the CD under the Chapter 5 models folder.

Add additional Pneumatic components in the Project exercises.

Assembly Techniques

Assembly modeling requires practice and time. Below are a few helpful techniques to address Standard Mates. These techniques are utilized throughout the development of all assemblies.

Mating Techniques:
• Plan your assembly and sub-assemblies in an assembly layout diagram. Group components together to form smaller sub-assemblies.
• Utilize symmetry in an assembly. Utilize Mirror Component and Component Pattern to create multiple instances (copies) of components. Reuse similar components with Save as copy and configurations.
• Use the Zoom and Rotate commands to select the geometry in the Mate process. Zoom to select the correct face.
• Apply various colors to features and components to improve display.
• Activate Temporary Axes and Show Planes when required for Mates, otherwise Hide All Types from the View menu.
• Select Reference planes from the FeatureManager for complex components. Expand the FeatureManager to view the correct plane.
• Remove display complexity. Hide components when visibility is not required.
• Suppress components when Mates are not required. Group fasteners at the bottom of the FeatureManager. Suppress fasteners and their assembly patterns to save rebuild time and file size.
• Utilize Section views to select internal geometry.
• Use the Move Component and Rotate Component commands before Mating. Position the component in the correct orientation.
• Create additional flexibility in a Mate. Distance Mates are modified in configurations and animations. Rename Mates in the FeatureManager.
• Verify the position of the components. Use Top, Front, Right, and Section views.

PNEUMATIC TEST MODULE Layout

The PNEUMATIC TEST MODULE assembly is comprised of four major sub-assemblies:

- LINKAGE assembly

- RESERVOIR assembly

- FRONT-SUPPORT assembly

- WHEEL-AND-AXLE assembly

Project 1 LINKAGE
assembly

Project 2 AIR
RESERVOIR assembly

Project 2 FRONT SUPPORT
assembly

Project 4 WHEEL-AND-AXLE
assembly

There are over one hundred components in the PNEUMATIC TEST MODULE assembly. Complex assemblies require planning. The Assembly Layout diagram provides organization for a complex assembly by listing sub-assemblies and parts.

Review the Assembly Layout diagram for the PNEUMATIC TEST MODULE assembly.

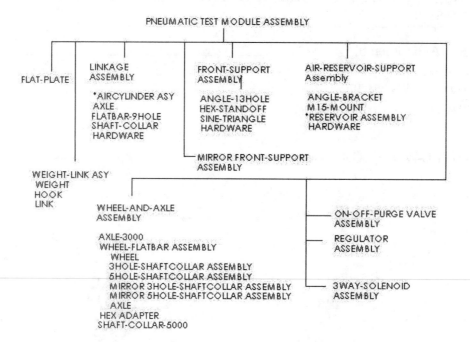

Physical space on the FLAT-PLATE is at a premium. Determine the requirements for hardware and placement after the mechanical components are assemble to the FLAT-PLATE part.

The FLAT-PLATE was created in the Project 2 exercises. The FLAT-PLATE is available on the enclosed CD in the book under the Chapter 5 models folder. If needed, copy the PLAT-PLATE from the CD to your working SW-TUTORIAL-2009 folder. View the available models in this folder. The LINKAGE assembly, FRONT-SUPPORT assembly and the AIR-RESERVOIR SUPPORT assembly were created in Project 1 and Project 2.

The ON-OFF-PURGE VALVE assembly, REGULATOR assembly and the 3WAY SOLENOID VALVE assembly require additional hardware and are addressed in the Project exercises.

The WHEEL-FLATBAR assembly consists of the following:

- WHEEL part

- 3HOLE-SHAFTCOLLAR assembly

- 5HOLE-SHAFTCOLLAR assembly

FLATBAR Sub-assemblies

There are two similar sub-assemblies contained in the WHEEL-FLATBAR assembly:

- 3HOLE-SHAFTCOLLAR assembly

- 5HOLE-SHAFTCOLLAR assembly

Create the 3HOLE-SHAFTCOLLAR assembly. Utilize parts and mating techniques developed in Project 1.

Utilize the Save as copy command and create the 5HOLE-SHAFTCOLLAR assembly.

Combine the 3HOLE-SHAFTCOLLAR assembly, 5HOLE-SHAFTCOLLAR assembly and the WHEEL part to create the WHEEL-FLATBAR assembly.

The FLATBAR-3HOLE and FLATBAR 5HOLE parts were created in the Project 1 exercises. If needed, copy the models from the Chapter 5 models folder on the CD to your working SW-TUTORIAL-2009 folder.

| **Activity: 3HOLE-SHAFTCOLLAR Assembly** |

Create the 3HOLE-SHAFTCOLLAR assembly.

1) Click **New** from the Menu bar.

2) Double-click **Assembly** from the Templates tab. The Begin Assembly PropertyManager is displayed.

3) Click the **Browse** button.

4) Select **Part** for Files of type in the SW-TUTORIAL-2009 folder.

5)   Double-click **FLATBAR-3HOLE**. The
         FLATBAR-3HOLE part was created in the
         Project 1 exercises. If you did not create this
         part, follow the below procedures; otherwise,
         skip the next few steps.

6)   Click **Open** from the Menu bar.

7)   Double-click **FLATBAR** from the SW-
         TUTORIAL-2009 folder.

8)   Click **Save As** from the Menu bar.

9)   Select the **SW-TUTORIAL-2009** folder.

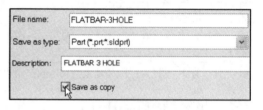

10) Enter **FLATBAR-3HOLE** for File name.

11) Enter **FLATBAR-3HOLE** for Description.

12) Click the **Save as copy** check box.

13) Click **Save**.

14) **Close** the FLATBAR model.

15) Click **Open** from the Menu bar.

16) Double-click **FLATBAR-3HOLE** from the SW-TUTORIAL-2009
         folder.

17) Right-click **LPATTERN1** from the FeatureManager.

18) Click **Edit Feature** from the Context toolbar. The LPattern1
         PropertyManager is
         displayed.

19) Enter **3** in the
         Number of Instances.

20) Click **OK** from
         the LPattern1
         PropertyManager.
         Note: If needed,
         delete the Design
         Table in the
         CommandManager.

21) Click **Extrude1** from the FeatureManager. View the dimensions in the Graphics window.

22) Click the **4.000**in, [**101.60**] dimension.

23) Enter **1.000**in, [**25.4**].

24) Click **Extrude2** from the FeatureManager. View the dimensions in the Graphics window.

25) Click the **9X** dimension text in the Graphics window. The Dimension PropertyManager is displayed.

26) Delete the **9X** text in the Dimension Text box.

27) Enter **3X** in the Dimension Text box.

28) Click **OK** ✔ from the Dimension PropertyManager.

29) Click **Save** 🖫.

30) Click **New** ⬜ from the Main menu.

31) Double-click **Assembly** from the Templates tab. The Begin Assembly PropertyManager is displayed.

32) Double-click **FLATBAR-3HOLE.**

33) Click **OK** ✔ from the Begin Assembly PropertyManager. The FLATBAR-3HOLE is fixed to the Origin.

Save the assembly.
34) Click **Save As** from the Menu bar.

35)   Enter **3HOLE-SHAFTCOLLAR** for File name.

36)   Enter **3HOLE-SHAFTCOLLAR** for
             Description.

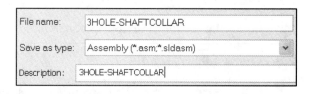

37)   Click **Save**.

Save the 3HOLE-SHAFTCOLLAR assembly.

38)   Click **Save** 💾.

Utilize a Concentric/Coincident ⬚ SmartMate between the
SHAFT-COLLAR and the FLATBAR-3HOLE.

Open the **SHAFT-COLLAR** part.

39)   Click **Open** 📂 from the Menu bar.

40)   Double-click **SHAFT-COLLAR** from the SW-TUTORIAL-
             2009 folder. SHAFT-COLLAR is the current document
             name.

41)   Press the **Left Arrow** key approximately 5 times to rotate
             the SHAFT-COLLAR to view the back circular edge.

42)   Click **Window**, **Tile Horizontally** from the Menu bar.

43)   Drag the **back circular edge** of the SHAFT-COLLAR to the
             left circular hole edge of the FLATBAR-3HOLE in the
             Assembly Graphics window as illustrated. The mouse

             pointer displays the Concentric/Coincident ⬚ icon.

44)   **Release** the mouse button. Note: Select the back circular
             edge of the SHAFT-COLLAR, not the face.

Save the 3HOLE-SHAFTCOLLAR assembly.

45)   **Close** ✖ the SHAFT-COLLAR window.

46)   **Maximize** ⬜ the 3HOLE-SHAFTCOLLAR assembly.

Fit the model to the Graphics window.
47)   Press the **f** key.

48)   Click **Save** 💾.

Create the 5HOLE-SHAFTCOLLAR assembly. Utilize the Save
As command with the Save as copy option. Recover from Mate
errors.

Save the 3HOLE-SHAFTCOLLAR assembly as the 5HOLE-
SHAFTCOLLAR assembly.

49)   Click **Save As** from the Menu bar.

50)   Check **Save as copy**.

51)   Enter **5HOLE-SHAFTCOLLAR** for
File name.

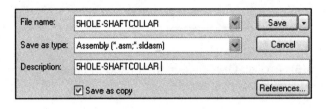

52)   Enter **5HOLE-SHAFTCOLLAR** for
Description.

53)   Click **Save**.

Close the model.

54)   Click **File**, **Close** from the Menu bar.

Open the new assembly.

55)   Click **Open** 📂 from the Menu bar.

56)   Select **Assembly** for Files of type.

57)   Double-click **5HOLE-SHAFTCOLLAR**. The 5HOLE-
SHAFTCOLLAR FeatureManager is displayed.

58)   Right-click **FLATBAR-3HOLE** from the FeatureManager.
Expand the Pop-up menu if needed.

59)   Click **Replace Components**. The Replace
PropertyManager is displayed.

60)   Click the **Browse** button.

61)   Double-click **FLATBAR-5HOLE**. Note: The FLATBAR-5HOLE
part was created in the Project 1 exercises.

62)   Check the **Re-attach mates** box.

63)   Click **OK** ✔ from the Replace PropertyManager. The Mate
Entities PropertyManager and the Wants Wrong dialog box is
displayed. There are two red Mate error marks displayed in the
Mate Entities box.

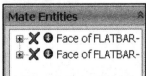

64)   The What's Wrong dialog box is displayed. Recover from the Mate errors. Click **Close** from the What's Wrong dialog box.

65)   Click **OK** ✅ from the Mated Entities PropertyManager.

66)   Click **Close** from the What's Wrong dialog box. View the location of the SHAFT-COLLAR in the Graphics window.

Recover from the Mate errors.

67)   **Expand** the Mates folder from the FeatureManager.

68)   Right-click the first mate, **Concentric #** from the Mates folder.

69)   Click **Edit Feature** from the Context toolbar. The Mate PropertyManager is displayed.

70)   Right-click the **Mate Face error** in the Mate Selections box as illustrated.

71)   Click **Delete**.

72)   Click the **inside face** of the left hole of the FLATBAR as illustrated. Concentric is selected by default.

73)   Click the **Green Check mark** ✅ .

74)   Click **OK** ✅ from the Mate PropertyManager.

75) Right-click the second mate, **Coincident #** from the
Mates folder.

76) Click **Edit Feature** from the Context toolbar. The Mate
PropertyManager is displayed.

77) Right-click the **Mate Face error** in the Mate Selections
box as illustrated.

78) Click **Delete** as illustrated.

79) Click the **front face** of the FLATBAR as illustrated. The
selected faces are displayed in the Mate Selections box.
Coincident is selected by default.

80) Click the **Green Check mark** .

81) Click **OK** from the Mate
PropertyManager.

82) **Expand** the Mate folder from the
FeatureManager. View the
corrected mates.

 The Mate Entities box will list red X's if the faces,
edges or planes are not valid. Expand the Mate Entities and
select new references in the Graphics window to redefine the
mates.

The FLATBAR-3HOLE is replaced with the FLATBAR-
5HOLE part. The Mates are updated.

Fit the model to the Graphics window.
83) Press the **f** key.

Save the 5HOLE-SHAFTCOLLAR assembly.
84) Click **Isometric view** from the Heads-up View toolbar.

85) Click **Save** .

Incorporate symmetry into the assembly. Divide large
assemblies into smaller sub-assemblies.

 The Multimedia CD illustrates the FLATBAR
configurations created in Project 2 to create the FLATBAR-
3HOLE and FLATBAR-5HOLE assemblies.

Utilize Design Tables to create multiple configurations of assemblies.

WHEEL-FLATBAR Assembly

The WHEEL-FLATBAR assembly consists of the following components:

- 3HOLE-SHAFTCOLLAR assembly

- 5HOLE-SHAFTCOLLAR assembly

- WHEEL part

Create the WHEEL-FLATBAR assembly. Mate the 3HOLE-SHAFTCOLLAR assembly 67.5 degrees counterclockwise from the Top Plane.

The 3HOLE-SHAFTCOLLAR assembly is concentric with holes on the second and forth bolt circle.

Mate the 5HOLE-SHAFTCOLLAR assembly 22.5 degrees clockwise from the Top Plane.

The 5HOLE-SHAFTCOLLAR assembly is concentric with holes on the second and forth bolt circle.

Activity: WHEEL-FLATBAR Assembly

Create the WHEEL-FLATBAR assembly.

86)   Click **New** ⬚ the Menu bar.

87)   Double-click **Assembly** from the Templates tab. The Begin Assembly PropertyManager is displayed.

Insert the WHEEL.

88)   Click the **Browse** button.

89)   Select **Part** for Files of type from the SW-TUTORIAL-2009 folder.

90)   Double-click **WHEEL**.

91)   Click **OK** ✔ from the Begin Assembly PropertyManager. The WHEEL part is fixed to the assembly Origin. If needed, click View, Origins from the Menu bar menu to displayed the Origin in the Graphics window.

Save the assembly.

92)   Click **Save As** from the Menu bar.

93)   Select the **SW-TUTORIAL-2009** folder.

94)   Enter **WHEEL-FLATBAR** for File name.

95)   Enter **WHEEL-FLATBAR** for Description.

96)   Click **Save**.

Display the Top Plane in the Front view.

97)   Click **Front view** ⬚ from the Heads-up View toolbar. View the WHEEL part.

Locate the first set of holes from the Right plane (-Y-axis). Left Hole1 and Left Hole2 are positioned on the second and forth bolt circle, 22.5° from the Right plane. Select Left Hole1. The x, y, z coordinates, -.287, -.693, .125 are displayed.

Tan^{-1} (-.287/.693) = 22.5°

As an exercise, utilize the Measure tool to determine the center-to-center distance between the Left Hole1 and Left Hole2. The center-to-center distance is .500in.

Insert two Concentric mates between Left Hole1 and Left Hole2 and the 3HOLE-SHAFTCOLLAR assembly holes. The FLATBAR-3HOLE center-to-center distance is also .500in.

☼ To determine tolerance issues, utilize two Concentric mates between components with mating cylindrical geometry. If the mating components center-to-center distance is not exact, a Mate error is displayed on the second Concentric mate.

Insert a Coincident mate between the back face of the 3HOLE-SHAFTCOLLAR assembly and the front face of the WHEEL.

Right Hole1 and Right Hole2 are 22.5° from the Top Plane.

Insert two Concentric mates between Right Hole1 and Right Hole2 and the 5HOLE-SHAFTCOLLAR assembly holes.

Insert a Coincident mate between the back face of the 5HOLE-SHAFTCOLLAR assembly and the front face of the WHEEL.

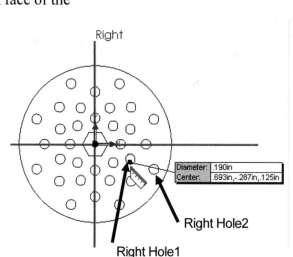

Activity: WHEEL-FLATBAR Assembly-Insert 3HOLE-SHAFTCOLLAR Assembly

Insert the 3HOLE-SHAFTCOLLAR assembly.

98) Click **Isometric view** 🔲 from the Heads-up View toolbar.

99) Click **Insert Components** 🔲 from the Assembly toolbar. The Insert Components PropertyManager is displayed.

100) Click the **Browse** button.

101) Select **Assembly** for Files of type from the SW-TUTORIAL-2009 folder.

102) Double-click the **3HOLE-SHAFTCOLLAR** assembly.

103) Click a **position** to the left of the WHEEL as illustrated.

Move and rotate the 3HOLE-SHAFTCOLLAR component.
104) Click the front face of the **3HOLE-SHAFTCOLLAR**.

105) Right-click **Move with Triad**.

106) Hold the **left mouse button** down on the X-axis (red).

107) Drag the **component** to the left.

108) Hold the **right mouse button** down on the Z-axis (blue).

109) Drag the **component** and rotate it about the Z-axis.

110) **Position** the component until the SHAFT-COLLAR part is approximately in front of the WHEEL Left Hole1.

111) Release the **right mouse** button.

112) Click a **position** in the Graphics window to deselect the face.

Insert the required mates.

113) Click the **Mate** ✎ tool from the Assembly toolbar. The Mate PropertyManager is displayed.

Insert a Concentric mate.

114) Click the **back top inside cylindrical face** of the SHAFT-COLLAR.

115) Click the **WHEEL Left Hole1** cylindrical face as illustrated. Concentric is selected by default. The selected faces are displayed in the Mate Selections box.

116) Click the **Green Check mark** ✔.

Insert the second Concentric mate.

117) Click the **back middle inside cylindrical face** of the FLATBAR.

118) Click the **WHEEL Left Hole2** inside cylindrical face as illustrated. Concentric is selected by default. The selected faces are displayed in the Mate Selections box.

119) Click the **Green Check mark** ✔.

Insert a Coincident mate.

120) Click the **FLATBAR-3HOLE back** face.

121) Click the front face of the **WHEEL**. Coincident is selected by default.

122) Click the **Green Check mark** ✔ .

123) Click **OK** ✔ from the Mate PropertyManager.

124) Click **Front view** 📄 from the Heads-up View toolbar.

Save the WHEEL-FLATBAR assembly.

125) Click **Save** 💾.

Mate Selections	
Face<5>@3HOLE-SHAFT	
Face<6>@WHEEL-1	

Activity: WHEEL-FLATBAR Assembly-Insert 5HOLE-SHAFTCOLLAR Assembly

Insert the 5HOLE-SHAFTCOLLAR assembly.

126) Click **Insert Components** 🖫 from the Assembly toolbar. The Insert Components PropertyManager is displayed.

127) Click the **Browse** button.

128) Double-click the **5HOLE-SHAFTCOLLAR** assembly from the SW-TUTORIAL-2009 folder.

129) Click a **position** to the right of the WHEEL.

Move the 5HOLE-SHAFTCOLLAR component.

130) Click the **5HOLE-SHAFTCOLLAR** front face.

131) Right-click **Move with Triad**.

132) Hold the **left mouse button** down on the X-axis (red). Drag the **component** to the right. View the results.

133) Click **Isometric view** 📦 from the Heads-up View toolbar.

134) Click **inside** the Graphics window.

Mate the 5HOLE-SHAFTCOLLAR assembly.

135)   Click the **Mate** ✎ tool from the Assembly toolbar. The Mate PropertyManager is displayed.

Insert a Concentric mate.

136)   Click the **back inside cylindrical face** of the first hole on the FLATBAR-5HOLE assembly.

137)   Click the **WHEEL Right Hole1** cylindrical face. Concentric is selected by default.

138)   Click the **Green Check mark** ✔.

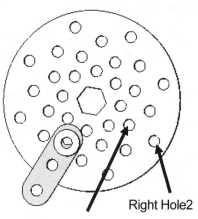

Right Hole2

Right Hole1

Insert a Concentric mate.

139)   **Move** the 5HOLE-SHAFTCOLLAR to view the back side.

140)   Click the **back inside cylindrical** face of the second hole on the FLATBAR-5HOLE assembly.

141)   Click the **WHEEL Right Hole2** cylindrical face. Concentric is selected by default.

142)   Click the **Green Check mark** ✔.

Right Hole2

Right Hole1

Insert a Coincident mate.

143) Click the **back face** of the FLATBAR-5HOLE.

144) Click the **front face** of the WHEEL. Coincident is the selected by default.

145) Click the **Green Check mark** ✓.

146) Click **OK** ✓ from the Mate PropertyManager.

Deactivate the Origins.

147) Click **View**, uncheck **Origin** from the Menu bar.

Measure the angle between the 3HOLE-SHAFTCOLLAR assembly and the 5HOLE-SHAFTCOLLAR assembly.

148) Click **Front view** 🔲 from the Heads-up View toolbar.

149) Click the **Measure** 📐 Measure... tool from the Evaluate tab in the CommandManager. The Measure dialog box is displayed.

150) Select the **two inside edges** of the FLATBAR assemblies. View the results.

151) If required, click the **Show XYZ Measurements button**. The items are perpendicular.

💡 The Measure tool provides the ability to display dual units. Click the **Units/Precision** $\frac{in}{mm}$ icon from the Measure dialog box. Set the desired units.

152) Close ✖ the Measure dialog box.

Apply the AssemblyXpert tool. The AssemblyXpert tool
displays statistics and checks the health of the current
assembly.

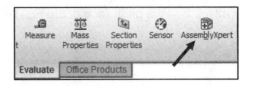

153) Click the AssemblyXpert 🎲
tool in the Evaluate toolbar.
The AssemblyXpert dialog
box is displayed. Review the
Status and description for the
assembly.

154) Click OK from the
AssemblyXpert dialog box.

Fit the model to the Graphics window.
155) Press the f key.

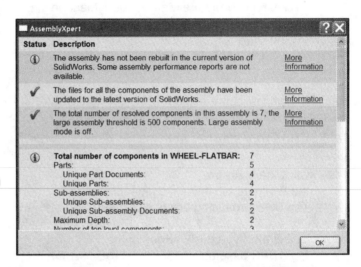

156) Click Isometric view 🔲 from
the Heads-up View toolbar.

Save the WHEEL-FLATBAR
assembly.

157) Click Save 💾.

WHEEL-AND-AXLE Assembly

The WHEEL-AND-AXLE assembly contains the
following items:

- WHEEL-FLATBAR assembly

- AXLE-3000 part

- SHAFTCOLLAR-500 part

- HEX-ADAPTER part

Create the WHEEL-AND-AXLE assembly. The AXLE-
3000 part is the first component in the assembly. A part
or assembly inserted into a new assembly is called a
component. The WHEEL-FLATBAR assembly rotates
about the AXLE part.

Combine the created new assemblies and parts to
develop the PNEUMATIC-TEST-MODULE assembly.

Activity: WHEEL-AND-AXLE Assembly

Create the WHEEL-AND-AXLE assembly.

158) Click **New** ⬜ from the Menu bar.

159) Double-click **Assembly** from the Templates tab.
The Begin Assembly PropertyManager is
displayed.

Insert the AXLE-3000 part.
160) Click the **Browse** button.

161) Select **Part** for Files of type from the
SW-TUTORIAL-2009 folder.

162) Double-click **AXLE-3000**. Note: AXLE-3000 was
created in the Project homework problems.

163) Click **OK** ✅ from the Begin Assembly
PropertyManager. The AXLE-3000 part is fixed
to the assembly Origin.

Save the assembly.
164)   Click **Save As** from the Menu bar.

165)   Enter **WHEEL-AND-AXLE** for File
name in the SW-TUTORIAL-2009
folder.

File name:	WHEEL-AND-AXLE
Save as type:	Assembly (*.asm;*.sldasm)
Description:	WHEEL-AND-AXLE

166)   Enter **WHEEL-AND-AXLE** for
Description.

167)   Click **Save**.

Insert a Coincident mate between the Axis of the AXLE-3000
and the Axis of the WHEEL. Insert a Coincident mate between
the Front Plane of the AXLE-3000 and the Front Plane of the
WHEEL. The WHEEL-FLATBAR assembly rotates about the
AXLE-3000 axis.

Display the Temporary Axes.
168)   Click **View**, check **Temporary Axes** from the Menu bar.

Insert the WHEEL-FLATBAR assembly.

169)   Click **Insert Components** from the Assembly toolbar. The
Insert Components PropertyManager is displayed.

170)   Click the **Browse** button.

171)   Double-click the **WHEEL-FLATBAR** assembly from the
SW-TUTORIAL-2009 folder.

172)   Click a **position** to the right of AXLE-
3000.

View the Reference WHEEL Axis.
173)   Click **View**, check **Axes** from the
Menu bar.

174)   Click **View**, uncheck **Origins** from the
Menu bar.

🔆   Reference geometry defines the
shape or form of a surface or a solid.
Reference geometry includes planes,
axes, coordinate systems, and points.

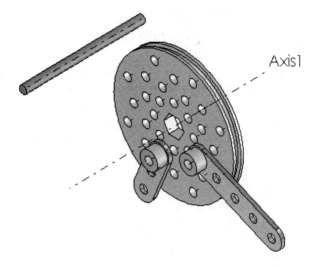

Insert a Coincident mate.

175) Click the **Mate** ✎ tool from the Assembly toolbar. The Mate PropertyManager is displayed.

176) Click **Axis1** in the Graphics window.

177) Click the **AXLE-3000 Temporary Axis**. Coincident is selected by default.

178) Click the **Green Check mark** ✔.

Insert a Coincident mate.

179) **Expand** WHEEL-AND-AXLE from the fly-out FeatureManager.

180) **Expand** AXLE-3000 from the fly-out FeatureManager.

181) **Expand** the Features folder.

182) Click **Front Plane** of AXLE-3000<1>.

183) **Expand** WHEEL from the fly-out FeatureManager.

184) **Expand** the Features folder.

185) Click **Front Plane** of the WHEEL. Coincident is selected by default.

186) Click the **Green Check mark** ✔.

187) Click **OK** ✔ from the Mate PropertyManager.

Rotate the WHEEL-FLATBAR assembly about AXLE-3000.
188) Click and drag the **WHEEL** around AXLE-3000.

Save the WHEEL-AND-AXLE assembly.

189) Click **Save** 🖫.

Activity: WHEEL-AND-AXLE Assembly-Insert the HEX-ADAPTER Part

Insert the HEX-ADAPTER part.

190) Click the **Insert Components** 🖐 tool from the
Assembly toolbar. The Insert Component
PropertyManager is displayed.

191) Click the **Browse** button.

192) Select **Part** for Files of type in the SW-TUTORIAL-
2009 folder.

193) Double-click **HEX-ADAPTER**.

194) Click a **position** to the left of the WHEEL as
illustrated. The HEX-ADAPTER is displayed
in the FeatureManager.

195) **Expand** the Mates folder. View the created
mates for the assembly. View the inserted
components: AXLE-3000, WHEEL-FLATBAR,
and HEX-ADAPTER.

Insert a Concentric mate. Mate the HEX-ADAPTER.

196)   Click the **Mate** ✎ tool from the Assembly toolbar. The Mate PropertyManager is displayed.

197)   Click the **HEX-ADAPTER** cylindrical face as illustrated.

198)   Click the **AXLE-3000** cylindrical face as illustrated. Concentric is selected by default. The selected faces are displayed in the Mate Selections box.

199)   Click **Aligned** 🔽🔽 from the Concentric1 PropertyManager to flip the HEX-ADAPTER, if required.

200)   Click **OK** ✔ from the Concentric PropertyManager.

Insert a Coincident mate.

201)   Click the **front face** of the WHEEL.

202)   Press the **left arrow key** to rotate the model.

203)   Click the **flat back circular face** of the HEX-ADAPTER as illustrated. Coincident is selected by default.

204)   Click the **Green Check mark** ✔.

Insert a Parallel mate.

205) **Rotate** the WHEEL-AND-AXLE assembly to view the back bottom edge of the HEX-ADAPTER.

206) **Zoom in** on the back bottom edge of the HEX-ADAPTER.

207) Click the **back bottom edge** of the WHEEL. Note: Do not select the midpoint.

208) Click the **top edge** of the HEX-ADAPTER. Do not select the midpoint. The selected edges are displayed in the Mate Selections box.

209) Click **Parallel** ⬉ as illustrated.

210) Click the **Green Check mark** ✔.

211) Click **OK** ✔ from the Mate PropertyManager.

Fit the model to the Graphics window.

212) Press the **f** key.

213) Click **Isometric view** 🔲 from the Heads-up View toolbar.

View the created mates.

214) **Expand** the Mates folder.

Save the WHEEL-AND-AXLE assembly.

215) Click **Save** 💾.

Activity: WHEEL-AND-AXLE Assembly-Insert SHAFTCOLLAR-500 Part

Insert the SHAFTCOLLAR-500 part.

216) Click the **Insert Components** 🖰 tool from the Assembly toolbar. The Insert Component PropertyManager is displayed.

217) Click the **Browse** button.

218) Select **Part** for Files of type from the SW-TUTORIAL-2009 folder.

219) Double-click **SHAFTCOLLAR-500**.

220) Click a **position** behind the WHEEL-AND-AXLE assembly as illustrated.

Insert a Concentric mate.

221) Click **View**, uncheck **Temporary Axes** from the Menu bar.

222) Click **View**, uncheck **Axes** from the Menu bar.

223) Click the **Mate** ✎ tool from the Assembly toolbar. The Mate PropertyManager is displayed.

224) Click the **front inside cylindrical face** of the SHAFTCOLLAR-500 part.

225) Click the **cylindrical face** of the AXLE-3000 part. Concentric is selected by default.

226) Click the **Green Check mark** ✔.

Insert a Coincident mate.

227) Click the **front face** of the SHAFTCOLLAR-500 part.

228) Click the **back face** of the WHEEL. Coincident is selected by default.

229) Click the **Green Check mark** ✔.

230) Click **OK** ✔ from the Mate PropertyManager.

Display an Isometric view.

231) Click **Isometric view** from the Heads-up View toolbar.

View the created Mates.

232) **Expand** the Mates folder. View the created mates.

Save the WHEEL-AND-AXLE assembly.

233) Click **Save** 💾.

Close all files.

234) Click **Windows**, **Close All** from the Menu bar.

Determine the static and dynamic behavior of mates in each sub-assembly before creating the top level assembly.

Review the WHEEL-AND-AXLE Assembly

You combined the WHEEL-FLATBAR sub assembly, the AXLE-3000 part, the HEX-ADAPTER part and the SHAFTCOLLAR-500 part to create the WHEEL-AND-AXLE assembly.

The WHEEL-FLATBAR sub-assembly rotated about the AXLE-3000 part. The WHEEL-FLATBAR assembly combined the 3HOLE-SHAFTCOLLAR assembly and the 5HOLE-SHAFTCOLLAR assembly. The 5HOLE-SHAFTCOLLAR assembly was created from the 3HOLE-SHAFTCOLLAR assembly by replacing the FLATBAR component and recovering from two Mate errors. Additional components are added to the WHEEL-AND-AXLE assembly in the project exercises.

PNEUMATIC-TEST-MODULE Assembly

Create the PNEUMATIC-TEST-MODULE assembly. The first component is the FLAT-PLATE. The FLAT-PLATE is fixed to the Origin ⬐. The FLAT-PLATE part was created in the Project 2 exercises: and is located on the enclosed CD and supports the other components.

Modify the LINKAGE assembly. Insert the HEX-STANDOFF part. Insert the LINKAGE assembly into the PNEUMATIC-TEST-MODULE assembly.

Insert the AIR-RESERVOIR-SUPPORT assembly. Utilize the Linear Component Pattern, and Feature Driven Component Pattern tools. Insert the FRONT-SUPPORT assembly. Utilize the Mirror Components tool to create a mirrored version of the FRONT-SUPPORT assembly.

Insert the WHEEL-AND-AXLE assembly. Utilize Component Properties and create a Flexible State. Utilize the ConfigurationManager to select the Flexible configuration for the AirCylinder assembly.

Work between multiple part and sub-assembly documents to create the final assembly. Illustrations indicate the active document.

Activity: PNEUMATIC-TEST-MODULE Assembly

Create the PNEUMATIC-TEST-MODULE assembly.

235) Click **New** 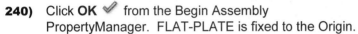 from the Menu bar.

236) Double-click **Assembly** from the
Templates tab. The Begin Assembly
PropertyManager is displayed.

Insert the FLAT-PLATE part.
237) Click the **Browse** button.

238) Select **Part** for Files of type from the
SW-TUTORIAL-2009 folder.

239) Double-click **FLAT-PLATE**. Note:
FLAT-PLATE was created in a Project 2
exercise.

240) Click **OK** from the Begin Assembly
PropertyManager. FLAT-PLATE is fixed to the Origin.

Save the assembly.
241) Click **Save As** from the Menu bar.

242) Enter **PNEUMATIC-TEST-MODULE** for File name.

243) Enter **PNEUMATIC-TEST-MODULE** for
Description.

244) Click **Save**.

Click **View**, **Origins** from the Menu bar
menu to display the Origin in the Graphics
window.

Activity: Modify the LINKAGE Assembly

Modify the LINKAGE assembly created in Project 1.
245) Click **Open** from the Menu bar.

246) Select **Assembly** for Files of type from the SW-TUTORIAL-2009 folder.

247) Double-click **LINKAGE**. The LINKAGE assembly is displayed.

Insert the HEX-STANDOFF part into the LINKAGE assembly.

248) Click the **Insert Components** tool from the Assembly toolbar. The Insert Component PropertyManager is displayed.

249) Click the **Browse** button.

250) Select **Parts** for Files of type from the SW-TUTORIAL-2009 folder.

251) Double-click **HEX-STANDOFF**.

252) Click a **position** to the front of the half Slot Cut as illustrated.

View the Temporary Axes.

253) Click **View**, check **Temporary Axes** from the Menu bar.

254) Click **View**, check **Axes** from the Menu bar.

Insert a Coincident mate.

255) Click the **Mate** ✎ tool from the Assembly toolbar. The Mate PropertyManager is displayed.

256) Click the **HEX-STANDOFF** tapped hole Temporary Axis.

257) Click the **half Slot Cut Axis1**. The selected entities are displayed in the Mate Selections box. Coincident is selected by default.

258) Click the **Green Check mark** ✓ .

💡 If an assembly or component is loaded in a Lightweight 🔲 state, right-click the **assembly name** or **component name** from the FeatureManager. Click **Set Lightweight to Resolved**.

Insert a Coincident mate.
259)   Click the **HEX-STANDOFF** top face.

260)   Click the **BRACKET bottom face**.
Coincident is selected by default.
The selected faces are displayed in
the Mate Selections box.

261)   Click the **Green Check mark** ✔.

Insert a Parallel mate.
262)   Click the **HEX-STANDOFF** front
face.

263)   Click the **BRACKET front face**. The
selected faces are displayed in the
Mate Selections box.

264)   Click **Parallel** ＼ as illustrated.

265)   Click the **Green Check mark** ✔.

266)   Click **OK** ✔ from the Mate
PropertyManager.

Fit the model to the Graphics window.
267)   Press the **f** key.

268)   Click **Isometric view**
from the Heads-up View
toolbar.

269)   Click **Save** 🖫.

View the created Mates.
270)   **Expand** the Mates folder.
View the created mates.

Insert the second HEX-STANDOFF.

271) Click the **Insert Components** tool from the Assembly toolbar. The Insert Component PropertyManager is displayed.

272) Click the **Browse** button.

273) Select **Parts** for Files of type from the SW-TUTORIAL-2009 folder.

274) Double-click **HEX-STANDOFF**.

275) Click a **position** to the back right of the back half Slot Cut as illustrated.

Insert a Concentric mate.

276) Click the **Mate** tool from the Assembly toolbar. The Mate PropertyManager is displayed.

277) Click the **second HEX-STANDOFF** Tapped Hole Temporary Axis.

278) Click the **back half Slot Cut Axis2**. Coincident is selected by default.

279) Click the **Green Check mark**.

Insert a Coincident mate.

280) Click the **second HEX-STANDOFF top** face.

281) Click the **BRACKET bottom face**. Coincident is selected by default.

282) Click the **Green Check mark**.

Insert a Parallel mate.

283) Click the **second HEX-STANDOFF** face as illustrated.

284) Click the **BRACKET back right** face.

285) Click **Parallel** \\ as illustrated.

286) Click the **Green Check mark** ✔.

287) Click **OK** ✔ from the Mate PropertyManager.

💡 Use Selection Filter toolbar to select the correct face, edge, Axis, etc.

Fit the model to the Graphics window.

288) Press the **f** key. Click **Isometric view** from the Heads-up View toolbar.

289) Click **Save** 💾.

In the Project 1 exercises, you created the LINKAGE-2 assembly. Insert the second AXLE. Insert the two SHAFT-COLLAR parts as an exercise at the end of this Project.

Insert the second AXLE.

290) Click the **Insert Components** tool from the Assembly toolbar.

291) Click the **Browse** button.

292) Select **Parts** for Files of type from the SW-TUTORIAL-2009 folder.

293) Double-click **AXLE**.

294) Click a **position** to the front bottom of the FLATBAR as illustrated.

Insert a Concentric mate.

295) Click the **Mate** 📎 Assembly tool. The Mate PropertyManager is displayed.

296) Click the **second AXLE cylindrical** face.

297) Click the **FLATBAR bottom hole** face as illustrated. Concentric is selected by default.

298) Click the **Green Check mark** ✔.

Insert a Coincident mate.

299) Click the second **AXLE Front Plane** from the fly-out FeatureManager.

300) Click the **LINKAGE assembly Front Plane** from the fly-out FeatureManager. Coincident is selected by default. The selected Front Planes are displayed in the Mate Selections box.

301) Click the **Green Check mark** ✔.

302) Click **OK** ✔ from the Mate PropertyManager.

Fit the model to the Graphics window.

303) Press the **f** key.

304) Click **Isometric view** 🔲 from the Heads-up View toolbar.

Save the LINKAGE assembly.

305) Click **Save** 💾.

Insert the first SHAFT-COLLAR on the second AXIS.

306) Click the **Insert Components** Assembly tool.

307) Click the **Browse** button.

308) Select **Part** type from the SW-TUTORIAL-2009 folder.

309) Double-click **SHAFT-COLLAR**.

310) Click a **position** to the back of the second AXLE as illustrated.

Enlarge the view.
311) Zoom-in on the **SHAFT-COLLAR** and the **AXLE** to enlarge the view.

Insert a Concentric mate.
312) Click the **Mate** Assembly tool. The Mate PropertyManager is displayed.

313) Click the inside **hole face** of the SHAFT-COLLAR.

314) Click the **long cylindrical face** of the AXLE. Concentric is selected by default. The selected faces are displayed in the Mate Selections box.

315) Click the **Green Check mark** .

Insert a Coincident mate.

316) Click the **front face** of the SHAFT-COLLAR.

317) Press the **left arrow key** approximately 5 times to rotate the model to view the back face of the first FLATBAR.

318) Click the **back face** of the FLATBAR. Coincident is selected by default.

319) Click the **Green Check mark** .

320) Click **OK** from the Mate PropertyManager.

Display the Isometric view.

321) Click **Isometric view** from the Heads-up View toolbar.

Insert the second SHAFT-COLLAR.

322) Click the **Insert Components** Assembly tool. The Insert Component PropertyManager is displayed.

323) Click the **Browse** button.

324) Select **Part** for Files of type from the SW-TUTORIAL-2009 folder.

325) Double-click **SHAFT-COLLAR**.

326) Click a **position** to the front of the AXLE as illustrated.

Enlarge the view.

327) **Zoom in** on the second SHAFT-COLLAR and the AXLE to enlarge the view.

Insert a Concentric mate.

328) Click the **Mate** Assembly tool. The Mate PropertyManager is displayed.

329) Click the inside **hole face** of the second SHAFT-COLLAR. Note: The icon face feedback symbol.

330) Click the **long cylindrical face** of the AXLE. Concentric is selected by default.

331) Click the **Green Check mark** ✔.

Insert a Coincident mate.
332) Press the **f** key to fit the model to the Graphics window.

333) **Zoom in** on the front face of the second FLATBAR.

334) Click the **front face** of the second FLATBAR.

335) Click the **back face** of the second SHAFT-COLLAR. Coincident is selected by default.

336) Click the **Green Check mark** ✔.

337) Click **OK** ✔ from the Mate PropertyManager.

Display the Isometric view.
338) Click **Isometric view** 🔲 from the Heads-up View toolbar.

Save the LINKAGE assembly.
339) **Rebuild** the model.

340) Click **View**, uncheck **Axis** from the Menu bar.

341) Click **View**, uncheck **Temporary Axis** from Menu bar.

342) Click **Save** 🖫. Note: As an exercise, insert SCREWs between the AirCylinder assembly and the two HEX-STANDOFFs as illustrated.

SCREWs

Activity: PNEUMATIC-TEST-MODULE-Insert LINKAGE Assembly

Insert the LINKAGE assembly into the PNEUMATIC-TEST-MODULE assembly.

343) Click **Window, Tile Horizontally** from the Menu bar. Note: The PNEUMATIC-TEST-MODULE assembly should be open.

344) Rotate the two **FLATBARs** approximately 45°.

345) Click and drag the **LINKAGE** assembly icon into the PNEUMATIC-TEST-MODULE assembly.

346) Click a **position** above the FLAT-PLATE as illustrated.

347) **Maximize** the PNEUMATIC-TEST-MODULE Graphics window.

348) Click **View**, uncheck **Origins** from the Menu bar. If required, click view, uncheck Planes from the Menu bar.

349) Click **Trimetric view** from the Heads-up View toolbar.

Insert a Concentric mate.

350) Click the **Mate** Assembly tool. The Mate PropertyManager is displayed.

351) Click the **Front HEX-STANDOFF Tapped** Hole face as illustrated.

352) Click the **FLAT-PLATE Hole** face in the 5th row, 4th column as illustrated. Concentric is selected by default. The selected faces are displayed in the Mate Selections box.

353) Click the **Green Check mark** .

Insert a Parallel mate.

354) Click the **PNEUMATIC-TEST-MODULE Front Plane** from the fly-out FeatureManager.

355) Click the **LINKAGE assembly Front Plane** from the fly-out FeatureManager.

356) Click **Parallel**.

357) Click the **Green Check mark** ✓ .

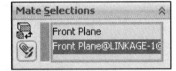

Insert a Coincident mate.

358) Click the **Front HEX-STANDOFF** bottom face.

359) Click the **FLAT-PLATE top face**. Coincident is selected by default.

360) Click the **Green Check mark** ✓ .

361) Click **OK** ✓ from the Mate PropertyManager.

Display the Isometric view.

362) Click **Isometric view** 🟦 from the Heads-up View toolbar.

Save the PNEUMATIC-TEST-MODULE assembly.

363) Click **Save** 💾 .

The LINKAGE assembly is fully defined, and located on the FLAT-PLATE part. Insert the AIR-RESERVOIR-SUPPORT assembly. The AIR-RESERVOIR-SUPPORT assembly was created in the Project 2 exercises. Note: The AIR-RESERVOIR SUPPORT is also located in the book's CD.

Activity: PNEUMATIC-TEST-MODULE Insert AIR-RESERVOIR-SUPPORT

Insert the AIR-RESERVOIR-SUPPORT assembly.

364) Click the **Insert Components** Assembly tool. The Insert Component PropertyManager is displayed.

365) Click the **Browse** button.

366) Select **Assembly** for Files of type from the SW-TUTORIAL-2009 folder.

367) Double-click the **AIR-RESERVOIR-SUPPORT** assembly. Note: The AIR-RESERVOIR SUPPORT assembly is supplied on the CD in the book: Chapter 5 models folder.

368) Click a **position** above the FLAT-PLATE as illustrated.

369) Click the **Rotate Component** Assembly tool. The Rotate Component PropertyManager is displayed. The Rotate icon is displayed in the Graphics window.

370) Click and drag the **AIR-RESERVOIR-SUPPORT** until the tank is parallel with the AirCylinder assembly as illustrated.

371) Click **OK** from the Rotate Component PropertyManager.

Insert a Concentric mate.

372) Click the **Mate** 📎 Assembly tool. The Mate PropertyManager is displayed.

373) Click the **FLAT-PLATE back left** inside hole face as illustrated.

374) Click the fourth **ANGLE-BRACKET** inside hole face. Concentric is selected by default.

375) Click the **Green Check mark** ✔.

Insert a Coincident mate.

376) Click the **ANGLE-BRACKET bottom face**.

377) Click the **FLAT-PLATE top face**. Coincident is selected by default.

378) Click the **Green Check mark** ✔.

Insert a Parallel mate.

379) Click **Left view** 🔲 from the Heads-up View toolbar.

380) Click the **ANGLE-BRACKET** narrow face.

381) Click the **FLAT-PLATE narrow face**.

382) Click **Parallel** ⟍.

383) Click the **Green Check mark** ✔.

384) Click **OK** ✔ from the Mate PropertyManager.

Display the Isometric view.

385)   Click **Isometric view** from the Heads-
          up View toolbar.

Save the PNEUMATIC-TEST-MODULE assembly.

386)   Click **Save** .

Component Patterns in the Assembly

There are three methods to define a pattern in
an assembly.

- Linear

- Circular

- Feature Driven

A Feature Driven Component Pattern
utilizes an existing feature pattern.

A Linear / Circular Component pattern
utilizes geometry in the assembly to arrange
instances in a Linear or Circular pattern.

The SCREW part fastens the ANGLE-
BRACKET part to the FLAT-PLATE part.
Mate one SCREW to the first instance on
the ANGLE-BRACKET Linear Pattern.

Utilize the Feature Driven Component Pattern tool to
create instances of the SCREW. Suppress the
instances.

Utilize the Linear Component Pattern tool to copy the
Feature Driven Pattern of SCREWS to the second
ANGLE-BRACKET part.

Drag the part by specific geometry to create a mate.

Activity: PNEUMATIC-TEST-MODULE-Component Pattern

Open the SCREW part.

387)   Click **Open** ⬚ from the Menu bar.

388)   Double-click **SCREW** from the SW-TUTORIAL-2009 folder.

389)   Unsuppress the **Fillet1** and **Chamfer1** feature.

390)   Click **Window, Tile Horizontally** to display the SCREW and the PNEUMATIC-TEST-MODULE assembly.

Insert and mate the SCREW.

391)   Click the **bottom circular edge** of the SCREW.

392)   Drag the **SCREW** into the PNEUMATIC-TEST-MODULE assembly window. Note: Zoom in on the top circular edge of the ANBLE-BRACKET left hole.

393)   Release the mouse pointer on the **top circular edge** of the ANGLE-BRACKET left hole. The mouse pointer displays the ⬚ Coincident/Concentric feedback symbol.

394)   **Return** to the PNEUMATIC-TEST-MODULE assembly window. Click **Left view** ⬚ from the Heads-up View toolbar.

The SCREW part is position in the left hole with a Coincident/Concentric mate.

Create a Feature Driven Component Pattern.

395)   Click the **Feature Driven Component Pattern** ⬚ tool from the Consolidate Assembly toolbar. The Feature Driven PropertyManager is displayed.

396)   Click the **SCREW** component in the Graphics window. SCREW<1> is displayed in the Components to Pattern box.

397)   Click inside the **Driving Feature** box. **Expand** the AIR-RESERVOIR-SUPPORT assembly in the PNEUMATIC-TEST-MODULE fly-out FeatureManager.

398)   **Expand** ANGLE-BRACKET <1>. **Expand** the Features folder.

399)   Click **LPattern1** in the fly-out FeatureManager. Note: The SCREW is the seed feature.

400) Click **OK** ✔ from the Feature Driven PropertyManager. Six instances are displayed in the Graphics window. DerivedLPattern1 is displayed in the FeatureManager.

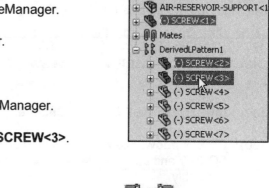

401) Click **SCREW<1>** from the FeatureManager.

402) Hold the **Ctrl** key down.

403) **Expand** DerivedLPattern1 from the FeatureManager.

404) Click the first two entries: **SCREW<2>** and **SCREW<3>**.

405) Release the **Ctrl** key.

406) Right-click **Suppress**. The first three SCREWs are not displayed.

💡 The Feature Driven PropertyManager contains an option to skip instances of a feature component in a pattern.

Activity: PNEUMATIC-TEST-MODULE-Linear Component Pattern

Create a Linear Component Pattern.

407) Click **Front view** 📦 from the Heads-up View toolbar.

408) Click the **Linear Component Pattern** 🔡 tool from the Assembly toolbar. The Linear Pattern PropertyManager is displayed.

409) Click inside the **Pattern Direction** box for Direction 1.

410) Click the long front edge of the **FRONT-PLATE** as illustrated. Edge<1> is displayed in the Pattern Direction box. The direction arrow points to the right.

411) Enter **177.80**mm, [7in] for Spacing.

412) Enter **2** for Instances.

413) Click inside the **Components to Pattern** box.

414) Click **DerivedLPattern1** from the fly-out FeatureManager.

415) Click **OK** ✔ from the Linear Pattern PropertyManager.

416) Click **Top view** ⊞ from the Heads-up View toolbar. View the results.

The Linear Component Pattern feature is displayed in the second ANGLE-BRACKET part. LocalLPattern1 is displayed in the FeatureManager.

Save the PNEUMATIC TEST MODULE assembly.

417) Click **Isometric view** 🟦 from the Heads-up View toolbar. View the FeatureManager and the created features in their states.

418) Click **Save** 🖫.

Hide the AIR-RESERVOIR-SUPPORT
assembly.

419) Right-click **AIR-RESERVOIR-
SUPPORT<1>** in the
FeatureManager.

420) Click **Hide components** 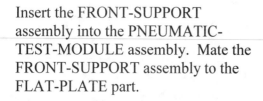.
Note: Utilize the Show
components tool to display a
component that has been hidden.

Hide the LINKAGE assembly.

421) Right-click **LINKAGE<1>** in the
FeatureManager.

422) Click **Hide components** .

Insert the FRONT-SUPPORT
assembly into the PNEUMATIC-
TEST-MODULE assembly. Mate the
FRONT-SUPPORT assembly to the
FLAT-PLATE part.

Utilize the Mirror Components tool to
create a mirrored copy of the
FRONT-SUPPORT assembly.

🔆 You can create new components
by mirroring existing part or sub-
assembly components. The new components can either
be a copy or a mirror of the original components. A
mirrored component is sometimes called a "right-hand"
version of the original "left-hand" version.

🔆 Access the Mirror Components tool from the
Consolidated Linear Component Pattern drop-down menu.

Activity: PNEUMATIC-TEST-MODULE-Insert FRONT-SUPPORT Assembly

---

Insert and mate the FRONT-SUPPORT assembly.

423) Click the **Insert Components** 🗂 tool from the Assembly toolbar. The Insert Component
PropertyManager is displayed.

424) Click the **Browse** button. Select **Assembly** for Files of type.

425) Double-click **FRONT**-**SUPPORT**.

Hide the SCREWs in the FRONT-SUPPORT.
426) Click a **position** above the FLAT-
        PLATE as illustrated.

427) Right-click **FRONT-SUPPORT** in
        the FeatureManager.

428) Click **Open Assembly**.

429) **Hide** the SCREW parts and HEX-
        NUTS if required in the assembly.

430) Click **Save** .

Return to the PNEUMATIC-TEST-
MODULE assembly.
431) Press **Ctrl Tab**.

432) Select the **PNEUMATIC-TEST-MODULE**
        document.

433) Click **Save** .

434) Click **Yes** to the Message, "Save the document
        and referenced models now?"

The PNEUMATIC-TEST-MODULE is displayed.
The SCREW and HEX-NUT components are hidden
in the FRONT-SUPPORT assembly.

Insert a Concentric mate.
435) Click the **Mate** Assembly tool. The Mate
        PropertyManager is displayed.

436) Click the **FLAT-PLATE hole face** in the 3rd row,
        right most column (17th column).

437) Click the **HEX-STANDOFF Tapped Hole as**
        illustrated. Concentric is selected by default.

438) Click the **Green Check mark** .

Insert a Coincident mate.
439) Click the bottom face of the **HEX-STANDOFF** part.

440) Click the top face of the **FLAT-PLATE**. The selected faces are displayed in the Mate Selections box. Coincident is selected by default.

441) Click the **Green Check mark** .

Insert a Parallel mate.
442) Click the **FRONT-SUPPORT Front Plane** from the fly-out FeatureManager.

443) **Show** the LINKAGE assembly.

444) Click the **LINKAGE Front Plane** from the fly-out FeatureManager.

445) Click **Parallel** .

446) Click the **Green Check mark** .

447) Click **OK** from the Mate PropertyManager.

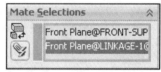

448) **Hide** the LINKAGE assembly.

Save the PNEUMATIC-TEST-MODULE assembly.
449) Click **Save** .

Mirrored Components

Create new components by mirroring existing parts or sub-assemblies. New components are created as copied geometry or mirrored geometry.

A mirrored component is sometimes called a "right-hand" version of the original "left hand" version.

The copied or mirrored component changes, when the original component is modified.

A mirrored component creates a new document. The default document prefix is mirror. A copied component does not create a new document.

Suppressed components in the original sub-assembly are not mirrored or copied. The SCREW parts in the FRONT-SUPPORT assembly are not copied.

Left Hand Version (Original)   Right Hand Version (Mirrored)

Instance Component

Mirrored Component

Instance Component

Front

PNEUMATIC-TEST-MODULE

Activity: PNEUMATIC-TEST-MODULE Assembly: Mirrored Component

Insert a Mirrored Component.

450) Click the **Mirror Components** 🔲 tool from the Consolidated Assembly toolbar. The Mirror Components PropertyManager is displayed.

Step 1: The Selections box is displayed. The first Step requires the mirrored plane, the components to mirror, and the components to copy.

451) **Expand** the PNEUMATIC-TEST-MODULE fly-out FeatureManager.

452) Click the **FLAT-PLATE Front Plane**. The Front Plane is displayed in the Mirror plane box.

453) Click the **FRONT-SUPPORT** assembly from the fly-out FeatureManager. The FRONT-SUPPORT assembly is displayed in the Components to Mirror box.

454) **Expand** the FRONT-SUPPORT entry in the Components to Mirror box.

455) Check the **FRONT-SUPPORT-1** box.

456) Check the **Recreate mates to new components** box.

457) Click **Next** .

Step 2: The Filenames box is displayed. "Mirror" is the default prefix utilized in the mirror part and assembly. MirrorFRONT-SUPPORT is the new assembly name.

458) Accept Mirror as the default prefix. Click **Next** .

Step 3: The Orientation box is displayed. The instanced components check box is automatically selected. A preview of the mirrored TRIANGLE and HEX-STANDOFF components are displayed.

459) Check the **Preview mirrored components** box. The ANGLE-13HOLE part is displayed in a preview in the Graphics window.

460) Click **OK** from the Mirror Components PropertyManager.

461) Click **OK** from the New SolidWorks Document dialog box. Assembly is the default template.

🔆 Select suppressed components and their mates to be mirrored in the Components to Mirror box.

The MirrorFRONT-SUPPORT, TRIANGLE, ANGLE-13HOLE, and SCREW components are mated.

Utilize the Fix option to mate the MirrorFRONT-SUPPORT to its current location in the PNEUMATIC-TEST-MODULE. No other mates are required.

Activity: PNEUMATIC-TEST-MODULE-Fix the MIRRORFRONT-SUPPORT

Fix the MirrorFRONT-SUPPORT.
462) Right-click **MirrorFRONT-SUPPORT** from the FeatureManager.

463) Click **Fix**. The MirrorFRONT assembly is fixed in the PNEUMATIC-TEST-MODULE assembly. The MirrorFRONT-SUPPORT does not move or rotate.

Display the LINKAGE assembly.
464) Right-click **LINKAGE** in the FeatureManager.

465) Click **Show components**.

Save the PNUEMATIC-TEST-MODULE assembly.

466) Click **Save** 💾.

🔆 Reuse geometry in the assembly. Utilize the Mirror Component tool to create a left and right version of parts and assemblies.

Component Properties

Component Properties control the flexibility of the sub-assembly when inserted into an assembly. Components do not translate or rotate after insertion into the assembly.

The FLATBAR parts in the LINKAGE assembly do not rotate after insertion into the PNEUMATIC TEST MODULE assembly. The LINKAGE assembly is in the Rigid State.

Insert the WHEEL-AND-AXLE assembly into the PNEUMATIC-TEST-MODULE assembly. Modify the Mate state of the LINKAGE assembly from the Rigid State to the Flexible State. The LINKAGE assembly is free to rotate.

Modify the Mate State of the AirCylinder assembly from the Rigid State to the Flexible State. The AirCylinder assembly is free to translate.

By default, when you create a sub-assembly, it is rigid. Within the parent assembly, the sub-assembly acts as a single unit and its components do not move relative to each other.

Activity: PNEUMATIC-TEST-MODULE Assembly-Insert WHEEL-AND-AXLE Assembly

---

Insert the WHEEL-AND-AXLE assembly.

467) Click the **Insert Components** tool from the Assembly toolbar. The Insert Component PropertyManager is displayed.

468) Click the **Browse** button.

469) Select **Assembly** for Files of type.

470) Double-click the **WHEEL-AND-AXLE** assembly from the SW-TUTORIAL-2009 folder.

471) Click a **position** above the FLAT-PLATE part as illustrated.

Insert a Concentric mate.

472) Click the **Mate** tool from the Assembly toolbar.

473) Click the **AXLE-3000 cylindrical** face.

474) Click the inside **TRIANGLE top hole** face. The selected faces are displayed in the Mate Selections box. Concentric is selected by default.

475) Click the **Green Check mark** ✓ .

Insert a Coincident mate.

476) Click the **WHEEL-AND-AXLE Front Plane** from the fly-out FeatureManager.

477) Click the **LINKAGE Front Plane** from the fly-out FeatureManager. Coincident is selected by default.

478) Click the **Green Check mark** ✓ .

479) Click **OK** ✓ from the Mate PropertyManager.

A Concentric mate is required between the left hole of the FLATBAR-3HOLE and right AXLE of the LINKAGE assembly.

DO NOT INSERT A CONCENTRIC MATE AT THIS TIME!

A Concentric mate will result in Mate errors.

The WHEEL-AND-AXLE is free to rotate in the PNEUMATIC-TEST-MODULE assembly. The LINKAGE assembly interferes with the WHEEL-AND-AXLE. The LINKAGE assembly is not free to rotate or translate. Mate errors will occur.

Sub-assemblies within the LINKAGE assembly are in a Rigid Mate state when inserted into the PNEUMATIC-TEST-MODULE assembly. Remove the Rigid Mate state and insert a Concentric mate between the LINKAGE assembly and the WHEEL-AND-AXLE.

Activity: PNEUMATIC-TEST-MODULE Assembly-Remove Rigid state

Remove the Rigid State.

480) Right-click the **LINKAGE** assembly from the FeatureManager.

481) Click **Component Properties** from the Context toolbar. The Component Properties dialog box is displayed.

482) Check **Flexible** in the Solve as box.

483) Click **OK** from the Component Properties dialog box. Note the icon next to the LINKAGE assembly in the FeatureManager.

484) Right-click the **AirCylinder** assembly from the FeatureManager.

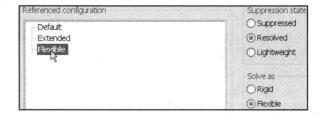

485) Click **Component Properties**.

486) Check **Flexible** in the Solve as box.

487) Click **Flexible** in the Referenced configuration box.

488) Click **OK** from the Component Properties dialog box.

Hide the FRONT-SUPPORT assembly.

489) Right-click **FRONT-SUPPORT** from the FeatureManager.

490) Click **Hide components**.

Move the LINKAGE assembly.

491) Click and drag the **front FLATBAR-9HOLE** downward. The FLATBAR-9HOLE rotates about the left AXLE.

492) Click a **position** below the WHEEL-AND-AXLE. Click **inside** the Graphics window to deselect.

Insert a Concentric mate.

493)   Click the **Mate** ✎ tool from the Assembly toolbar.

494)   Click the second bottom **AXLE** face of the LINKAGE assembly.

495)   Click the **bottom hole** of the FLATBAR-3HOLE as illustrated. Concentric is the default.

496)   Click the **Green Check mark** ✓.

497)   Click **OK** ✓ from the Mate PropertyManager.

Save the PNEUMATIC-TEST-MODULE assembly.

498)   Click **Isometric view** 🧊 from the Heads-up View toolbar.

499)   Click **Save** 💾.

The AirCylinder assembly is inserted in a Rigid state by default. The AirCylinder contains three configurations:

- Default

- Extended

- Flexible

Open the AirCylinder assembly. Modify the configuration to Flexible.

Open the LINKAGE assembly. Modify the AirCylinder Component Properties from Default to Flexible.

Activity: PNEUMATIC-TEST-MODULE Assembly - Review AirCylinder Configurations

Review the AirCylinder configurations.

500)   Right-click **LINKAGE** from the PNEUMATIC-TEST-MODULE FeatureManager.

501)   Click **Open Assembly** from the Context toolbar.

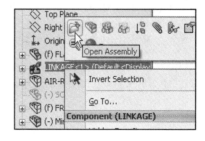

502) Right-click **AirCylinder** in the LINKAGE FeatureManager.

503) Click **Open Assembly**.

504) Click the **Configuration Manager** tab at the top of the AirCylinder FeatureManager. Three configurations are displayed: *Default*, *Extended* and *Flexible*. The current Default configuration sets the Piston Rod at 0 mm.

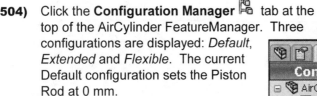

Display the Extended Configuration.
505) Double-click **Extended**. The Piston Rod of the AirCylinder extends 25mm.

Display the Flexible Configuration.
506) Double-click **Flexible**.

507) Click the **Rod-Clevis** in the Graphics window.

508) Click and drag the **Piston Rod** from left to right.

509) Click a **position** near its original location. The AirCylinder remains in the Flexible configuration for the rest of this project.

Update the LINKAGE assembly.
510) Click **Window**, **LINKAGE** from the Menu bar. The current configuration of the AirCylinder part in the LINKAGE assembly is Default. Modify the configuration.

511) Right-click **AirCylinder** from the LINKAGE assembly FeatureManager.

512) Click **Component Properties**.

513) Click **Flexible** for Solve as.

514) Click **Flexible** for Referenced configuration.

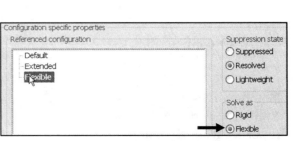

515) Click **OK**. The AirCylinder displays the Flexible configuration next to its name in the FeatureManager.

A Rebuild icon is displayed in the Assembly FeatureManager and a flexible rebuild icon at the sub-assembly level when the AirCylinder assembly is in the Flexible state.

Update the PNEUMATIC-TEST-MODULE.
516) Click **Window**, **PNEUMATIC-TEST-MODULE** assembly from the Menu bar.

Move the ROD-CLEVIS.
517) Click and drag the **ROD-CLEVIS** to the right. The WHEEL rotates in a counterclockwise direction.

518) Click and drag the **ROD-CLEVIS** to the left. The WHEEL rotates in a clockwise direction.

Display the AIR-RESERVOIR-SUPPORT assembly.
519) Right-click **AIR-RESERVOIR-SUPPORT** in the FeatureManager.

520) Click **Show components**.

Display the second FRONT-SUPPORT assembly.
521) Right-click **FRONT-SUPPORT** in the FeatureManager.

522) Click **Show components**.

523) **Display** the SCREWs in the FRONT-SUPPORT.

Save the PNEUMATIC-TEST-MODULE.

524)   Click **Isometric view** from the Heads-up View toolbar.

525)   Click **Save** .

526)   Click **Yes** to update referenced documents.

Close all documents.

527)   Click **Windows**, **Close All** from the Menu bar.

Explore additional parts and assemblies at the end of this project. Add the WEIGHT, HOOK and FLATBAR parts.

A Rebuild icon is displayed in the Assembly FeatureManager and a flexible rebuild icon at the sub-assembly level when the AirCylinder assembly is in the Flexible state.

Additional details on Show components, Hide components, Linear Component Pattern, Circular Component Pattern, Feature Driven Component Pattern, Mirror Components, Configurations, Configuration Manager are available in SolidWorks Help. Select Help, SolidWorks Help topics.

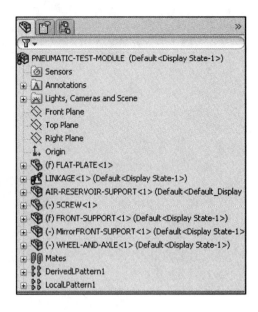

Review the PNEUMATIC-TEST-MODULE Assembly

The PNEUMATIC TEST MODULE assembly was created by combining five major mechanical sub-assemblies.

The PNEUMATIC TEST MODULE assembly utilized the FLAT-PLATE as the first component. The LINKAGE assembly, AIR-RESERVOIR-SUPPORT assembly, FRONT-SUPPORT assembly, MirrorFRONT-SUPPORT assembly and the WHEEL-AND-AXLE assembly were mated to the FLAT-PLATE part.

Work at the lowest assembly level. The LINKAGE assembly required two HEX-STANDOFF parts. The HEX-STANDOFF components were inserted into the LINKAGE assembly. The LINKAGE assembly was inserted into the PNEUMATIC-TEST-MODULE assembly.

The AIR-RESERVOIR-SUPPORT assembly was inserted into the PNEUMATIC-TEST-MODULE assembly. The SCREW component utilized a Feature Driven Component Pattern tool and the Linear Component Pattern tool to create multiple copies.

The FRONT-SUPPORT assembly was inserted into the PNEUMATIC-TEST-MODULE assembly. The Mirror Components tool created a mirrored version of the FRONT-SUPPORT assembly.

The WHEEL-AND-AXLE assembly was inserted into the PNEUMATIC-TEST-MODULE assembly. Component Properties created a Flexible state mate.

The LINKAGE assembly, "AirCylinder" is in a Flexible state.

In the section, create the final ROBOT assembly. Either use your created assemblies and components, or use the created assemblies and components provided in the Chapter 5 models folder on the enclosed CD.

Work from your hard drive. Copy the folders from the CD to your hard drive.

Final ROBOT Assembly

The final ROBOT assembly is comprised of three major sub-assemblies and the HEX-STANDOFF component:

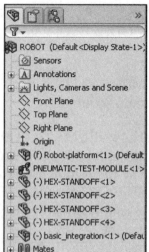

- Robot Platform assembly

- PNEUMATIC-TEST-MODULE assembly

- Basic_integration assembly

- 4 – HEX-STANDOFF components

 The LINKAGE assembly is in a Flexible state.

 A Rebuild icon is displayed in the final ROBOT Assembly FeatureManager and a flexible rebuild icon at the sub-assembly level when the AirCylinder assembly is in the Flexible state.

All assemblies and components for the final ROBOT assembly are provided in the Chapter 5 models folder on the enclosed CD.

The Robot-platform assembly was provided by **GEARS Educational Systems** (www.gearseds.com).

Combine the created new assemblies and components to develop the final ROBOT assembly. In this next section, work from the Chapter 5 models folder located on the CD in the book. If needed, copy all models from to the CD to your hard drive. Create the SW-TUTORIAL-2009/Chapter 5 models folder.

Note: Step-by-step instructions are not provided in this section for the mates.

Activity: Create the ROBOT Assembly

Create the final ROBOT assembly.

528)   Click **New** ⬜ from the Menu bar.

529)   Double-click **Assembly** from the Templates tab. The Begin Assembly PropertyManager is displayed.

Insert the Robot-platform assembly.
530)   Click the **Browse** button.

531)   Select **Assembly** for Files of type from the SW-TUTORIAL-2009/Chapter 5 models folder. Note: The Chapter 5 models folder is located on the CD in the book.

532)   Double-click **Robot-platform**.

533)   Click **OK** ✔ from the Begin Assembly PropertyManager. The Robot-platform is fixed to the assembly Origin.

Save the Assembly.
534)   Click **Save As** from the Menu bar.

535)   Enter **ROBOT** for File name in the SW-TUTORIAL-2009/Chapter 5 models folder.

536)   Enter **Final ROBOT Assembly** for Description.

537)   Click **Save**.

Insert the PNEUMATIC-TEST-MODULE assembly.

538)   Click **Insert Components** 🖱 from the Assembly toolbar. The Insert Components PropertyManager is displayed.

539)   Click the **Browse** button.

540) Double-click the **PNEUMATIC-TEST-MODULE** assembly from the SW-TUTORIAL-2009/Chapter 5 models folder.

541) Click a **position** above the Robot-platform.

💡 If an assembly or component is loaded in a Lightweight 🖼 state, right-click the **assembly name** or **component name** from the FeatureManager. Click **Set Lightweight to Resolved**.

Insert 4 HEX-STANDOFF components.

542) Click **Insert Components** 🔧 from the Assembly toolbar. The Insert Components PropertyManager is displayed.

543) Click the **Browse** button.

544) Select **Part** for Files of type from the SW-TUTORIAL-2009/Chapter 5 models folder.

545) Double-click **HEX-STANDOFF**.

546) **Pin** the Insert Components PropertyManager.

547) Click **four positions** as illustrated for the four HEX-STANDOFF components.

548) **Un-Pin** the Insert Components PropertyManager.

549) Click **OK** ✓ from the Insert Components PropertyManager.

Insert Coincident and Concentric mates between the four HEX-STANDOFF components and the PNEUMATIC-TEST-MODULE and the Robot-platform as illustrated. View the location of the HEX-STANDOFF components on the PNEUMATIC-TEST-MODULE assembly.

View the location of the HEX-STANDOFF
components on the Robot-platform as
illustrated.

550) **Expand** the Mates folder. View
the created mates.

Insert the basic_integration assembly.

551) Click the **Browse** button.

552) Select **Assembly** for Files of type from the
SW-TUTORIAL-2009/Chapter 5 models
folder.

```
⊟ 🔗 Mates
    ⟋ Coincident1 (PNEUMATIC-TEST-MODULE<1>,HEX-STANDOFF<1>)
    ◎ Concentric1 (PNEUMATIC-TEST-MODULE<1>,HEX-STANDOFF<2>)
    ⟋ Coincident2 (PNEUMATIC-TEST-MODULE<1>,HEX-STANDOFF<2>)
    ◎ Concentric2 (PNEUMATIC-TEST-MODULE<1>,HEX-STANDOFF<3>)
    ⟋ Coincident3 (PNEUMATIC-TEST-MODULE<1>,HEX-STANDOFF<3>)
    ◎ Concentric3 (PNEUMATIC-TEST-MODULE<1>,HEX-STANDOFF<4>)
    ⟋ Coincident4 (PNEUMATIC-TEST-MODULE<1>,HEX-STANDOFF<4>)
    ◎ Concentric5 (Robot-platform<1>,HEX-STANDOFF<1>)
    ◎ Concentric6 (Robot-platform<1>,HEX-STANDOFF<3>)
    ◎ Concentric7 (Robot-platform<1>,HEX-STANDOFF<4>)
    ◎ Concentric8 (Robot-platform<1>,HEX-STANDOFF<2>)
    ⟋ Coincident7 (Robot-platform<1>,HEX-STANDOFF<3>)
```

553) Double-click **basic_integration**.

554) Click a position to the **left** of the
assembly as illustrated.

Insert Coincident and Concentric mates
between the two screws in the
basic_integration assembly and the
PNEUMATIC-TEST-MODULE
assembly.

555) **Expand** the Mates folder. View the
created mates.

Save the ROBOT assembly.

556) Click **Save** 🖫. You are finished with the final
ROBOT assembly.

```
◎ Concentric10 (PNEUMATIC-TEST-MODULE<1>,basic_integration<1>)
⟋ Coincident9 (PNEUMATIC-TEST-MODULE<1>,basic_integration<1>)
⟋ Coincident10 (PNEUMATIC-TEST-MODULE<1>,basic_integration<1>)
◎ Concentric12 (PNEUMATIC-TEST-MODULE<1>,basic_integration<1>)
```

Project Summary

In this Project, you created and worked with multiple documents in sub-assemblies and assemblies. You developed sound assembly modeling techniques that utilized Standard mates, fixed components, symmetry, component patterns, and mirrored components.

The WHEEL-AND-AXLE assembly combined the WHEEL-FLATBAR assembly with the AXLE-3000 part, SHAFTCOLLAR-500 part and HEX-ADAPTER part.

The WHEEL-FLATBAR assembly combined the 3HOLE-SHAFTCOLLAR assembly and 5HOLE-SHAFTCOLLAR assembly.

The PNEUMATIC-TEST-MODULE assembly combined four major mechanical sub-assemblies. The final ROBOT assembly was comprised of three major sub-assemblies and the HEX-STANDOFF component.

Organize your assemblies. For an exercise, create an assembly Layout Diagram of the final ROBOT assembly to determine the grouping of components and assemblies.

Project Terminology

Mates: A mate is a Geometric relationship between components in an assembly.

Circular Pattern: A Circular Pattern repeats features or geometry in a polar array. A Circular Patten requires an axis of revolution, the number of instances and an angle.

Component Pattern: There are two methods to define a component pattern in an assembly. A Derive Component Pattern utilizes an existing feature pattern. A Local Component pattern utilizes geometry in the assembly to arrange instances in a Linear or Circular pattern.

Component Properties: The properties of a component, part or assembly are controlled through Component Properties. The Rigid/Flexible Mate State property and Configuration property were explored in this project. Component Properties are used to define visibility and color.

ConfigurationManager: The ConfigurationManager on the left side of the Graphics window is utilized to create, select, and view the configurations of parts and assemblies.

Dome: A Dome feature creates a spherical or elliptical feature from a selected face.

Loft: A Loft feature blends two or more profiles. Each profile is sketched on a separate plane.

Mirror Component: A mirror component creates a mirrored or copied part or assembly. A mirrored component is sometimes called a "right-hand" version of the original "left hand" version.

Replace: The Replace command substitutes one or more open instances of a component in an assembly with a different component.

Revolved Cut: A Revolved Cut removes material. A sketched profile is revolved around a centerline. The Revolved Cut requires a direction and an angle of revolution.

Swept: A Swept feature adds/removes material by moving a profile along a path. A basic Swept feature requires two sketches. The first sketch is called the path. The second sketch is called profile. The profile and path are sketched on perpendicular planes.

Engineering Journal

1. Engineers research, specify and test the components utilized in their designs. The PNEUMATIC TEST MODULE assembly was partially completed in this project. Additional pneumatic components are required.

Knob

The Regulator utilizes a plastic knob to control the pressure from the Air Reservoir.

The Knob controls the Pressure at P2 by adjusting the screw loading on the setting Spring. The Main valve is held open, allowing flow from the inlet, P1 to the outlet, P2. When the air consumption rate drops, the force at P2 increases. This increase in force causes the Diaphragm to drop maintaining the constant pressure through the valve.

Regulator Assembly
Courtesy of SMC
Corporation of America

Images Courtesy of SMC Corporation of America

Utilize the internet to research different types of Air Regulators. What design parameters are required for the Regulator before placing an order to purchase one?

_____
_____
_____
_____

2. Pneumatic Applications.

Plastic components are utilized in a variety of applications. The ON/OFF/PURGE value utilizes plastic components for the Knob and Inlet and Outlet ports.

The ON/OFF/PURGE valve controls the airflow from the Regulator. The valve knob indiates the direction of flow. The valve is Off when the knob is perpendicular to the direction of flow.

ON/OFF/PURGE Valve
Courtesy of SMC
Corporation of America

The valve is On when the knob is parallel to the direction of flow.

Write a 2 step operating procedure to instruct your customer how to operate the valve. Indicate the position of the value and the state of the air in each step.

Valve Operating Procedure

1 _____

_____

_____

2 _____

_____

Questions

1. What function does the Save as copy check box perform when saving a part under a new name?

2. True or False. Never reuse geometry from one part to create another part.

3. Describe 5 Assembly techniques utilized in this project.

4. True or False. A fixed (f) component cannot move and is locked to the Origin.

5. Describe the purpose of an Assembly Layout diagram.

6. Describe the difference between a Feature Driven Component Pattern and a Linear Component Pattern.

7. Describe the difference between copied geometry and mirrored geometry utilizing the Mirror Components tool.

8. True of False. An assembly contains one or more configurations.

9. Review the Design Intent section in the Introduction. Identify how you incorporated design intent into the assembly.

10. Review the Keyboard Short Cut keys in the Appendix. Identify the Short Cut keys you incorporated into this project. What is the g key used for?

Exercises

Exercise 5.1: Regulator-Standoff Assembly.

The Regulator assembly is a pneumatic component. The Regulator assembly is available in the pneumtatic component folder or from the Chapter 4 Homework folder which are on the CD in the book.

The Regulator assembly cannot be directly fastened to the PNEUMATIC-TEST-MODULE assembly. The slotted holes in the bracket do not fit directly onto the FLAT-PLATE.

- Insert two HEX-STANDOFF parts.
  Note: Use the View, Temporary Axis option.

- Insert two SCREWs as illustrated.

Exercise 5.2: VALVE-BRACKET Assembly.

The ON-OFF-PURGE-VALVE assembly cannot be directly fastened to the FLAT-PLATE.

- Create the Servo-Bracket part on the Top Plane.

The VALVE-BRACKET assembly consists of the ON-OFF-PURGE-VALVE assembly, the Servo-Bracket and two HEX-STANDOFF parts.

The ON-OFF-PURGE VALVE assembly is available in the pneumtatic component folder and the Chapter 4 Homework folder on the Multi-media CD.

- The Servo Bracket Part is machined from 0.09in, [2.7mm] Stainless Steel flat stock.

- The ⌀4.2mm, [.165in] Mounting Holes fasten to the back Slot Cuts of the Servo Bracket.

- The Servo-Bracket default units are inches. The Purge-Valve Assembly default units are millimeters.

- Engineers and designers work with components in multiple units such as inches and millimeters. Utilize Tools, Options, Document Properties, Units to check default units and precision.

Servo Bracket   Purge-Valve Assembly

The Servo-Bracket Part illustration represents part dimensions, only.

Servo Bracket
Part Dimensions

- Locate the center circle at the part Origin.

- Utilize a Mirror Feature.

- Utilize a Distance
  Mate to align the
  Mounting Holes
  of the ON-OFF-
  PURGE-VALVE
  Valve to the Slot
  Cuts of the Servo
  Bracket.

Detail A

The valve knob
indicates the
direction of flow.
The valve is off when the knob is perpendicular to the direction
of flow.

The valve is on when the knob is parallel to the direction of flow.

Review the ON-OFF-PURGE-VALVE Configurations and Mates. The Angle Mate
controls the orientation of the Knob.

Valve OFF   Valve ON

Exercise 5.3: **FLATBAR Design Table**.

- Create FLATBAR configurations with a Design Table.

The configurations contain 11, 13, 15, and 17 holes. Note the 0.09in dimension.

	A	B	C	D	E	F	G
1	Design Table for: FLATBAR						
2		D1@Sketch1	D2@Sketch1	D1@Extrude1	D1@Sketch3	D3@LPattern1	D1@LPattern1
3	Default	4.000	0.25	0.09	0.19	0.5	9
4	11HOLE	5.000	0.25	0.09	0.19	0.5	11
5	13HOLE	6.000	0.25	0.09	0.19	0.5	13
6	15HOLE	7.000	0.25	0.09	0.19	0.5	15
7	17HOLE	8.000	0.25	0.09	0.19	0.5	17
8							
9							
10							

Sheet1

Exercise 5.4: **SOLENOID-VALVE Assembly and PNEUMATIC-TEST-MODULE Assembly**.

The 3Way SOLENOID-VALVE utilizes a plastic housing to protect the internal electronic components. The 3Way Solenoid value controls the electrical operation of to the AirCylinder.

The Solenoid acts like a switch. The SOLENOID-VALVE is assembled to the PNEUMATIC-TEST-MODULE with cable ties.

Insert the following components into PNEUMATIC TEST MODULE assembly:

- SOLENOID-VALVE assembly.
- VALVE-BRACKET assembly.
- REGULATOR-STANDOFF assembly.
- WEIGHT-AND-LINK assembly.

3WAY SOLENOID VALVE
Courtesy of SMC Corporation of America

Exercise 5.5: Drive Motor Mount assembly.

- Create the Drive Motor Mount Assembly. The Drive Motor Mount assembly is utilized on a MARS Rover Training Robot (courtesy of Gears Educational Systems). Create the Drive Motor Mount assembly from the components located on the enclosed CD in the book.

- Create an Exploded view that represents how the components would be assembled in manufacturing.

ITEM NO.	PART NUMBER	QTY.
1	4-40_5-8_socket_capsc	8
2	4-40_nut	8
3	90_deg_semi_tube	1
4	4_40_washer	8
5	chamf-1-25_tube	1
6	semi-tube_master4	1
7	pittmam_motor	1
8	hex_axle_adapter	1
9	solid_swivell_arm2	1
10	wheel assembly	1
11	hex_nut	1
12	#10_1.5_cap screw	2
13	#10_nut	2

Exercise 5.6: **GEAR-DRIVE Assembly.**

Create the GEAR-DRIVE assembly.

DC MOTOR

The DC Motor shaft drives the
36TOOTH-GEAR. The TIRE, WHEEL,
60TOOTH-GEAR parts are all located
on the same axle rod and rotate at the
same angular velocity.

The TIRE, 60TOOTH-GEAR,
36TOOTH-GEAR and SHAFT -
PLATE2 parts and BearingPlate-
Bushing assembly are located on the CD
contained with the text. Copy these
components to the SW-TUTORIAL file
folder.

GEAR-DRIVE Assembly
Courtesy of Gears Educational Systems, LLC

You created the other components in the
projects and exercises.

Design unknowns:

- The AXLE-ROD length required to mount the WHEEL, TIRE and 60TOOTH-
  GEAR.

- Clearance distance between the 60TOOTH-GEAR and the WHEEL-TIRE assembly.
  Stack multiple LARGE-WASHER parts for the clearance distance.

- Mating Distance between the 36TOOTH-GEAR and the 60TOOTH-GEAR.

Utilize your skills to create the following documents:

- Draw an assembly layout listing all parts, sub-assemblies and assemblies on paper.

- In SolidWorks create a top level assembly and sub-assemblies.

- In SolidWorks create a top level assembly drawing and sub-assembly drawings with
  Bill of Materials.

- In SolidWorks create individual part drawings for machined parts.

- In SolidWorks create exploded view and animation of the GEAR-DRIVE.

Note: Balloons have been enlarged. Actual GearsEds (www.gearseds.com) purchased
parts may vary from the model file.

- The IM15-MOUNT PLATE was created in the Project 2 exercises.

The gears in the assembly utilize imported
geometry.

Parts List for GEAR-DRIVE assembly:

ITEM NO.	PART NUMBER:	DESCRIPTION:	QTY:
1	GIDS-SC-10003	SHAFT-PLATE2	1
2	GIDS-SC-10017	AXLE-ROD	1
3	GIDS-SC-60036	36-TOOTH, 24-PITCH GEAR	1
4	GIDS-SC-10014	WHEEL	1
5	GIDS-SC-10013	HEX-ADAPTER	2
6	GIDS-SC-10012-3-16	LARGE-WASHERS	?
7	GIDS-SC-60060	60-TOOTH, 24-PITCH GEAR	1
8	GIDS-SC-10004	TIRE-RUBBER	1
9	GIDS-SC-10010	BEARING PLATE-BUSHING ASM	1
10	GIDS-SC-10015	HEX-STANDOFF	2
11	GIDS-SC-10016-SW	SMALL WASHER ¼ IN	8
12	GIDS-SC-10016-MS	MACHINE SCREW 10-24X3/8	6
13	GIDS-SC-10012-3-16	SMALL SHAFT-COLLAR	1
14	GIDS-SC-10009	IM15-MOUNT PLATE	1
15	GIDS-MC-11515	MOTOR DC	1

Answers will vary. Simplify a large design problem. Create multiple sub-assemblies.

Notes:

Project 6

Introduction to the Certified SolidWorks Associate Exam

Below are the desired outcomes and usage competencies based on the completion of Project 6.

Given:
A = 63, B = 50, C = 100
Material: Copper
Units: MMGS
Density: .0089 g/mm^3
All HOLES THROUGH ALL

Origin

Desired Outcomes:	Usage Competencies:
• Procedure and process knowledge	• Familiarity of the CSWA exam.
• Exam categories:	• Comprehension of the skill sets to past the CSWA exam.
o Basic Theory and Drawing Theory, Part Modeling, Advanced Part Modeling, Assembly Modeling and Advanced Modeling Theory and Analysis	• Awareness of the question types. • Capability to locate additional CSWA exam information.

Notes:

Notes:

Project 6 – Certified SolidWorks Associate CSWA Exam

Project Objective

Provide a basic introduction into the curriculum and categories of the Certified SolidWorks Associate CSWA exam. Awareness to the exam procedure, process, and required model knowledge needed to take and past the CSWA exam. The five exam categories are:

- Basic Theory and Drawing Theory

- Part Modeling

- Advanced Part Modeling

- Assembly Modeling

- Advanced Modeling Theory and Analysis (SimulationXpress/COSMOSXpress)

Introduction

SolidWorks Corporation offers two levels of certification representing increasing levels of expertise in 3D CAD design as it applies to engineering: *Certified SolidWorks Associate CSWA* and the *Certified SolidWorks Professional CSWP*.

The CSWA certification indicates a foundation in and apprentice knowledge of 3D CAD design and engineering practices and principles. The main requirement for obtaining the CSWA certification is to take and pass the 3 hour, seven question on-line proctored exam at a Certified SolidWorks CSWA Provider, "university, college, technical, vocational, or secondary educational institution" and to sign the SolidWorks Confidentiality Agreement.

Passing this exam provides students the chance to prove their knowledge and expertise and to be part of a world wide industry certification standard.

⌖ At this time, the CSWA exam is given in both SolidWorks 2007 and SolidWorks 2008.

Intended Audience

The intended audience for the CSWA exam is anyone with a minimum of 6 - 9 months of SolidWorks experience and basic knowledge of engineering fundamentals and practices. SolidWorks recommends that you review their SolidWorks Tutorials on Parts, Assemblies, Drawings, and SolidWorks SimulationXpress/COSMOSXpress as a prerequisite and have at least 45 hours of classroom time learning SolidWorks or using SolidWorks with basic engineering design principles and practices.

To prepare for the CSWA exam, it is recommended that you first perform the following:

- Take a CSWA exam preparation class or review a text book written for the CSWA exam.

- Complete the SolidWorks Tutorials

- Practice creating models from the isometric working drawings sections of any Technical Drawing or Engineering Drawing Documentation text books.

- Complete the sample CSWA exam in a timed environment, available at www.solidworks.com.

Additional references to help you prepare are as follows:

- SolidWorks Users Guide, SolidWorks Corporation, 2009.

- Certified SolidWorks 2008 Associate CSWA Exam Book, Delmar Thomson 2008.

- Bertoline, Wiebe, Miller, Fundamentals of Graphics Communication, Irwin, 1995.

- Earle, James, Engineering Design Graphics, Addison Wesley, 1999.

- Hibbler, R.C, Engineering Mechanics Statics and Dynamics, 8th ed, Prentice Hall, Saddle River, NJ.

- Hoelscher, Springer, Dobrovolny, Graphics for Engineers, John Wiley, 1968.

- Jensen, Cecil, Interpreting Engineering Drawings, Glencoe, 2002.

- Jensen & Helsel, Engineering Drawing and Design, Glencoe, 1990.

- Lieu, Sorby, Visualization, Modeling, and Graphics for Engineering, Delmar Thomson, 2007.

- Madsen, David, Engineering Drawing and Design, Delmar Thomson, 2007.

- Planchard & Planchard, Drawing and Detailing with SolidWorks, SDC Pub., Mission, KS 2008.

💡 View the Certified SolidWorks Associate CSWA exam pdf file on the enclosed CD for a sample exam!

CSWA Exam Content

The CSWA exam is divided into five key categories. Questions on the timed exam are provided in a random manor. The following information provides general guidelines for the content likely to be included on the exam. However, other related topics may also appear on any specific delivery of the exam. In order to better reflect the contents of the exam and for clarity purposes, the guidelines below may change at any time without notice.

Basic Theory and Drawing Theory (2 Questions - Total 10 Points)

- Identify and apply basic concepts in SolidWorks

- Recognize 3D modeling techniques:

  - Understand how parts, assemblies, and drawings are related

  - Identify the feature type, parameters, and dimensions

  - Identify the correct standard reference planes: Top, Right, and Front

  - Determine the design intent for a model

- Identify and understand the procedure for the following:

  - Assign and edit material to a part

  - Apply the Measure tool to a part or an assembly

  - Locate the Center of mass, and Principal moments of inertia relative to the default coordinate location, and Origin.

  - Calculate the overall mass and volume of a part

- Use SolidWorks Help:

  - Contents, Index, and Search tabs

- Identify the process of creating a simple drawing from a part or an assembly:

- Identify the procedure to create a named drawing view:

  - Model, Projected, Auxiliary, Section, Aligned Section, Detail, Standard, Broken-out Section, Break, Crop, and Alternate Position

- Specify Document Properties:

  - Select Unit System

  - Set Precision

Part Modeling (1 Question - Total 30 Points)

- Read and understand an Engineering document:

  - Identify the Sketch plane, part Origin location, part dimensions, geometric relations, and design intent of the sketch and feature

- Build a part from a detailed dimensioned illustration using the following SolidWorks tools and features:

  - 2D & 3D sketch tools

  - Extruded Boss/Base

  - Extruded Cut

  - Fillet

  - Mirror

  - Revolved Base

  - Chamfer

  - Reference geometry

  - Plane

  - Axis

  - Calculate the overall mass and volume of the created part

- Locate the Center of mass for the created part relative to the Origin

Advanced Part Modeling (1 Question -Total 20 Points)

- Specify Document Properties

- Interpret engineering terminology:

  - Create and manipulate a coordinate system

- Build an advanced part from a detailed dimensioned illustration using the following tools and features:

  - 2D & 3D Sketch tools

  - Extruded Boss/Base

  - Extruded Cut

  - Fillet

  - Mirror

  - Revolved Boss/Base

  - Linear & Circular Pattern

  - Chamfer

  - Revolved Cut

- Locate the Center of mass relative to the part Origin

- Create a coordinate system location

- Locate the Center of mass relative to a created coordinate system

Assembly Modeling (1 Question - Total 30 Points)

- Specify Document Properties

- Identify and build the components to construct the assembly from a detailed illustration using the following features:

  - Extruded Boss/Base

  - Extruded Cut

  - Fillet

  - Mirror

  - Revolved Boss/Base

  - Revolved Cut

  - Linear Pattern

- Chamfer

- Hole Wizard

- Identify the first fixed component in an assembly

- Build a bottom-up assembly with the following Standard mates:

  - Coincident, Concentric, Parallel, Perpendicular, Tangent, Angle, and Distance

  - Aligned, Anti-Aligned options

- Apply the Mirror Component tool

- Locate the Center of mass relative to the assembly Origin

- Create a coordinate system location

- Locate the Center of mass relative to a created coordinate system

- Calculate the overall mass and volume for the created assembly

- Mate the first component with respect to the assembly reference planes

Advanced Modeling Theory and Analysis (2 Questions - Total 10 Points)

- Understand basic Engineering analysis definitions

- Understand the procedure and process to apply COSMOSXpress/SolidWorks SimulationXpress to a simple part

- Understand the functions and differences of the following SolidWorks analysis tools:

  - COSMOSXpress/SimulationXpress, COSMOSWorks Designer/SolidWorks Simulation, COSMOSWorks Professional/SolidWorks Simulation Professional, COSMOSMotion/SolidWorks Motion, and COSMOSFloWorks/SolidWorks Flow Simulation.

Why the CSWA exam?

The CAD world has many different certifications available. Some of these certifications are sponsored by vendors and some by consortiums of different vendors. Regardless of the sponsor of the certifications, most CAD professionals today recognize the need to become certified to prove their skills, prepare for new job searches, and to learn new skill, while at their existing jobs.

Specifying a CSWA or CSWP certification on your resume is a great way to increase your chances of landing a new job, getting a promotion, or looking more qualified when representing your company on a consulting job.

Obtain the CSWA Certification

For Educational customers, SolidWorks Corporation requires that you take and pass the 3 hour on-line proctored exam in a secure environment at a designated CSWA Provider and to sign the SolidWorks Confidentiality Agreement. A CSWA Provider can be a university, college, technical, vocational, or secondary educational institution. Contact your local SolidWorks Value Added Reseller (VAR) or instructor for information on CSWA Providers.

Commercial customers can obtain information on taking the CSWA exam through the SolidWorks Customer Portal.

There are five key categories in the CSWA exam. The minimum passing grade is 70 out of 100 points. There are two questions in both the Basic Theory and Drawing, and Advanced Modeling Theory and Analysis Categories, (multiple choice, single answer or fill in the blank) and one question in each of the Part modeling, Advanced Part Modeling and Analysis, and the Assembly Modeling categories. The single questions are on an in-depth illustrated dimension model. All questions are in a multiple choice single answer or fill in the blank format. There is no partial credit on exam questions.

Prepare to pass the CSWA exam

Taking a SolidWorks class at a university, college, technical, vocational, or secondary educational institution or time in industry using SolidWorks does not mean that you will automatically pass the CSWA exam. In fact, the CSWA exam purposefully attempts to make the questions prove that you know the material well by making you apply the concepts in a real world situation. The CSWA exam questions tend to be a fair amount more involved than just creating a single sketch, part, or simple assembly. The exam requires that you know and apply the knowledge to different scenarios.

How does an institution become a CSWA Provider?

A Certified SolidWorks Associate CSWA Provider is any university, college, technical, vocational, or secondary educational institution. All CSWA Providers must complete the CSWA Provider application: Visit www.solidworks.com. The educational institution provides the following to administer the CSWA exam:

• Valid SolidWorks Maintenance agreement

• Recommended computer hardware with the required internet access

• Printer for CSWA certificates

- Proctor to administer the CSWA exam

- Reviewed CSWA "Terms and Conditions" document

Educational institution instructors or administrators can contact their Value Added Reseller for additional information.

Exam day

Candidates must acknowledge the SolidWorks CSWA Certification and Confidentiality Agreement online at the authorized CSWA Provider site prior to taking the exam. Candidates will not be able to proceed with the exam and a refund will not be provided. Signing this legal agreement is required to be officially certified.

Gather personal information prior to exam registration:

- Legal name (from government issued ID)

- CSWA Certification exam event code from the Provider

- Valid email address

- Method of payment

Students will not be able to use notes, books, calculators, PDA's, cell phones, or materials not authorized by a SolidWorks Certified Provider or SolidWorks during the exam.

The CSWA exam, at this time, is provided in the following languages: English, Brazilian Portuguese, Chinese-S, Chinese-T, French, German, Italian, Japanese, Spanish, and Korean.

Exams may contain non-scored items to collect performance data on new items. Non-scored items are not used in determining the passing score nor are reported in a subsection of the score report. All non-scored items are randomly placed in the exam with sufficient time calculated and given to complete the entire exam.

At the completion of the computer-based on-line exam, candidates receive a score report along with a score breakout by exam section and the passing score for the given exam. Note: All students are required to sign and return all supplied papers/notes that were taken during the exam to the onsite proctor before leaving the testing room.

What do I get when I pass the exam?

After a candidate passes the CSWA exam and signs the required agreements an email is sent to you to visit the following website: www.virtualtester.com/solidworks.

Certified candidates are authorized to use the appropriate CSWA SolidWorks certification logo indicating certification status. Prior to use, they must read and acknowledge the SolidWorks Certification Logo Agreement. Logos can be downloaded through the CSWA Certification Tracking System.

The CSWA Certification Tracking System provides a record of both exam and certification status. Candidates and certification holders are expected to keep contact information up to date for receiving notifications from SolidWorks.

VirtualTester is a system for delivering and managing multiple choice tests over the internet. The system consists of a web service complete with company and user database, question editor and a client.

The VirtualTester website: www.virtualtester.com/solidworks provides the following menu options:

At the time of this book, the following dialog box with *Actions*, *Downloads*, *Search* and *More* is provided.

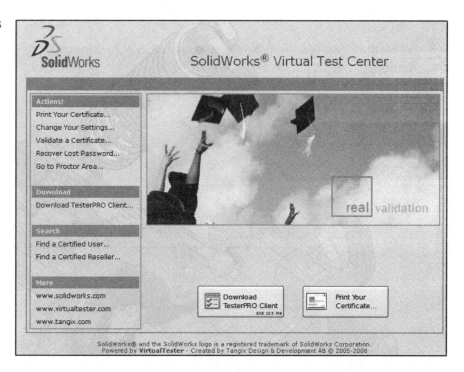

Use the login credentials sent by email from virtualtester.com. If you do not receive the email, check your spam filters, junk email filters, etc. to receive the email.

A certificate suitable for framing is provided with your name and CSWA Certification ID.

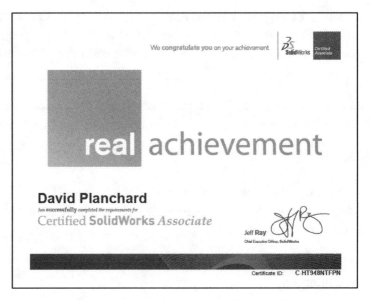

View the Certified SolidWorks Associate CSWA exam pdf file on the enclosed CD for a sample exam!

Basic Theory and Drawing Theory

Basic Theory and Drawing Theory is one of the five categories on the CSWA exam. There are two questions on the CSWA exam in this category. Each question is worth five points. The two questions are in a multiple choice single answer or fill in the blank format and requires general knowledge and understanding of the SolidWorks User Interface, FeatureManager, ConfigurationManager, Sketch toolbar, Feature toolbar, Drawing view methods, and basic 3D modeling techniques and engineering principles. Spend no more than 10 minutes on each question in this category for the exam. Manage your time.

Sample Questions in the category

In the Basic Theory and Drawing Theory category, an exam question could read:

Question 1: Identify the Sketch plane for the Extrude1 feature.

A: Top Plane

B: Front Plane

C: Right Plane

D: Left Plane

Origin

The correct answer is A.

Question 2: Identify the Sketch plane for the Extrude1 feature.

A: Top Plane

B: Front Plane

C: Right Plane

D: Left Plane

Origin

The correct answer is B.

Question 3: Identify the Sketch plane for the Extrude1 feature.

A: Top Plane

B: Front Plane

C: Right Plane

D: Left Plane

The correct answer is B.

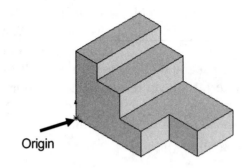

Origin

Question 4: Identify the Sketch plane for the Extrude1 feature.

A: Top Plane

B: Front Plane

C: Right Plane

D: Left Plane

The correct answer is A.

Origin

Question 5: Identify the number of instances in the illustrated model.

A: 7

B: 5

C: 8

D: None

The correct answer is B.

Question 6: Identify the number of instances in the illustrated model.

A: 7

B: 4

C: 8

D: None

The correct answer is B.

Question 7: Identify the material category for 6061 Alloy.

A: Steel

B: Iron

C: Aluminum Alloys

D: Other Alloys

E: None of the provided

The correct answer is C.

Question 8: In an assembly, the (-) symbol means?

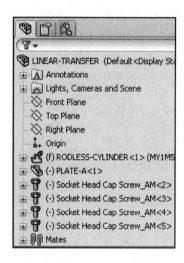

A: Reference is unlocked

B: The reference is broken

C: A floating component

D: A fixed component

The correct answer is C.

Question 9: In an assembly, the symbol before a component <1> indicates?

A: First inserted instance of the component

B: First inserted instance of a drawing

C: Nothing

D: External reference broken

The correct answer is A.

Question 10: What is the default part file format in SolidWorks?

A: *.sldfop

B: *.sldprt

C: *.hjyy

D: *.pprt

The correct answer is B.

Question 11: Which is a valid assembly format in SolidWorks?

A: *.tiffe

B: *.jpgg

C: * .assmy

D: * .stl

The correct answer is D.

Question 12: Identify the view procedure. To create the following view, you need to insert a:

- A: Open Spline

- B: Closed Spline

- C: 3 Point Arc

- D: None of the above

The correct answer is B.

Question 13: Identify the illustrated view type.

- A: Crop view

- B: Section view

- C: Projected view

- D: None of the above

The correct answer is A.

Question 14: Identify the illustrated Drawing view.

- A: Projected View

- B: Alternative Position View

- C: Extended View

- D: Aligned Section View

The correct answer is B.

Question 15: Identify the illustrated Drawing view.

- A: Crop View

- B: Break View

- C: Broken-out Section View

- D: Aligned Section View

The correct answer is B.

Question 16: Identify the illustrated Drawing view.

- A: Section View

- B: Crop View

- C: Broken-out Section View

- D: Aligned Section View

The correct answer is A.

Question 17: Identify the view procedure. To create the following view, you need to insert a:

- A: Rectangle Sketch tool

- B: Closed Profile: Spline

- C: Open Profile: Circle

- D: None of the above

The correct answer is a B.

Part Modeling

Part Modeling is one of the five categories on the CSWA exam. This category covers the knowledge to identify the part Origin, design intent, and key features to build a simple part from a detailed dimensioned illustration.

There is one question on the CSWA exam in this category. The question is in a multiple choice single answer or fill in the blank format. The question is worth thirty points. You are required to build a model, with six or more features and to answer a question either on the overall mass, volume, or the location of the Center of mass relative to the default part Origin. Spend no more than 40 minutes on the question in this category. This is a timed exam. Manage your time.

☀ The main difference between the Part Modeling category and the Advanced Part modeling category is the complexity of the sketches and the number of dimensions and geometric relations along with an increase in the number of features.

Sample Questions in the category

In the Part Modeling category, an exam question could read:

Question 1: Build the illustrated from the provided information. Calculate the Center of mass to the part Origin with the provided information.

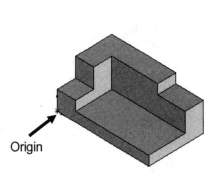

Origin

Given:
A = 100
B = 40
Material: Brass
Density = .0085 g/mm^3
Units: MMGS

Think about the steps that are required to build this model. There are numerous ways to build models. The CSWA is a three hour timed exam. Work efficiently.

- A: X = 43.36 millimeters, Y = 15.00 millimeters, Z = -37.69 millimeters

- B: X = 1.63 inches, Y = 1.01 inches, Z = -0.04 inches

- C: X = 44.44 millimeters, Y = -15.00millimeters, Z = -37.02 millimeters

- D: X = 1.66 inches, Y = 1.04 inches, Z = -1.04 inches

The correct answer is A.

Mass = 1105.00 grams

Volume = 130000.00 cubic millimeters

Surface area = 23400.00 millimeters^2

Center of mass: (millimeters)
  X = 43.46
  Y = 15.00
  Z = -37.69

As an exercise, recalculate the Center of mass using the IPS unit system.

View the provided Part FeatureManagers. Both FeatureManagers create the same illustrated model. In Option1, there are four sketches and four features that are used to build the model.

In Option2, there are three sketches and three features that are used to build the model. Which FeatureManager is better? In a timed exam, optimize your time and use the least amount of features through mirror, pattern, symmetry, etc.

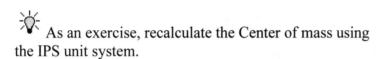

All models for Project 6 are located on the CD in the book.

Question 2: Build the illustrated model from the provided information. Locate the Center of mass relative to the default coordinate system, Origin.

Origin

Given:
A = 4.00, B = 2.50
Material: Alloy Steel
Density = .278 lb/in^3
Units: IPS
Decimal places = 2

- A: X = -1.63 inches, Y = 1.48 inches, Z = -1.09 inches

- B: X = 1.63 inches, Y = 1.01 inches, Z = -0.04 inches

- C: X = 43.49 inches, Y = -0.86 inches, Z = -0.02 inches

- D: X = 1.63 inches, Y = 1.01 inches, Z = -0.04 inches

Origin

Center of mass relative
to the part Origin

The correct answer is B.

In the Part Modeling category of the exam; you are required to read and understand an engineering document, set document properties, identify the correct Sketch planes, apply the correct Sketch and Feature tools, and apply material to build a simple part.

Note the Depth/Deep ⊽ symbol with a 1.50 dimension associated with the hole. The hole Ø.562 has a three decimal place precision. Hint: Insert three features to build this model: Extruded Base, and two Extruded Cuts. Insert a 3D sketch for the first Extruded Cut feature. You are required to have knowledge in 3D sketching for the exam.

Question 3: Build the illustrated model from the provided information. What is the volume of the part?

Origin

Given:
A = .75, B = 2.50
Material: 2014 Alloy
Density = .10 lb/in^3
Units: IPS
Decimal places = 2

A: 18.88 cubic inches

B: 19.55 cubic inches

C: 17.99 cubic inches

D: 16.25 cubic inches

The correct answer is D.

 To build this model, insert two features: Extruded Base, Extruded Cut. Apply a closed four point 3D sketch as the profile for the Extruded Cut feature. The part Origin is located in the lower left front corner of the model.

 All models for Project 6 are located on the CD in the book.

Question 4: Build the illustrated model
from the provided information. Locate
the Center of mass of the part?

Given:
A = 40, B = 20
All Thru Holes
Material: Copper
Density = .0089 g/mm^3
Units: MMGS

- A: X = 0.00 millimeters, Y = 19.79
  millimeters, Z = 0.00 millimeters

- B: X = 0.00 inches, Y = 19.79 inches, Z = 0.04 inches

- C: X = 19.79 millimeters, Y = 0.00 millimeters, Z = 0.00
  millimeters

- D: X = 0.00 millimeters, Y = 19.49 millimeters, Z = 0.00
  millimeters

- The correct answer is A.

Question 5: Build the illustrated model
from the provided information. Locate the
Center of mass of the part.

Given:
A = Ø12
Material: Cast Alloy Steel
Density = .0073 g/mm^3
Units: MMGS

- A: X = 10.00 millimeters, Y = -79.79 millimeters,
  Z: = 0.00 millimeters

- B: X = 9.79 millimeters, Y = -0.13 millimeters,
  Z = 0.00 millimeters

- C: X = 9.77 millimeters, Y = -0.10 millimeters,
  Z = -0.02 millimeters

- D: X = 10.00 millimeters, Y = 19.49 millimeters,
  Z = 0.00 millimeters

- The correct answer is B.

Question 6: Build the illustrated model
from the provided information. Locate
the Center of mass of the part.

```
38 DIA
57 DIA SF
1 DEEP
2 HOLES
```

Given:
A = 76, B = 127
Material: 2014 Alloy
Density: .0028 g/mm^3
Units: MMGS
ALL ROUNDS EQUAL 6MM

There are numerous ways to build this model.
Think about the various features that create the model.
Hint: Insert seven features to build this model: Extruded Base,
Extruded Cut, Extruded Boss, Fillet, Extruded Cut, Mirror, and an
second Fillet. Apply symmetry.

In the exam, create the left half of the model first, and then apply
the Mirror feature. This is a timed exam.

- A: X = 49.00 millimeters, Y = 45.79 millimeters, Z = 0.00 millimeters

- B: X = 0.00 millimeters, Y = 19.79 millimeters, Z = 0.04 millimeters

- C: X = 49.21 millimeters, Y = 46.88 millimeters, Z = 0.00 millimeters

- D: X = 48.00 millimeters, Y = 46.49 millimeters, Z = 0.00 millimeters

The correct answer is C.

Mass = 3437.29 grams

Volume = 1227602.20 cubic millimeters

Surface area = 101091.11 millimeters^2

Center of mass: (millimeters)
   X = 49.21
   Y = 46.88
   Z = 0.00

Question 7: Build the illustrated model from the provided information. Locate the Center of mass of the part.

Think about the various features that create this model. Hint: Insert five features to build this part: Extruded Base, two Extruded Bosses, Extruded Cut, and Rib. Insert a Reference plane to create the Extruded Boss feature.

Origin

Given:
A = Ø3.00, B = 1.00
Material: 6061 Alloy
Density: .097 lb/in^3
Units: IPS
Decimal places = 2

- A: X = 49.00 inches, Y = 45.79 inches, Z = 0.00 inches

- B: X = 0.00 inches, Y = 19.79 inches, Z = 0.04 inches

- C: X = 49.21 inches, Y = 46.88 inches, Z = 0.00 inches

- D: X = 0.00 inches, Y = 0.73 inches, Z = -0.86 inches

The correct answer is D.

Advanced Part Modeling

Advanced Part Modeling is one of the five categories on the CSWA exam. The main difference between the Advanced Part modeling and the Part Modeling category is the complexity of the sketches and the number of dimensions and geometric relations along with an increase number of features.

There is one question on the CSWA exam in this category. The question is worth twenty points and is in a multiple choice single answer or fill in the blank format. The question is either on the location of the Center of mass relative to the default part Origin or to a new created coordinate system and all of the mass properties located in the Mass Properties dialog box: total overall mass, volume, etc.

Sample Questions in the category

In the Advanced Part Modeling category, an exam question could read:

Question 1: Build the illustrated model from the provided information. Locate the Center of mass of the part.

Origin

Given:
A = 2.00, B = Ø.35
Material: 1060 Alloy
Density: 0.097 lb/in^3
Units: IPS
Decimal places = 2

⚡ Built the model with seven features: Extruded Base, two Extruded Bosses, two Extruded Cuts, Chamfer, and Fillet. Think about the steps that you would take to build the illustrated part. Identify the location of the part Origin. Start with the back base flange. Review the provided dimensions and annotations in the part illustration.

⚡ The key difference between the Advanced Part Modeling and the Part Modeling category is the complexity of the sketches and the number of features, dimensions, and geometric relations. You may also need to locate the Center of mass relative to a created coordinate system location.

```
Mass = 0.59 pounds

Volume = 6.01 cubic inches

Surface area = 46.61 inches^2

Center of mass: ( inches )
   X = 0.00
   Y = 0.00
   Z = 1.51
```

- A: X = 1.00 inches, Y = 0.79 inches, Z = 0.00 inches

- B: X = 0.00 inches, Y = 0.00 inches, Z = 1.04 inches

- C: X = 0.00 inches, Y = 1.18 inches, Z = 0.00 inches

- D: X = 0.00 inches, Y = 0.00 inches, Z = 1.51 inches

The correct answer is D.

⚡ All models for Project 5 are located on the CD in the book.

```
Advanced Part Modeling-Question1
  A  Annotations
     1060 Alloy
     Front Plane
     Top Plane
     Right Plane
     Origin
     Extrude1
     Extrude2
     Extrude3
     Extrude4
     Extrude5
     Chamfer1
     Fillet1
```

Question 2: Build the
illustrated model from the
provided information.
Locate the Center of mass
of the part.

Hint: Create the part
with eleven features and a
Reference plane:
Extruded Base, Plane1,
two Extruded Bosses, two
Extruded Cuts, Extruded
Boss, Extruded Cut,

Given:
A = 3.500, B = 4.200, C = 2.000,
D =1.750, E = 1.000
Material: 6061 Alloy
Density: 0.097 lb/in^3
Units: IPS
Decimal places = 3

Extruded-Thin, Mirror, Extruded Cut, and
Extruded Boss.

Think about the steps that you would take to build the
illustrated part. Create the rectangular Base feature. Create
Sketch2 for Plane1. Insert Plane1 to create the Extruded
Boss feature: Extrude2. Plane1 is the Sketch plane for
Sketch3. Sketch3 is the sketch profile for Extrude2.

- A: X = 1.59 inches, Y = 1.19 inches, Z = 0.00 inches

- B: X = -1.59 inches, Y = 1.19 inches, Z = 0.04 inches

- C: X = 1.00 inches, Y = 1.18 inches, Z = 0.10 inches

- D: X = 0.00 inches, Y = 0.00 inches, Z = 1.61 inches

The correct answer is A.

Density = 0.10 pounds per cubic inch

Mass = 1.37 pounds

Volume = 14.05 cubic inches

Surface area = 79.45 inches^2

Center of mass: (inches)
    X = 1.59
    Y = 1.19
    Z = 0.00

Question 3: Build the illustrated model from the provided information. Locate the Center of mass of the part. Note the coordinate system location of the model as illustrated.

A = 110, B = 65, C = 5 X 45Ø CHAMFER
Material: 5MM, 6061 Alloy
Density: .0027 g/mm^3
Units: MMGS
ALL HOLES 6MM

Where do you start? Build the model. Insert thirteen features: Extruded-Thin1, Fillet, two Extruded Cuts, Circular Pattern, two Extruded Cuts, Mirror, Chamfer, Extruded Cut, Mirror, Extruded Cut, and Mirror.

Think about the steps that you would take to build the illustrated part. Review the provided information. The depth of the left side is 50mm. The depth of the right side is 60mm

Create Coordinate System1 to locate the Center of mass.

Coordinate system: +X, +Y. +Z

🔅 The SolidWorks software displays positive values for (X, Y, Z) coordinates for a reference coordinate system. The CSWA exam displays either a positive or negative sign in front of the (X, Y, Z) coordinates to indicate direction as illustrated, (-X, +Y, -Z).

- A: X = -53.30 millimeters, Y = -0.27 millimeters, Z = -15.54 millimeters

- B: X = 53.30 millimeters, Y = 0.27 millimeters, Z = 15.54 millimeters

- C: X = 49.21 millimeters, Y = 46.88 millimeters, Z = 0.00 millimeters

- D: X = 45.00 millimeters, Y = -46.49 millimeters, Z = 10.00 millimeters

The correct answer is A.

Question 4: Build the illustrated model from the provided information. Locate the Center of mass of the part.

Hint: Insert twelve features and a Reference plane: Extruded-Thin1, two Extruded Bosses, Extruded Cut, Extruded Boss, Extruded Cut, Plane1, Mirror, five Extruded Cuts.

Think about the steps that you would take to build the illustrated part. Create an Extrude-Thin1 feature as the Base feature.

Given:
A = Ø19
Material: Gray Cast Iron
Density: .0072 g/mm^3
Units: MMGS
ALL HOLES THROUGH UNLESS
OTHERWISE NOTED

- A: X = -53.30 millimeters, Y = -0.27 millimeters, Z = -15.54 millimeters

- B: X = 53.30 millimeters, Y = 1.27 millimeters, Z = -15.54 millimeters

- C: X = 0.00 millimeters, Y = 34.97 millimeters, Z = 46.67 millimeters

- D: X = 0.00 millimeters, Y = 34.97 millimeters, Z = -46.67 millimeters

```
Mass = 2536.59 grams

Volume = 352304.50 cubic millimeters

Surface area = 61252.90 millimeters^2

Center of mass: ( millimeters )
    X = 0.00
    Y = 34.97
    Z = -46.67
```

The correct answer is D.

☀ Due to software rounding, you may view a negative -0.00 coordinate location in the Mass Properties dialog box.

Question 5: Build the illustrated model from the provided information. Locate the Center of mass of the part.

Origin

Origin

Given:¶
A·=·63,·B·=·50,·C·=·100¶
Material:·Copper¶
Units:·MMGS¶
Density:·.0089·g/mm^3¶
All·HOLES·THROUGH·ALL¶

Hint: Insert thirteen features to build this model: Extruded Base, nine Extruded Cuts, two Extruded Bosses, and a Chamfer. Note: The center point of the top hole is located 30mm from the top right edge.

Think about the steps that you would take to build the illustrated part. Review the centerlines that outline the overall size of the part.

- A: X = 26.81 millimeters, Y = 25.80 millimeters, Z = -56.06 millimeters

- B: X = 43.30 millimeters, Y = 25.27 millimeters, Z = -15.54 millimeters

- C: X = 26.81 millimeters, Y = -25.75 millimeters, Z = 0.00 millimeters

- D: X = 46.00 millimeters, Y = -46.49 millimeters, Z = 10.00 millimeters

The correct answer is A.

This example was taken from the SolidWorks website, www.solidworks.com/cswa as an example of an Advanced Part on the CSWA exam. This model has thirteen features and twelve sketches. There are numerous ways to create the models in this chapter.

Assembly Modeling

Assembly Modeling is one of the five categories on the CSWA exam. In the last two section of this chapter, a simple or advanced part was the focus. The Assembly Modeling category addresses an assembly with numerous sub-components.

Knowledge to build simples parts and to insert Standard mates is required in this category for the CSWA exam. There is one question on the CSWA exam in this category. The question is worth thirty points. The question is in a multiple choice single answer or fill in the blank format.

Spend no more than 40 minutes on the question in this category. This is a timed exam. Manage your time. At this time, there are no sheet metal assembly questions or question using Advanced mates on the CSWA exam.

Sample Questions in the category

In the Assembly Modeling category, an exam
question could read:

Question 1: Build this assembly. Locate the Center
of mass of the model with respect to the illustrated
coordinate system.

The assembly contains the following: One Clevis
component, three Axle components, two 5 Hole
Link components, two 3 Hole Link components,
and six Collar components. All holes Ø.190 THRU
unless otherwise noted. Angle A = 150deg.
Angle B = 120deg. Note: The location of the
illustrated coordinate system: (+X, +Y, +Z).

The following information is provided:

- Clevis, (Item 1): Material: 6061 Alloy. The two 5 Hole Link components are positioned with equal Angle mates, (150deg) to the Clevis component.

- Axle, (Item 2): Material: AISI 304. The first Axle component is mated Concentric and Coincident to the Clevis. The second and third Axle components are mated Concentric and Coincident to the 5 Hole Link and the 3 Hole Link components respectively.

- 5 Hole Link, (Item 3): Material: 6061 Alloy. Material thickness = .100in. Radius = .250in. Five holes located 1in. on center. The 5 Hole Link components are position with equal Angle mates, (120deg) to the 3 Hole Link components.

- 3 Hole Link, (Item 4): Material: 6061 Alloy. Material thickness = .100in. Radius = .250in. Three holes located 1in. on center. The 3 Hole Link components are positioned with equal Angle mates, (120deg) to the 5 Hole Link components.

- Collar, (Item 5): Material: 6061 Alloy. The Collar components are mated Concentric and Coincident to the Axle and the 5 Hole Link and 3 Hole Link components respectively.

Think about the steps that you would take to build the illustrated assembly. Identify and build the required parts. Identify the first fixed component. Position the Base component features in the part so they are in the correct orientation in the assembly. Insert the required Standard mates. Locate the Center of mass of the model with respect to the illustrated coordinate system. In this example, start with the Clevis part.

Remember: The illustrated assembly contains the following: One Clevis component, three Axle components, two 5 Hole Link components, two 3 Hole Link components, and six Collar components. All holes Ø.190 THRU unless otherwise noted.
Angle A = 150deg.
Angle B = 120deg.

- A: X = 1.59 inches, Y = 1.19 inches, Z = 0.00 inches

- B: X = -1.59 inches, Y = 1.19 inches, Z = 0.04 inches

- C: X = 1.00 inches, Y = 1.18 inches, Z = 0.10 inches

- D: X = 1.79 inches, Y = 0.25 inches, Z = 2.61 inches

The correct answer is A.

Question 2: Build this assembly. Locate the Center of mass using the illustrated coordinate system.

The assembly contains the following: One WheelPlate component, two Bracket100 components, one Axle40 component, one Wheel1 component, and four Pin-4 components.

- WheelPlate, (Item 1): Material: AISI 304. The WheelPlate contains 4-Ø10 holes. The holes are aligned to the left Bracket100 and the right Bracket100 components. All holes are through-all. The thickness of the WheelPlate = 10 mm.

- Bracket100, (Item 2): Material: AISI 304. The Bracket100 component contains 2-Ø10 holes and 1- Ø16 hole. All holes are through-all.

- Wheel1, (Item 3): Material AISI 304: The center hole of the Wheel1 component is Concentric with the Axle40 component. There is a 3mm gap between the inside faces of the Bracket100 components and the end faces of the Wheel hub.

- Axle40, (Item 4): Material AISI 304: The end faces of the Axle40 are Coincident with the outside faces of the Bracket100 components.

- Pin-4, (Item 5): Material AISI 304: The Pin-4 components are mated Concentric to the holes of the Bracket100 components, (no clearance). The end faces are Coincident to the WheelPlate bottom face and the Bracket100 top face.

Identify and build the required parts. Identify the first fixed component. This is the Base component of the assembly. Position the Base component features in the part so they are in the correct orientation in the assembly. Insert the required Standard mates. Locate the Center of mass of the illustrated model with respect to the referenced coordinate system. The referenced coordinate system is located at the bottom, right, midpoint of the Wheelplate. In this example, start with the WheelPlate part.

- A: X = 26.81 millimeters, Y = 25.80 millimeters, Z = -56.06 millimeters

- B: X = 0.00 millimeters, Y = 25.27 millimeters, Z = -15.54 millimeters

- C: X = 0.00 millimeters, Y = 37.14 millimeters, Z = -50.00 millimeters

- D: X = 0.00 millimeters, Y = -46.49 millimeters, Z = -50.00 millimeters

The correct answer is C.

 All models for Project 4 are located on the CD in the book.

Advanced Modeling Theory and Analysis

Advanced Modeling Theory and Analysis is one of the five categories on the CSWA exam. There are two questions on the CSWA exam in this category. Each question is worth five points. The two questions are in a multiple choice single answer or fill in the blank format.

As in the Part Modeling category of the exam, you are not required to perform an analysis on a part or assembly, but are required to understand general engineering analysis terminology and how COSMOSXpress/SolidWorks Simulation works.

COSMOSXpress/SolidWorks Simulation Interface

COSMOSXpress/SolidWorks Simulation guides you through six steps to define material properties, restraints, loads, analyze the model, view the results, and the optional Optimization. The interface consists of the following tabs:

- **Welcome tab**: Allows you to set the default units and to specify a folder for saving the analysis results.

- **Material tab**: Applies material properties to the part. The material can be assigned from the material library or you can input the material properties.

- **Restraint tab**: Applies restraints to faces of the part.

- **Load tab**: Applies forces and pressures to faces of the part.

- **Analyze tab**: Provides the ability to either display the analysis with the default settings or to change the settings.

- **Optimize tab**: Optimizes a model dimension based on a specified criterion.

- **Results tab**: Displays the analysis results in the following ways:

  - Shows critical areas where the factor of safety is less than a specified value.

  - Displays the stress distribution in the model with or without annotation for the maximum and minimum stress values.

  - Displays resultant displacement distribution in the model with or without annotation for the maximum and minimum displacement values.

  - Shows deformed shape of the model.

  - Generates an HTML report.

  - Generates eDrawings files for the analysis results

- **Start Over button**: Deletes existing analysis data and results and starts a new analysis session.

- **Update button**: Runs COSMOSXpress/SolidWorks Simulation analysis if the restraints and loads are resolved. Otherwise, it displays a message and you need to resolve the invalid restraints or loads. The Update button is displayed if you modify geometry after applying loads or restraints. It also is displayed if you modify material properties, restraints, loads, or geometry after completing the analysis. Once any of these values are changed, an exclamation mark is displayed on the Analyze and Results tabs. An exclamation mark on the Restraint or Load tab indicates that a restraint or load became invalid after a change in geometry

You can use COSMOSXpress/SolidWorks Simulation only on an active part document. If you create a new part document or open an existing document with COSMOSXpress/SolidWorks Simulation active, COSMOSXpress/SolidWorks Simulation automatically saves the analysis information and closes the current analysis session.

Sample Questions in the category

In the Advanced Modeling Theory and Analysis category, an exam question could read:

Question 1: Under what COSMOSXpress/SolidWorks Simulation menu tab do you set system units?

- A = Material tab

- B = Restraint tab

- C = Welcome tab

- D = Load tab

The correct answer is C. Either SI or the IPS system units.

Questions 2: Under what COSMOSXpress/SolidWorks Simulation menu tab can you modify the Mesh period of the part?

- A = Restraint tab

- B = Material tab

- C = Analyze tab

- D = Welcome tab

The correct answer is C = Analyze tab.

Questions 3: Yield strength is typically determined at _____ strain.

- A = 0.1%
- B = 0.2%
- C = 0.02%
- D = 0.002%

The correct answer is B.

Questions 4: There are four key assumptions made in Linear Static Analysis: 1: Effects of inertia and damping is neglected, 2. The response of the system is directly proportional to the applied loads, 3: Loads are applied slowly and gradually, and_____ .

- A = Displacements are very small. The highest stress is in the linear range of the stress-strain curve.

- B = There are no loads.

- C = Material is not elastic.

- D = Loads are applied quickly.

The correct answer is A.

Questions 5: How many degrees of freedom does a physical structure have?

- A = Zero.

- B = Three – Rotations only.

- C = Three – Translations only.

- D = Six – Three translations and three rotations.

The correct answer is D.

Questions 6: Brittle materials has little tendency to deform (or strain) before fracture and does not have a specific yield point. It is not recommended to apply the yield strength analysis as a failure criterion on brittle material. Which of the following failure theories is appropriate for brittle materials?

- A = Mohr-Columb stress criterion.

- B = Maximum shear stress criterion.

- C = Maximum von Mises stress criterion.

- D = Minimum shear stress criterion.

The correct answer is A.

Questions 7: You are performing an analysis on your model. You select three faces and apply a 40lb load. What is the total force applied to the model?

- A = 40lbs.

- B = 20lbs.

- C = 120lbs.

- D: Additional information is required.

The correct answer is C.

Questions 8: In an engineering analysis, you select a face to restrain. What is the affect?

- A = The face will not translate but can rotate.

- B = The face will rotate but can not translate.

- C = You can not apply a restraint to a face.

- D = The face will not rotate and will not translate.

The correction answer is D.

Questions 8: A material is orthotropic if its mechanical or thermal properties are not unique and independent in three mutually perpendicular directions.

- A = True.

- B = False.

The correction answer is B.

Definition Review

Buckling:

Is a failure mode characterized by a sudden failure of a structural member subjected to high compressive stresses, where the actual compressive stresses at failure are smaller than the ultimate compressive stresses that the material is capable of withstanding. This mode of failure is also described as failure due to elastic instability.

Coefficient of Thermal Expansion:

Is defined as the change in length per unit length per one degree change in temperature (change in normal strain per unit temperature).

Creep:

A term used to describe the tendency of a solid material to slowly move or deform permanently under the influence of stresses. It occurs as a result of long term exposure to levels of stress that are below the yield strength or ultimate strength of the material. Creep is more severe in materials that are subjected to heat for long periods, and near the melting point.

Degrees of Freedom:

Are the set of independent displacements and/or rotations that specify completely the displaced or deformed position and orientation of the body or system. This is a fundamental concept relating to systems of moving bodies in mechanical engineering, aeronautical engineering, robotics, structural engineering, etc. There are six degrees of freedom: Three translations and three rotations.

Density:

Is mass per unit volume. Density units are lb/in^3 in the English system, and kg/m^3 in the SI system.

Density is used in static, nonlinear, frequency, dynamic, buckling, and thermal analyses. Static and buckling analyses use this property only if you define body forces (gravity and/or centrifugal).

Ductile:

A mechanical property which describes how able the material lends itself to be formed into rod-like shapes before fracture occurs. Examples of highly ductile metals are silver, gold, copper, and aluminum. The ductility of steel varies depending on the alloying constituents. Increasing levels of carbon decreases ductility, i.e. the steel becomes more brittle.

Elastic Modulus:

For a linear elastic material, the elastic modulus is the stress required to cause a unit strain in the material. In other words stress divided by the associated strain. The modulus of elasticity was first introduced by Young and is often called the Young's Modulus.

Fatigue:

Is the progressive and localized structural damage that occurs when a material is subjected to cyclic loading. The maximum stress values are less than the ultimate tensile stress limit, and may be below the yield stress limit of the material.

Fixed Restraint:

For solids this restraint type sets all translational degrees of freedom to zero. For shells and beams, it sets the translational and the rotational degrees of freedom to zero. For truss joints, it sets the translational degrees of freedom to zero. When using this restraint type, no reference geometry is needed.

Force:

Is a push or pull upon an object resulting from the object's interaction with another object. Whenever there is an interaction between two objects, there is a force upon each of the objects. When the interaction ceases, the two objects no longer experience the force. Forces only exist as a result of an interaction.

For example, if you select 3 faces and specify a 50 lb force, COSMOSXpress applies a total force of 150 lbs (50 lbs on each face).

Knowing how a design will perform under different conditions allows engineers to make changes prior to physical prototyping, thus saving both time and money.

Linear Static Analysis:

Linear static analysis allows engineers to test different load conditions and their resulting stresses and deformation. What is stress? Stress is a measure of the average amount of force exerted per unit area. It is a measure of the intensity of the total internal forces acting within a body across imaginary internal surfaces, as a reaction to external applied forces and body forces.

Deformation is a change in shape due to an applied force. This can be a result of tensile (pulling) forces, compressive (pushing) forces, shear, bending or torsion (twisting). Deformation is often described in terms of strain.

When loads are applied to a body, the body deforms and the effect of loads is transmitted throughout the body. The external loads induce internal forces and reactions to render the body into a state of equilibrium.

Linear Static analysis calculates *displacements*, *strains*, *stresses*, and *reaction forces* under the effect of applied loads. Linear static analysis makes the following assumptions:

1. The induced response is directly proportional to the applied loads.

2. The highest stress is in the linear range of the stress-strain curve characterized by a straight line starting from the origin.

3. The maximum calculated displacement is considerably smaller than the characteristic dimension of the part. For example, the maximum displacement of a plate must be considerably smaller than its thickness and the maximum displacement of a beam

must be considerably smaller than the smallest dimension of its cross-section. Inertia is neglected.

4. Loads are applied slowly and gradually until they reach their full magnitudes. Suddenly applied loads cause additional displacements, strains, and stresses.

Below are three simple graphics of Stress vs. Strain:

(a) Full sharp-yielding stress strain curve

(b) Full gradual-yielding stress strain curve

Inertia:

Describes the motion of matter and how it is affected by applied forces. The principle of inertia as described by Newton in Newton's First Law of Motion states: "An object that is not subject to any outside forces moves at a constant velocity, covering equal distances in equal times along a straight-line path." In even simpler terms, inertia means "A body in motion tends to remain in motion, a body at rest tends to remain at rest."

Material Strength:

In materials science, the strength of a material refers to the material's ability to resist an applied force.

Mohr-Columb Stress Criterion:

The Mohr-Columb stress criterion is based on the Mohr- Columb theory also known as the Internal Friction theory. This criterion is used for brittle materials with different tensile and compressive properties. Brittle materials do not have a specific yield point and hence it is not recommended to use the yield strength to define the limit stress for this criterion.

Orthotropic Material:

A material is orthotropic if its mechanical or thermal properties are unique and independent in three mutually perpendicular directions. Examples of orthotropic materials are wood, many crystals, and rolled metals. For example, the mechanical properties of wood at a point are described in the longitudinal, radial, and tangential directions. The longitudinal axis (1) is parallel to the grain (fiber) direction; the radial axis (2) is normal to the growth rings; and the tangential axis (3) is tangent to the growth rings.

Poisson's Ratio:

Extension of the material in the longitudinal direction is accompanied by shrinking in the lateral directions. For example, if a body is subjected to a tensile stress in the X-direction, then Poisson's Ratio NUXY is defined as the ratio of lateral strain in the Y-direction divided by the longitudinal strain in the X-direction. Poisson's ratios are dimensionless quantities. If not defined, the program assumes a default value of 0.

Shear Modulus:

Also called modulus of rigidity, is the ratio between the shearing stress in a plane divided by the associated shearing strain. Shear Moduli are used in static, nonlinear, frequency, dynamic and buckling analyses.

Thermal Conductivity:

Indicates the effectiveness of a material in transferring heat energy by conduction. It is defined as the rate of heat transfer through a unit thickness of the material per unit temperature difference. The units of thermal conductivity are Btu/in sec $^{\circ}$F in the English system and W/m $^{\circ}$K in the SI system.

Thermal conductivity is used in steady state and transient thermal analyses.

Tensile Strength:

Tensile strength is the maximum load sustained by the specimen in the tension test, divided by the original cross sectional area.

von Mises yield Criterion:

A scalar stress value that can be computed from the stress. In this case, a material is said to start yielding when its von Mises stress reaches a critical value known as the yield strength. The von Mises stress is used to predict yielding of materials under any loading condition from results of simple uniaxial tensile tests. The von Mises stress satisfies the property that two stress states with equal distortion energy have equal von Mises stress.

Yield Strength:

The stress at which the metal yields or becomes permanently deformed is an important design parameter. This stress is the elastic limit below which no permanent shape changes will occur.

The elastic limit is approximated by the yield strength of the material, and the strain that occurs before the elastic limit is reached is called the elastic strain. The yield strength is defined in three ways, depending on the stress-strain characteristics of the steel as it begins to yield. The procedures in SAE J416, ASTM E8, and ASTM A370.

COSMOSXpress uses this material property to calculate the factor of safety distribution. COSMOSXpress assumes that the material starts yielding when the equivalent (von Mises) stress reaches this value.

Appendix

Engineering Changer Order (ECO)

D&M	Engineering Change Order	ECO # _____ Page 1 of __

	☐ Hardware	Author
	☐ Software	Date
Product Line	☐ Quality	Authorized Mgr.
	☐ Tech Pubs	Date

Change Tested By
Reason for ECO(Describe the existing problem, symptom and impact on field)

D&M Part No.	Rev From/To	Part Description	Description	Owner

ECO Implementation/Class		Departments	Approvals	Date	
All in Field	☐	Engineering			
All in Test	☐	Manufacturing			
All in Assembly	☐	Technical Support			
All in Stock	☐	Marketing			
All on Order	☐	DOC Control			
All Future	☐				
Material Disposition		ECO Cost			
Rework	☐	DO NOT WRITE BELOW THIS LINE (ECO BOARD ONLY)			
Scrap	☐	Effective Date			
Use as is	☐	Incorporated Date			
None	☐	Board Approval			
See Attached	☐	Board Date			

This text follows the ASME Y14 Engineering Drawing and Related Documentation Practices for drawings. Display of dimensions and tolerances are as follows:

TYPES of DECIMAL DIMENSIONS (ASME Y14.5M)			
Description:	**UNITS: MM**	**Description:**	**UNITS: INCH**
Dimension is less than 1mm. Zero precedes the decimal point.	0.9 0.95	Dimension is less than 1 inch. Zero is not used before the decimal point.	.5 .56
Dimension is a whole number. Display no decimal point. Display no zero after decimal point.	19	Express dimension to the same number of decimal places as its tolerance. Add zeros to the right of the decimal point. If the tolerance is expressed to 3 places, then the dimension contains 3 places to the right of the decimal point.	1.750
Dimension exceeds a whole number by a decimal fraction of a millimeter. Display no zero to the right of the decimal.	11.5 11.51		

TABLE 1 TOLERANCE DISPLAY FOR INCH AND METRIC DIMENSIONS (ASME Y14.5M)		
DISPLAY:	**UNITS: INCH:**	**UNITS: METRIC:**
Dimensions less than 1	.5	0.5
Unilateral Tolerance	$1.417^{+.005}_{-.000}$	$36^{0}_{-0.5}$
Bilateral Tolerance	$1.417^{+.010}_{-.020}$	$36^{+0.25}_{-0.50}$
Limit Tolerance	.571 .463	14.50 11.50

SolidWorks Keyboard Shortcuts

Listed below are some of the pre-defined keyboard shortcuts in SolidWorks:

Action:	Key Combination:
Model Views	
Rotate the model horizontally or vertically:	**Arrow** keys
Rotate the model horizontally or vertically 90 degrees.	**Shift** + **Arrow** keys
Rotate the model clockwise or counterclockwise	**Alt** + left of right **Arrow** keys
Pan the model	**Ctrl** + **Arrow** keys
Magnifying glass	**g**
Zoom in	**Shift + z**
Zoom out	**z**
Zoom to fit	**f**
Previous view	**Ctrl + Shift + z**
View Orientation	
View Orientation menu	**Spacebar**
Front view	**Ctrl + 1**
Back view	**Ctrl + 2**
Left view	**Ctrl + 3**
Right view	**Ctrl + 4**
Top view	**Ctrl + 5**
Bottom view	**Ctrl + 6**
Isometric view	**Ctrl + 7**
NormalTo view	**Ctrl + 8**
Selection Filters	
Filter edges	**e**
Filter vertices	**v**
Filter faces	**x**
Toggle Selection Filter toolbar	**F5**
Toggle selection filters on/off	**F6**
File menu items	
New SolidWorks document	**Ctrl + n**
Open document	**Ctrl + o**
Open From Web Folder	**Ctrl + w**
Make Drawing from Part	**Ctrl + d**
Make Assembly from Part	**Ctrl + a**
Save	**Ctrl +s**
Print	**Ctrl + p**
Additional shortcuts	
Access online help inside of PropertyManager or dialog box	**F1**
Rename an item in the FeatureManager design tree	**F2**
Rebuild the model	**Ctrl + b**
Force rebuild – Rebuild the model and all its features	**Ctrl + q**
Redraw the screen	**Ctrl + r**

Cycle between open SolidWorks document	Ctrl + Tab
Line to arc/arc to line in the Sketch	a
Undo	Ctrl + z
Redo	Ctrl + y
Cut	Ctrl + x
Copy	Ctrl + c
Additional shortcuts	
Paste	Ctrl + v
Delete	**Delete**
Next window	Ctrl + F6
Close window	Ctrl + F4
View previous tools	s
Selects all text inside an Annotations text box	Ctrl + a

 In a sketch, the **Esc** key un-selects geometry items currently selected in the Properties box and Add Relations box. In the model, the **Esc** key closes the PropertyManager and cancels the selections.

Use the **g** key to activate the Magnifying glass tool. Use the Magnifying glass tool to inspect a model and make selections without changing the overall view.

Use the **s** key to view/access previous command tools in the Graphics window.

Windows Shortcuts

Listed below are some of the pre-defined keyboard shortcuts in Microsoft Windows:

Action:	Keyboard Combination:
Open the Start menu	Windows Logo key
Open Windows Explorer	Windows Logo key + E
Minimize all open windows	Windows Logo key + M
Open a Search window	Windows Logo key + F
Open Windows Help	Windows Logo key + F1
Select multiple geometry items in a SolidWorks document	Ctrl key (Hold the Ctrl key down. Select items.) Release the Ctrl key.

Helpful On-Line Information

The SolidWorks URL: http://www.solidworks.com contains information on Local Resellers, Solution Partners, Certifications, SolidWorks users groups, and more.

Access 3D ContentCentral using the Task Pane to obtain engineering electronic catalog model and part information.

Use the SolidWorks Resources tab in the Task Pane to obtain access to Customer Portals, Discussion Forums, User Groups, Manufacturers, Solution Partners, Labs, and more.

Helpful on-line SolidWorks information is available from the following URLs:

- http://www.dmeducation.net

    Information on the CSWA Certification, software updates, design tips, and new book releases.

- http://www.mechengineer.com/snug/

    News group access and local user group information.

- http://www.nhcad.com

    Configuration information and other tips and tricks.

- http://www.solidworktips.com

    Helpful tips, tricks on SolidWorks and API.

- http://www.topica.com/lists/SW

    Independent News Group for SolidWorks discussions, questions and answers.

Certified SolidWorks Professionals (CSWP) URLs provide additional helpful on-line information.

- http://www.scottjbaugh.com   Scott J. Baugh

- http://www.3-ddesignsolutions.com   Devon Sowell

- http://www.zxys.com   Paul Salvador

- http://www.mikejwilson.com   Mike J. Wilson

- http://www.dimontegroup.com   Gene Dimonte & Ed Eaton

*On-line tutorials are for educational purposes only. Tutorials are copyrighted by their respective owners.

Notes:

Index

CD-ROM Included!
Over 100 sample practice tutorials

OFFICIAL CERTIFIED SOLIDWORKS® ASSOCIATE CSWA EXAM GUIDE

THE ONLY AUTHORIZED CSWA EXAM PREPARATION GUIDE

David C. Planchard and Marie P. Planchard (CSWP)

Users wanting further preparation for the SolidWorks Certification Exam should purchase the **Official Certified SolidWorks Associate CSWA Exam Guide**.

Available on Amazon.com.